THE
FIFTY-EIGHTH
CENTURY

THE FIFTY-EIGHTH CENTURY

A Jewish Renewal Sourcebook

edited by

SHOHAMA WIENER

JASON ARONSON INC.
Northvale, New Jersey
London

This book was set in 11 pt. Stempel Schneidler by Alabama Book Composition, Deatsville, Alabama.

Library of Congress Cataloging-in-Publication Data

The Fifty-eighth century : a Jewish renewal sourcebook / edited by
   Shohama Wiener.
      p.   cm.
   Includes index.
   ISBN 1-56821-947-4 (alk. paper)
      1. Spiritual life—Judaism.   2. Judaism—20th century.   3. Jewish
   women—Religious life.   4. New age movement.   I. Wiener, Shohama.
   BM723.F48   1996
   296.7'1—dc20   96-9446
                                                                      CIP

Manufactured in the United States of America. Jason Aronson Inc. offers books and cassettes. For information and catalog write to Jason Aronson Inc., 230 Livingston Street, Northvale, New Jersey 07647.

To our beloved teacher and rebbe,
Rabbi Zalman Schachter-Shalomi,
guiding light of Jewish Renewal
in our generation.

The contributors,
and
Shohama Wiener, Editor

Contents

Part III
Created Them: On Gender and Relationship   181

Contributors

Joe August has played a leading role in promoting the use of Torah text and ritual for masculine renewal. He has organized and led ALEPH's annual northeast regional men's retreats and has led Jewish men's activities at several Kallahs, the Tikkun Conference and Elat Chayyim. He lives in Woodstock, New York with his wife, Tsurah.

Karen Barth earned her MBA at Harvard and is a management consultant with McKinsey & Company, specializing in strategic planning, innovation, and change management. She has worked extensively on a *pro bono* basis for Jewish organizations and has developed and taught a course "Time and Torah: Jewish Time Management" with her husband, Rabbi Samuel Barth.

Samuel Barth is Dean and Lecturer in Codes and Liturgy at The Academy for Jewish Religion, the pluralistic seminary in New York City. He also serves as Rabbi of the Park Slope Jewish Center. He is completing a doctorate in liturgy, at The Jewish Theological Seminary, where he was formerly Assistant Dean of the Rabbinical School. He has taught widely in the United States and Europe.

Mordechai Beck, an artist and writer, is a founder-member of Kehillat Yedidyah, a neo-Orthodox community in Jerusalem. His works of fiction, essays, and artwork appear in Israel, North America, and England.

Moshe ben Asher has rabbinic ordination from Reb Zalman, and has been a community organizer for 25 years. Since 1987 he has organized congregations to bring their faith into action. **Khulda**

bat Sarah is also a congregational organizer. They are married, and are now working together to form a nonprofit organization for covenantal community organizing and outreach training.

Marc Bregman has been teaching at the Jerusalem campus of the Hebrew Union College, where he is associate professor of Rabbinic Literature. He has published numerous articles and creative writing in journals worldwide. His forthcoming book, *The Sign of the Serpent*, (Mohr-Siebeck, Tübingen) is a detailed analysis of part of the Tanhuma-Yelammdenu genre of midrashic literature.

Sylvia Boorstein teaches Vipassana and Metta meditation in the United States, Canada, and Israel. She is a founding teacher at Spirit Rock Meditation Center in Woodacre, California, and a senior teacher at Insight Meditation Society in Barre, Massachusetts. A practicing psychotherapist in Northern California, Sylvia is the author of *It's Easier Than You Think: The Buddhist Way to Happiness* (Harper, 1995).

Barbara E. Breitman, M.S.W., is a psychotherapist in Philadelphia, an instructor at the University of Pennsylvania School of Social Work and at the Reconstructionist Rabbinical College. She has facilitated workshops at P'nai Or Kallahs, Elat Chayyim, and Omega. She is a longtime activist for Jewish Renewal and Jewish feminism, and is currently chair of the board of ALEPH.

Lawrence Bush edits *Reconstructionism Today*, a quarterly magazine of the Reconstructionist movement, and also works as a consultant for the Reform movement. Larry has authored three books of fiction and co-wrote *Jews, Money and Social Responsibility: Developing a "Torah of Money" for Contemporary Life* (The Shefa Fund, 1993).

David Carson is co-author of the best-selling *Medicine Cards: The Discovery of Power Through the Ways of Animals* (Bear & Company, 1988), which has sold over a half a million copies. A renowned Choctaw shamanic teacher, David has been invited to share the mystical wisdom of the Native American traditions across the United States, Europe, and most recently, Russia.

Mitchell Chefitz is a rabbi, and director of Havurah of South Florida in Miami, Florida. He is a past chairperson of the National Havurah Committee, and an editor of the N.H.C. D'var Torah column. He teaches and writes on matters of Jewish spirituality.

Bernard DeKoven has brought the spirit of play and the wisdom of games to business, education, and recreation. He is the author of *Connected Executives* and *The Well-Played Game*. He has designed computer games for Children's Television Workshop, a virtual world game for the Time-Warner Network, and organized community celebrations for hundreds of thousands of people.

Lakme Batya Elior is a psychotherapist as well as a teacher of Jewish feminine spirituality. She is co-author with Gershon Winkler of *The Place Where You Are Standing Is Holy: A Jewish Theology on Human Relationships* (Jason Aronson). She is also a teacher of Focusing, a way of accessing inner teachings and creativity, and has taught seminars and workshops across the country.

Zev-Hayyim Feyer, founder of Elu v'Elu, Atlanta Jewish Renewal congregation, and editor of *Shokhen Ad Marom*, a Jewish Renewal Siddur, is known throughout the United States and Canada as a "teller of songs and singer of stories," presenting classes and seminars on Kabbalah, Self-Esteem, Spiritual Stories, and Comparative Religion.

Russell Fox is a *hasid* of Reb Zalman, a rabbinical student at the Academy for Jewish Religion, a scholar, and a writer. He also serves as the spiritual leader of Congregation Beth Torah in Willingboro, New Jersey, and has been active in the P'nai Or Havura in Philadelphia.

Cindy Gabriel spends much of her energy supporting Jewish women in reclaiming and celebrating the Jewish contexts of their lives. She has started women's Rosh Chodesh groups in three communities. She was coordinator of the 1995 ALEPH Kallah, and is Rocky Mountain States Coordinator of the National Havurah Committee.

Ya'acov Gabriel is Rabbi of Congregation Har Shalom, a Jewish renewal community in Fort Collins, Colorado, and a *hasid* of Reb Zalman's. He lives his Judaism through singing, and has written over 180 niggunim and liturgical pieces, and recorded six albums of his music.

Yehudit Goldfarb, Ph.D., is a founder and spiritual leader of the Aquarian Minyan, the originator of *Otiyot Khayyot*—Hebrew Letter Movements for Healing and Renewal, and the Associate Editor of *Agada*. She teaches courses in Judaic and Chinese mystical writings, dance midrash, and T'ai Chi.

Edward Hoffman, Ph.D., is a licensed clinical psychologist in the New York City area. He is the author of nine books in psychology and Jewish studies including *The Way of Splendor, The Heavenly Ladder,* and most recently, *Opening the Inner Gates: New Paths in Kabbalah and Psychology* (Shambhala).

Eve Penner Ilsen, M.A., is a therapist and master teacher, singer, and storyteller, whose subjects range from personal mythology and Jewish mysticism to transformational imagery. In addition to her own work, she has taught all over the world with Reb Zalman, and together they created a Wisdom School. They were married early in 1995.

Reuel Falcon Karpov received writing awards, including the Academy of American Poets, for work leading to her University of Wisconsin Ph.D. In 1989 she became one of the first women rabbis in the Conservative movement to hold her own pulpit. She is now completing the editing of a Passover Haggadah including *minhagim* and *kavanot* from global Jewish traditions to be published by Jason Aronson. She is in her eighth year of serving a Conservative pulpit, and also serves as Professor of both Hebrew and English at the State University of New York.

Nathan Katz, Ph.D., is a professor and chair of Religious Studies at Florida International University and has studied and taught in South Asia for eight years. He is author/editor of numerous books about Buddhism, Hinduism, and Indian Judaism and has pioneered dialogues between Jews, Buddhists, and Hindus.

Shoni Labowitz is a nationally known lecturer, spiritual counselor, and creator of healing rituals. She has studied Buddhism, Eastern philosophies, and Kabbalah, has an M.A. from Vermont College and rabbinic ordination from Reb Zalman. She is co-rabbi with her husband Phillip at Temple Adath Or in Fort Lauderdale, and founder of Living Waters, a spiritual health spa based on Mystical Judaism.

Ma Jaya Sati Bhagavati is an American spiritual teacher, founder of the River Fund, and director of Neem Karoli Baba Kashi Ashram, an interfaith community in Roseland, Florida. She was born into an Orthodox Jewish family and is particularly devoted to helping people in need, the sick, the poor, and the dying.

Leah Novick is a rabbi and West Coast author and spiritual teacher whose work has been focused on restoring the Divine Feminine and the human feminine to the study and practice of Judaism. Her main writings are on "Shekhinah" and the righteous women teachers who have represented the Divine Presence throughout our history.

Nehemia Polen is a rabbi, and Associate Dean of Students and Assistant Professor of Jewish Thought at Boston Hebrew College. His book *The Holy Fire* (Jason Aronson, 1994) is on the Holocaust theology of Rabbi Kalonymus Shapira of Piaseczno (1889–1943), one of the last masters of Hasidism in Poland.

Marcia Prager, a teacher, artist, and storyteller, is a graduate of the Reconstructionist Rabbinical College and has received *smikha* from Reb Zalman. She teaches classes at the Jewish Renewal Life Center, works with rabbinical students as director of professional development for ALEPH, and is Rabbi-Chaver for the P'nai Or chavurot in Philadelphia, Pennsylvania, and Princeton, New Jersey.

Simcha Paull Raphael, Ph.D., received ordination as a rabbinic pastor from Reb Zalman. In 1980–81 he was founding Executive Director of B'nai Or Religious Fellowship. He teaches in the Religion Department and is chaplain at La Salle University, Philadelphia, Pennsylvania. He is author of *Jewish Views of the Afterlife* (Jason Aronson, 1994).

Jack Riemer is the editor of *Torah Fax* of the *National Rabbinic Network, The World of the High Holy Days,* and *Jewish Reflections on Death.* He is co-editor of *So That Your Values Live On.* His most recent book is *Wrestling with the Angel* (Schocken, 1995).

Carol Rose is a writer, educator, and spiritual counselor who lives in Winnipeg, Canada, with her husband Neal and five children. Her poetry and essays are widely published, and she has just completed a manuscript entitled *Jerusalem: Another Version of the Story.*

Dawn Rose is part-time adjunct instructor of feminist studies and modern thought at the Reconstructionist Rabbinical College and the Jewish Theological Seminary. A doctoral candidate in Jewish Philosophy at the latter institution, her dissertation-in-progress is entitled *Resources in Jewish Feminist Theology.*

Neal Rose is an ordained rabbi and professor of religion at the University of Manitoba, Winnipeg, Canada. He also has a private practice in marriage and family therapy in which he utilizes myth, ritual, and storytelling. He and his wife, Carol, are first generation B'nai Or.

Harold M. Schulweis is Rabbi of Valley Beth Shalom in Encino, California and Founding Chairperson of the Jewish Foundation for Christian Rescuers. He is author of *For Those Who Can't Believe, In God's Mirror,* and *Evil and the Morality of God.*

Howard Schwartz, Ph.D., is a professor of English at the University of Missouri, St. Louis, and a widely published author and editor. Included in his edited works are *Elijah's Violin & Other Jewish Fairy Tales, Miriam's Tambourine: Jewish Folktales from Around the World, Lilith's Cave, Gabriel's Palace,* and *The Dream Assembly: Tales of Rabbi Zalman Schachter-Shalomi.*

Diane M. Sharon, Ph.D., is a *hasid* of Reb Zalman's and a writer, scholar, and teacher. Her doctorate from the Jewish Theological Seminary is in Bible and Ancient Semitic Languages. She is a seeker with interest in all religious traditions—East and West, ancient and modern.

Shohama Wiener, D. Min., editor of this book, is president of The Academy for Jewish Religion (NYC), the multi-denominational seminary that ordains both rabbis and cantors. Following her ordination as rabbi by the AJR, she received honorary ordination from Reb Zalman. She is co-editor of *Worlds of Jewish Prayer* (Jason Aronson, 1993), and writes and teaches widely on Jewish spirituality, meditation, and healing.

Batya D. Moskowitz Wininger, M.A., C.S.C., C.S.W., is a psychotherapist and shamanic practitioner in Brooklyn, New York, offering counseling, healing, and workshops through her Mother Earth Healing Center. Her master's degrees in Cultural Anthropology and Clinical Social Work inform her work/play with people with respect to their souls' journeys through life.

Gershon Winkler is a storyteller, humorist, and circuit-riding rabbi for the Four Corners region of New Mexico and Colorado. He is also the author of eight books ranging from juvenile adventure novels to works on Jewish folklore and mysticism. He holds ordinations from the late Rabbi Ben Zion Bruk and from Reb Zalman.

Yosef Wosk, Ph.D., has lived and studied in Canada, Israel, and the United States. Ordained as a rabbi by Yeshiva University, he has served a number of communities. Yosef has graduate degrees from Harvard (Th.M.), Boston (Ph.D.), William Lyon (Ph.D.), and Yeshiva (M.S.) Universities.

Joel Ziff, Ed.D., is a psychologist in private practice in Newton, Massachusetts and serves on the faculty at Lesley College and the Interface Foundation. He is the author of *Mirrors in Time: Psychotherapeutic Process in the Jewish Holy Day Cycle* (Jason Aronson, 1996) and *A Protocol for Multi-Modality Counseling*, a training manual for practitioners.

Introduction

This volume, *The Fifty-Eighth Century: A Jewish Renewal Sourcebook*, contains insights and pointers for making Judaism alive and relevant in our daily lives. These ideas are rooted in the philosophy and theology of the Jewish Renewal movement. Jewish Renewal, inspired to a great extent by Rabbi Zalman Schachter-Shalomi, began some thirty years ago to look for ways to open up once again the channels of our tradition to the life of the spirit, mystical realities, and the emerging consciousness of a new world paradigm. In the Jewish calendar, the year we are in is 5756—therefore this is, from the Jewish perspective, the fifty-eighth century.

The beginning of this century, the year 5700, 1940 in the Western calendar, marked the Holocaust, the genocide of six million and the destruction of European Jewish culture. The world was not the same after that, and could never be made the same. The fifty-eighth century marks a break in our history as dramatic and in need of a collective response as the destruction of the second Temple by the Romans in the year 70 B.C.E. We are entering a new paradigm in the course of human history, demanding a new relationship with the divine, the earth, our communities, and other peoples and traditions. This calls for a reformatting of the social, spiritual, and psychological "technology" we use to bring the connection to the Divine into our lives.

Jewish Renewal speaks to those Jews who have been turned off by the aridness and spiritual emptiness of much of mainstream Jewish life, by offering a contemporary view of ancient Jewish mystical tradition. It is infused by an awareness of gender issues and the environment, the validity of other spiritual traditions, and the interconnectedness of all things. This has resulted in the

1

creation of new kinds of Jewish communities, new modalities of prayer and study, new kinds of teachers and leaders, and a reconnection of Judaism to areas of meaning in our age, which are serving more and more as models and inspiration throughout a broad spectrum of the Jewish world.

As more and more people are exposed to Jewish Renewal, there is increasing curiosity and desire to "bring this home," to anchor the inspiration found in Jewish Renewal events, workshops, and books into our awareness and daily lives. *Renewal is a process—a way of looking at the spiritual life rather than a fixed body of rules and practices.* The articles, essays, and stories you will find within can help you in the process of building your own system of Jewish spiritual practice in three ways: some are intended to serve as inspiration for the mind and to let the spirit and imagination soar; some are stories of personal journeys which can serve as generic examples for your own lifepath; and yet others propose specific practices which you can try out and elaborate on as you wish.

This volume, an anthology of how to bring Jewish Renewal into our lives, includes essays, stories, and personal narratives along the following four themes:

1. Our personal journey into the paradigm shift
2. Renewing our relationship to Jewish text
3. Renewing our understanding of gender roles
4. Revisioning the relationship of Judaism and other religions

We are constantly growing and evolving, if we are healthy, both as individuals and as collective humanity. Part I of this anthology contains stories about and inspirations for a personal relationship with God. These range from some challenging thinking about reincarnation and the Holocaust by Zev-Hayyim Feyer to the humorous introspective view of theology in "Serious and Silly" by Bernard DeKoven. Yehudit Goldfarb shares with us her Jewish movement form based on the Hebrew letters; Mitchell Chefitz offers a practical theology for those wrestling with addiction; Joel Ziff explains a developmental view of the relationship with God that parallels psychological theory, while Shohama Wiener shares her personal theological transformations. Shoni Labowitz speaks of the spiritual side of being with the sick and the dying, Russell Fox speaks of his Godsent encounter with Reb Shlomo Carlebach, and Karen and Samuel Barth teach us how to make the way we spend our time reflect our spiritual priorities. Finally, Simcha Paull Raphael shares how Reb Zalman's dream of the rainbow tallit became a reality.

In Part II of this book are inspired new looks at Torah in its broadest meaning—as the body of oral and written Jewish thought ranging from the five books of Moses to writings of contemporary times. Barbara Breitman uses family systems theory to illuminate the binding of Isaac, while Nehemia Polen translates a teaching from the Piaseczno Rebbe, a Hasidic master who taught in Warsaw between the World Wars. In between we have a look by Jack Riemer at the story of David and Bathsheba through traditional, modern and offbeat eyes; an allegorical story about holiness by Moshe ben Asher and Khulda bat Sarah; an analysis by Howard Schwartz of the psychic symbolism in a series of tales of Shekhinah; an experiential journey into Kabbalistic meditation by Edward Hoffman; a contemporary midrash (story) of a visionary journey into the Zohar by Marc Bregman; a feminist interpretation of creation by Eve Ilsen; and a window into the world of the Hasidim by Neal Rose.

A major tenet of the revisioning we are engaged in revolves around male- and femaleness—adding women's voices to our texts and history, fashioning a contemporary view of women's and men's roles, and rethinking the Jewish position on sexual preference. These issues and more are dealt with in the third section of the book. Yosef Wosk describes a ritual commemorating the tragedy of a woman in the days of the prophets, while Leah Novick gives voice to the life of a holy woman, the Hasidic Rebbetzin Malka of Belz. Dawn Rose offers her perspective on identifying Jewish women's spirituality, Carol Rose gives us a way to re-vision our biblical mothers, and Reuel Karpov writes of the love relationship between a woman *leiner* (reader) of Torah and the words of the sacred text. Ya'acov and Cindy Gabriel share their pre-wedding agreement based on gender equality, Harold Schulweis argues for a new attitude toward homosexuality, and Joe August and Larry Bush look at the Jewish perspective on what it means to be a man.

There are many rich spiritual traditions in the world. Central to

Jewish Renewal philosophy is that each of them has a valuable function to fulfill, and that much of the spiritual light of the emerging paradigm is coming from the dialogue between the traditions. In the fourth section of the book we hear from Jews who have studied, sojourned in, or even found their homes in other spiritual traditions. Many have brought the essence of what they have learned back into Judaism, infusing Jewish Renewal with new approaches to spiritual practice. Mordechai Beck starts out by taking us along with Reb Zalman as he speaks of the importance of learning from other religions; Ma Jaya Sati Bhagavati gives us a moving account of how Reb Zalman gave her a new connection to her Jewish roots; Marcia Prager informs us about her spiritual work with Quakers; Batya Wininger explains shamanism and shares her journey as a Jewish shaman; Sylvia Boorstein offers us her personal story of parallel and complementary journeys into Judaism and Buddhism; Gershon Winkler together with Lakme Elior dialogue with David Carson, a Native American; Diane Sharon looks at the parallels between a Yogi and a Jewish mystic; and Nathan Katz discusses the dialogue between Hinduism and Judaism.

Many of the pieces in this book were written and all were offered in honor of Rabbi Schachter-Shalomi—Reb Zalman, as he is known to us all, for his pivotal role in the lives of many, his wisdom, and his caring spirit. He figures in many of the personal accounts you will read in these pages. Although the life of someone so multifaceted can hardly be done justice in these few pages, let us tell you something about him:

Born in 1924 to a family that embraced both tradition and modernity, Reb Zalman was educated in Vienna, in both secular and religious schools. The Nazi invasion caused him to flee to France, where he spent a year in internment camps. Afterwards, he made his way to the United States and enrolled in a Lubovitcher Yeshiva in Brooklyn, where he received rabbinical ordination in 1947.

Zalman showed great promise as a hasidic outreach worker, as indicated in this story which Zalman's mother of blessed memory shared with Andy Rose:

The family had recently arrived in Brooklyn from internment camps in Europe. Zalman was seventeen and had been studying at the Lubavitcher Yeshiva for a short time. Parnassa (income) was difficult for everyone, and some of the other boys in the Yeshiva had started working part-time in the diamond businesses run by local hasidim. So we thought that maybe Zalman should do the same to help out with expenses.

So he went to the Rebbe to ask permission. The Rebbe smiled, shook his head "no," and said, "These boys are working in diamonds. You are already working in diamonds—diamonds of life."

The Rebbe was right about Zalman's promise as a rebbe, but he had not foreseen that Zalman's thirst for universal answers would take him far beyond the hasidic world. Interspersed with his work as a congregational rabbi, Hillel chaplain, camp counselor, university professor, and grandfather of the Havurah and Jewish Renewal movements, Zalman has sought out colleagues of other faiths and intellectual disciplines, and re-imbued Judaism with insights brought from other religious traditions, and from science and psychology.

He is the author of countless articles and books, all having to do with the endless variety of ways to travel the spiritual path. A great visionary, Zalman loves to share his ideas and urge others to implement them in their own unique ways. He is inevitably on the cutting edge, always being both deeply traditional and egregiously outrageous. And always, he imparts God's love.

This book was several years in the collecting and editing. To all those who generously submitted articles in honor of Reb Zalman, we give thanks. To Arthur Kurzweil, for his vision and encouragement, we are deeply indebted. To the office staff at the Academy for Jewish Religion and at ALEPH: The Alliance for Jewish Renewal, we express our appreciation. Finally, we give thanks to the Holy One, the source of all inspiration and renewal, for allowing us to bring this collection to light.

Shohama Wiener, Editor
Russell Fox, Assistant Editor

PART I

A New Spirit: Personal Growth and Transformation

Mitchell Chefitz

A Half Hour with Dr. A.

Dr. A. is an alcoholic or perhaps an addict. I don't know which. It doesn't matter. He has an appetite over which he has no control.

Dr. A. is an in-patient in an addiction treatment program. His professional life hangs in the balance. Indeed his very life hangs in the balance. If he is not on the road to recovery by the time he completes the program, he may well just be on the road, looking for a new profession and a new family.

Dr. A. is Jewish, and I have a half hour with him.

Through his treatment program, Dr. A. has discovered that the path to recovery is primarily spiritual. There are no miracle anti-addiction pills. Psychotherapy will reduce stress, but it won't remove the addiction. The addiction is permanent; it will always be there. And since the recovery program is ultimately built on spiritual discipline, Dr. A. has a problem. He has no spiritual discipline. His faith is based upon science. If he cannot understand it, he cannot believe it. In my half hour with him, I am to provide a framework within which Dr. A. can develop a spiritual discipline.

"What can I do for you?" I ask him. He knows I am a rabbi, and he knows that the program chaplain has asked me to visit him, but he doesn't have the slightest idea of what to ask me to do for him. He still believes he can do it all for himself.

"They talk about a 'Higher Power' here. I don't know what it means."

"It means God. They are telling you that you need help from God to stay in recovery."

Such words are very strange to Dr. A. He tells me he has no history of relating to God. He went to Hebrew school for a few

9

years, celebrated his Bar Mitzvah, and has not been involved in a synagogue since.

We are sitting in the chaplain's small office, a few feet apart with nothing between us. To one side is a desk cluttered with papers, to the other a large standing fan left over from the time when the air-conditioning wasn't working. A light hangs in the corner. Schlock art adorns the walls.

"We have about twenty-five minutes left," I tell him. "In that time I have to give you a framework you can accept that will contain a Higher Power that can help you remain in recovery. We'll have to work fast. Remember everything I say. You don't have to accept any of it, just remember it and wrestle with it later. Ready?"

Dr. A. is ready. Perhaps for the first time in his life he is ready. And this is what I share with him:

"Do you see this fan? This fan did not make itself. It was created by somebody. We know something about who created the fan. He needed a breeze. And you see this desk. It was created by someone who needed a place to put all these papers. And this light, by someone who needed illumination. And this painting on the wall, by someone who needed to express himself artistically. Or maybe by someone who needed money and could make a painting and sell it. None of these things was made except to fulfill the need of the person who made it.

"Also we know that the fan did not make itself; the desk did not make itself; the light and the painting—they did not make themselves.

"So two things about a creation: A creation is made to fulfill the needs of the creator. And a creation does not make itself.

"The universe is a creation. We can say that pretty much as a matter of fact today. Quantum physics. . . ."

I interrupt my discourse to Dr. A. for a moment to comment on the words "quantum physics." I don't know much about quantum physics, though I spent a few years at M.I.T. I make sure to let Dr. A. know I was at M.I.T. It establishes my credentials. I don't tell him I left M.I.T. to study poetry at Berkeley. The words "quantum physics" are magical. Maimonides had to argue through hundreds of pages to counter Aristotle's premise that the universe is eternal. All I have to do is mention the words "quantum physics" and

Dr. A. readily accepts creation. He doesn't know any more quantum physics than I do, but he has a vague notion somewhere that a physicist has proven a Big Bang theory, which means the universe has a beginning. Dr. A. cannot follow the mathematics of the physicist. He is willing to take the idea of creation on faith—faith in the scientist. So Dr. A. is already a man of faith. He just doesn't know that yet. And since I have only twenty minutes left with him, I am not about to challenge his faith by challenging his knowledge of quantum physics. I let the words work their magic, and I continue.

". . . and if there is a creation, there is a Creator. Now before we continue I must apologize. I will be using human language to describe the Creator, but then I have no choice. It's the only language I have. So whatever words I use will be inadequate, but it's the best I can do.

"What do we know of a creator? A creator creates in order to fulfill its needs. And the creator is separate from its creation.

"So, if the creator of the desk creates to provide a place for its papers, and the creator of the fan creates to provide a breeze, why does the Creator of the universe create? Remember, the creator of the desk is separate from the desk, and the creator of the fan is separate from the fan, and the Creator of the universe is separate from the universe. That means, the Creator of the universe is not in space and time, because space and time is what the universe is. So what can there be within a universe of space and time that can meet the needs of a Creator beyond space and time . . . ?"

I don't expect Dr. A. to have an immediate answer. While he wrestles with the problem subliminally, I shift gears.

"One of the difficulties here is that you don't know how to ask God for help. A lot of it is our fault, we rabbis. We leave you with an infantile notion of God, and even if you come to synagogue, we keep treating you like infants. I'm sorry about that.

"When you were little your notion of God was probably something like a king sitting way up there on a throne. Robes and a long grey beard. If you have a weakness, it is difficult to go to a king. Kings don't like subjects who have weaknesses. They are likely to say, 'Off with its head!' So you don't ask for help from a king.

"And then, perhaps, your idea of God advanced to that of a

parent. No longer 'Our King' but 'Our Father, our King.' But it is difficult to go a parent with your weaknesses. The parent might say, 'No child of mine comes home with a bad report card! No child of mine is an alcoholic or an addict!' And the fear is that the parent will withhold love.

"So if your model of God is that of king or parent, it is difficult to approach God with a weakness and ask for help. But these are both childish notions of God. A more adult notion is that of partner.

"If you want to establish a partnership, you have to make full disclosure. Your prospective partner asks up front, 'What are your weaknesses?' There have to be some. Otherwise why would you need a partner? So you can go to a partner with weaknesses. And if the partner has something to compensate for your weakness, it's always available to you.

"Let's say you go to a prospective partner and say, 'I'm a great salesman. What I need is a great product.' The prospective partner comes back and says, 'I've got a great product. What I need is a great salesman.' You're in business.

"Now you go out into the marketplace, and a customer wants a thousand yellow widgets. You don't have any. So you call back to the main office and ask your partner for a thousand yellow widgets. If he has them in inventory, they're yours. Why would he keep them back? On the other hand, if he has to shut down the entire factory and retool to produce yellow instead of green, your order is not going to be filled.

"So, if you have an image of God as partner instead of king or parent, you can ask such a God for help. And if God has in inventory what you need, why should God keep it back? You've got it. Just don't expect God to shut down the entire world to fill your order."

Dr. A. is wrestling now with this new notion of God as partner. He is feeling a ray of hope. There is some potential for him in this model. But I have only thirteen minutes left, and he'll have to do his serious wrestling after I'm gone.

"Now, what is there in a universe made of space and time that can meet the needs of a Creator that is beyond space and time?" Has the subliminal process worked? Has he arrived at an answer?

He has already dismissed the desk and the fan. God does not

need a place to put papers. God does not need a breeze in hot weather. And he dismisses the light. Quantum physicist that he is, even the light is material. And God would need nothing material. Indeed, nothing that consists of space and time could fulfill the needs of a Creator beyond space and time.

But there is within the universe something beyond space and time, something which cannot be quantified. I poke him in the knee.

"This is your body. It is material and measurable. But your life, that's something beyond your body. Your personality, intellect, soul—whatever you want to call it.

"This whole universe is a cosmic soup that is constantly stirred and allows for the evolution of ever higher organisms that can absorb more and more life stuff—soul if you like. And this soul, which is not measurable in terms of space and time, grows or is refined by your life process. When you are born, you take on a given amount of it, and as you live you do something to it, and when you die, it is released from you.

"You might think of it this way: When you are born, you soak up some God stuff. As you live, you refine it. When you die, it is returned to God. And hopefully God is better off for it.

"You are a God refining factory."

Now there are some gross inaccuracies in the above argument. If God is beyond space and time, why does God have to wait for us to die to benefit from our life process, a process which is a function of time? God was, is, and will be all at once. But the mind aches when it wrestles with such extra-temporal problems. When one is racing through the entire framework of kabbalistic theology in half an hour, some of these difficulties are overlooked. Dr. A. will have to wrestle with them later.

"So there is a working partnership. God is beyond space and time. Soul processing is done within space and time. God creates a universe that evolves beings which are conscious of themselves and have the potential of becoming conscious of their relationship with God. Such beings can act on their souls and refine them. God is better off for the process.

"You are God's limited partner. And even a limited partner can ask the general partner for assistance when it is required. If the assistance is available, why should the general partner withhold it?"

Dr. A's hopes for spiritual recovery have soared enormously. However there is still a significant hurdle for him to overcome, and we have only nine minutes left.

How does the system work? How are our requests heard by God, and how does God respond? If Dr. A. were religious, he might have asked, "How does prayer work?" But Dr. A. is not religious, yet. He is a scientist. And science and religion, for another few minutes anyway, remain separate for him.

"How does it work?" he asks.

Does he really need to know how it works? Does he need to know how a television works before he will turn it on? And if he turns it on, and it does work, can he explain to me exactly how it does what it does?

Concerning the television, he has a model in mind that allows it to work. He cannot explain it fully, but he has enough faith in the system to push the buttons and enjoy the benefits. From me now, concerning prayer, all he needs is the model, enough so he can have faith in it and push the buttons and enjoy the benefits.

I lift a book from the desk and throw it into the air. The book falls back into my hand. "How does that work?" I ask in return.

"It's the law of gravity," he responds.

Ah, the law of gravity. It's so nice to have names to put on things. When we label something, in this instance the law of gravity, we think, because we can name it, we know what it is. We can indeed describe what happens. But in truth, we still don't know why it does what it does. Gravity, for all we use it and all we know about it, continues to be a mystery, as are all of the laws of nature. All of them mysteries. We call them laws because they are constant, they never change, not because we understand them.

"The laws of nature," I inform Dr. A., "are constant because the Creator never interrupts the transmission. If the transmission of the laws of nature should cease even for a moment, the universe would blink out of existence.

"Think of it as a radio transmitter that never stops broadcasting. When the broadcast started, the universe came into being. The universe is utterly dependent upon the continuation of that transmitter.

"Everything, everything material in the universe is a receiver of that transmitter. The book is a receiver, the desk is a receiver, and you are a receiver."

Dr. A. looks at the book, at the desk, at himself, all three receivers of natural law.

"The broadcast is constant and unchangeable. If it changed, then the laws of nature would change.

"What is being broadcast? Gravity is being broadcast. Thermodynamics is being broadcast. According to tradition, the laws of the Bible are being broadcast. All at once, all at the same time.

"Some of this law is very strong. You can't keep it out even for a moment. Like gravity. Some of the law isn't so strong. By exercise of your free will, you can keep it out. Like healing.

"Healing is a law. It reads like this: Whatever can regenerate will regenerate. Whatever can be healed will be healed.

"Do you see this cut on my finger?" I almost always have a cut on one of my fingers, usually from slicing a bagel. "This cut is healing. I don't know how it does that. You're a doctor. You don't know how it does that. You can describe it. You can advise me what to do to facilitate healing. But we both know, that as long as I don't let something get in the way, this finger will heal."

What has Dr. A been thinking these last few years as he has wrestled with his addiction? "Physician, heal thyself!" And what has he been feeling? Guilt or incompetence, because no matter how fine a physician he is, he has been unable to heal himself. But I have just told him he can't heal anyone. He can serve as a catalyst in the process; he can remove impediments to healing. But ultimately it is not he who does it, and he doesn't argue the point.

"The laws of healing are part of that transmission," I continue. "But if I should want to, I could keep them out. I could interfere with them.

"There are different kinds of healing. You have an appetite over which you have no control. The appetite might be for alcohol or cocaine or prescription drugs or too much food. You will always have that appetite. There is no way of getting rid of it. It is like a scratch inside you, and as long as the edges of that scratch gnaw away at your insides, there is no way that you can function well in this world. You can't be a good partner.

"So what do you do? You ask the general partner for help. You ask like this: I have this scratch inside me. It's gnawing away at my guts and I can't do anything about it. If you have something available in inventory that can help me, please send it now. I can't fulfill my end of the partnership very well without it.

"If the general partner has it, you're going to get it. It doesn't make any sense to withhold it. And you know that the general partner has it. You know that for a scientific fact. And you know that it is available. Otherwise you wouldn't be in this program. You know that people come into this program and leave in recovery. You know that the process of recovery is spiritual in nature. You know that it works. Before you ever came here, you checked this program out against other programs and chose this one because it had the highest success rate. Am I right?"

I am right. Dr. A. is a scientist to the end.

"The problem is that you don't have a model that will allow it to work, but we're almost there. There is a healing that can fill in that scratch if you let it."

I receive no compensation for the counseling I do at the addiction treatment center. I wouldn't think of negotiating a contract, because in the end I would have to pay them more than I could afford for the privilege!

Where else could I possibly find such attentive students? Dr. A. is absorbing every word. His mind is racing ahead, anticipating where I am going. From time to time he might argue, but his arguments will be right to the point and razor sharp.

I used to teach the same materials to a confirmation class. In ten weeks I could not teach a group of teenagers as much as Dr. A. will acquire in half an hour. High-school students were under the illusion that what they were learning in their secular programs—geometry, biology, Spanish III—was more important than what we had to teach in a religious curriculum. "What you are learning in high school is nice to know," I would tell them. "Most of you will learn it now and never use it again. What I have to share with you is need to know. Someday your life may depend on it." They didn't believe me, of course. I have since seen several of them in treatment.

Could I have done a more effective job of teaching them when they were teenagers? Teenagers do not readily accept the notion that they will ever die.

Dr. A. is not a teenager, and he knows very well that he can die. That's what makes him such a good student.

I recall once hearing words very similar to those I would use with the confirmation class. "Some of the information I am going to give you is nice to know," the instructor said. "Some of it is need to know. If you forget what is nice to know, no harm will come of it. If you forget what is need to know, you will die." I believed him, and I learned what I needed to know. That was in a U.S. Navy school shortly before I shipped out to Vietnam.

Dr. A. is waiting.

"Imagine for a moment a cut crystal glass, but let all the cuts be on the inside. What would that glass look like if you held it up to the light? You could see all the cuts, sharp and sparkling. But what if you filled the glass with water? The cuts would disappear. Light would pass through the glass and the water together, and you wouldn't be able to see the cuts at all.

"You are like that glass. You are cut on the inside. What you are asking for from God is not to remove the cuts. To do that, God would have to change the laws of nature, destroy the entire world. What is done is done. What you are asking for is that the glass be filled in, that whatever healing there is flow into you like water and fill in the cracks. And that healing is always available to you. It is pouring down on you like a deluge. But up to now you've kept your lid on, and the lid keeps the healing out.

"The lid is—'I ought to be able to do this myself.' As long as you think you can do it yourself, you refuse help. If you remove the lid, admit that you are powerless and cannot heal yourself, then the healing flows in and makes you whole. You and your partner together can control the appetite.

"You know, you have such chutzpah, such gall to think you can heal this yourself. You can't even heal a cut on your finger yourself. That's managed for you. And that's a trivial wound compared to this cut you have on the inside."

The half hour is gone. I hope to have another half hour with him in the next week. My hope is that he will have wrestled with the model, altered it, adapted it to meet his needs so that, when I am with him again, he will be ever so excited to show me where I am wrong.

Shoni Labowitz

Beyond Words, Beyond Life

When my mother of blessed memory was dying, Reb Zalman called from Philadelphia. He asked me to put the receiver of the phone on top of my head and he blessed me with the strength to let my mother go, to give her permission to die. Then he instructed me to look up the *ana b'koach* prayer in the Siddur and recite it as a mantra. I did as he instructed, only partially understanding the manifold meaning of what was happening. My soul understood. My heart was grieving and my mind was torn between what I knew and what I felt.

Five years later, as Chaplain for Hospice, I fully appreciated the blessing and instruction of Reb Zalman. I understood the concept and need for "letting go," moving into emptiness, and the power of praying with and for others. The following are a few stories of actual patient experiences that will illustrate this. One is a story that validates the power of the spoken word beyond cultural religious boundaries. Another story is of a disillusioned believer whose need for prayer shattered self-inflicted rage. The third story is of a young girl who faced her own mortality, and as a result of our having prayed together for just a few moments, she returned home to God, and I returned to my physical home more blessed than before.

Story One

Rose, a supervisor in a nursing home, thought it could never happen to her. It did. The first time I walked into her trailer I knew this was a special place. She was a very beautiful, tactile woman. I hopped up on her bed, made myself perfectly comfortable and

19

started massaging her feet while her loving husband ever so gently stroked her back. She was the kind of person who welcomed the warmth in others, and it was not too difficult to make Rose feel good. She was open and curious and wanted to know life's experiences. The conversation was very light and at times humorous. Rose was open and could "hang loose" about death. Her husband would listen and speak little for he was having a difficult time coping with Rose's impending demise.

The call came early one morning: Rose was in a coma, death was imminent and Joe paged me. I dressed quickly, hurried from my home, hair still shower-wet, started the car, plugged in the audio siddur and prayed for the wisdom to BE present. This was the first time I had ever been with someone dying, my first exposure to imminent expiration. I had only just begun working for Hospice. The only other death I was close to was my Mother's, yet I was not there at the time of her expiration. I had borrowed her car and the tire blew out at the moment my Mother died, preventing me from returning home on time. I asked my Mother's spirit to be with me and guide me now.

The trailer door was open and only faint whispers were heard. Joe and a neighbor were in the kitchen. It felt like I was walking into a sanctuary of God, somewhere between here and there. In the center of the sacred space was Rose's bed, the altar. The ethereal air was intoxicating. I approached Rose, her eyes closed, skin porcelain, barely breathing. She had been comatose for several days. We held hands with each other and with Rose and prayed from our hearts. Joe was broken, caught between not wanting to lose her and not wanting her to suffer.

My belief since that day (verified by the hundreds of people I've been with) is that, at time of death, we do not breathe our last breath until we've completed the mission for which we entered life. It need not be a monumental mission; most of the time it is so subtle and humble that only participating family members are aware of it. Rose had not yet completed that final mission. Rose had been the dominant caretaker of their relationship, and perhaps her final mission was to give Joe the reigns and his mission was to let her know he could handle it on his own. Up until that moment he was telling her how much he loved and needed her. Understanding the power of words and believing she could still hear him, he mustered up the courage to speak to her in a manner that would give her permission to let go.

I left him in the privacy of his beloved. He gave her permission and encouragement and reassured her he would be all right. What happened next, as Joe described it, was unforgettably beautiful. As he uttered the last words, Rose opened her eyes for the first time in three days, looked at him, squeezed his hand and died.

Rose and Joe were Catholic. Yet her soul was transforming, and religion and prayer knew no boundary. I called their priest. He arrived as Rose's body was being removed. I asked if there were any prayers that could be said at that moment. He had none, I had none, so we created ritual on the spot. As the stretcher wheeled her body past Joe and loved ones who had gathered, we blessed her soul, her journey. As the door closed, we encircled Joe and each person present gave him blessings, tears, and presence. It was a spontaneous rite for transition. One neighbor broke into song, another chanted, we all prayed, parish priest and rabbi friend—hand in hand, heart to heart, soul to soul to the God of all forms.

Story Two

The last time I visited, Mollie was caught in that delicate balance between life and death, and Al could no longer bear the suffering. I assured him that although one may be unconscious, one's soul still hears.

It was difficult for him to let her go, and he told the story of when his brother's life was in danger in the War. He recalled his brother belting out the Shema prayer at the top of his lungs on top a mountain. His brother was saved.

At moments of extreme emotion the mind releases its hold on the soul, and an awareness deeper than the rational mind takes over. This is what happened when Al handed me a Bible and asked if I would read from it for Mollie's sake. *V'talmud tora k'neged kulam.*

We went into the bedroom, combed Mollie's hair, propped up her unconscious body, freshened her gown and I read. The book opened to the portion where God was handing out the manna from heaven, directing Moses to tell the people not to take too much or too little. They were to take just what was needed at the present time. Turning to Al, I asked rhetorically, "Isn't that the lesson of life? We never know when it's too long or too short, too much or too little. The blessing is to accept it is just enough." He understood.

As Al was talking to Mollie on one side of the bed, I was praying on the other side. His heart, body, and soul cried out the silent scream and released her from the role of valiant soldier. Through tear-stained eyes we looked at each other, paused a moment and in synchronicity sang out the Shema Yisroel with full faith in the unknown known. That night Mollie died in peace.

As I became seasoned in death and dying, I learned to listen more than speak, to "be" more than "become," to let go of my self. It was Mollie's husband who helped teach me. He was very angry at God and would ask all those questions "why" that I could not answer. Mollie and Al were nearing their fiftieth year together— just the two of them, no children. It was a good, sweet life until Mollie's cancer of the nervous system. It took a while for us to bond; we were both treading in unfamiliar territory. I just wanted to be Al's friend and he needed one. There was no pushing religion, theology, or even an attempt to answer his questions. I heard with his ears, struggled with his struggle, and understood his wavering beliefs.

With Al's unrelenting support, Mollie fought until the end to survive this dreadful disease. Mollie rarely spoke, was seldom awake and mostly in pain. Whenever I entered her bedroom, it was for only a moment or two; she could handle no longer. There were times when Al would be preoccupied and she would point to her reform prayerbook and ask me to read. The page would open to a place chosen by God and I would recite the appropriate prayers.

Mostly I would sit in the living room overlooking the Atlantic Ocean and talk with Al. He was angry (especially at God), in denial and just wanted his Mollie back. His inner rage was a silent scream.

Mollie began deteriorating rapidly. On my frequent visits I would bring Al the "Jewish foods" he liked. He was so touched, he would cry. No one had ever brought him gifts other than his Mollie.

Story Three

The final story I will share with you is the shortest in physical form, the longest in spirit. It is about Laura. Laura was only twenty-three years in life and had a rare disease with which most people live for only ten to fifteen years. As death pursued Laura, Laura pursued life, with death as a familiar companion. She became a nurse, married, and lived to the fullest of her abilities. She far surpassed others who travel life only to stay seated in life's hallway, never to open the doors to broader awareness. Laura was a door opener, a pioneer traveler. I knew Laura well and yet only spent forty minutes with her on her dying day. Did we pray together? Very much. Every word was a prayer. Every word was God's name. Nothing was wasted. Nothing went unrevealed. What happened in those forty minutes? I could not tell you. I do not know in the sense one usually knows things. There was only an exchange of energy, instant recognition, and deep honoring. I left. Laura died. We were both blessed in the moment that is eternity. Would you believe it if I told you that Laura's spirit guides me in praying for others?

Death, after-death, before-life, life, after-life. It is all one.

Zev-Hayyim Feyer

Redeeming the Holocaust: A Returnee's View

An eye-opening article that interprets the Jewish doctrine of reincarnation as applied to the Holocaust—and sees that both the victims and the victimizers choose their roles. The author calls on us to forgive and move on.

A student once asked Rabbi Dov Baer, the Maggid of Mezeritz, how it was that an omnipotent and benevolent God permitted evil to exist in the world.

"I am not the one to answer that question," replied the Maggid. "Why don't you ask my student Zusya? I am sure that he will be able to explain it to you."

The student went to the House of Study and encountered Zusya, later to be known as Rabbi Zusya of Hanipol. "Reb Zusya," he said, "our teacher and master, the holy Maggid, said that you would be able to answer a question for me."

"What is your question, my brother?" replied Zusya.

"How is it," the student asked, "that Hashem, Who is all-good and all-powerful, permits evil to exist in the world?"

"Evil?" asked Zusya. "I don't understand what you mean. What evil are you talking about?"

"What evil!" exclaimed the student. "How can you, of all people, doubt the existence of evil? Your wife—may God forgive me for saying it—has the sharpest tongue this side of the grave. You have lived in such poverty all your life that you've never known how God was going to supply your next meal. Your children are well known to give you nothing but trouble. And that

25

skin disease of yours is so painful for us who need only look at it; it must be sheer agony for you to have to endure it day after day!"

"Is that what you mean?" replied Zusya. "Clearly, since that is what Hashem has granted me in this life, it is undoubtedly just what my soul needs for its growth. As our sages have said, 'A red halter is fitting for a white horse.'"

Zusya was a *tzaddik*, a saint we would call him in English. Whatever God sent his way, Zusya rejoiced in the knowledge that it was from God. Most of us are not so conscious as was Zusya. We are not so tuned in to God's presence, the *Shekhinah*, within us as was Zusya. Nevertheless, the Zusya attitude is what will enable us to accept and deal with the painful events that pass our way in life.

But the Holocaust?! The Holocaust seems to constitute evil and pain beyond even Zusya's saintliness. And yet, does it? Or is it possible that the world's soul needed so great a trauma that God had no other option than to present it to us?

There is a theory—advanced by the kabbalistic tradition—that the soul, far from perishing at the termination of bodily life, not only lives on, but is, in fact, recycled, returned, reincarnated so that it may continue to work toward its own perfection. One may even go so far as to say that it is the ultimate destiny of all souls to be reunited with their Creator, however many lifetimes of work it may require.

Operating from this theory, let us examine what is undoubtedly the greatest trauma which we as Jews and we as human beings have suffered in all our history.

The Holocaust did not spring into existence from nothing. It was not born full-grown like Hera from the forehead of Zeus; it developed over many centuries, and this development was observed from Heaven. God having granted humanity free will, the mentality which made the Holocaust possible, could not be stopped by divine intervention. Only great changes in human nature could block the headlong slide.

Under the circumstances, souls preparing for their return in the nineteenth and early-twentieth centuries were told of the situation and given a choice. Four roles would be necessary, unless human attitudes could be radically changed:

- Some would have to sacrifice themselves, be the victims of the Holocaust.
- Some would have to stand apart and far off while it happened.
- Some would have to survive and bear the pain.
- Some would have to take on the most difficult task of all and be the sacrificers.

Each of the four tasks was assigned. Fourteen million souls accepted the roles of victims, and millions of others took each of the other roles. Today, when most of the survivors are gone and when many of the victims have returned and reached adulthood once again, we have a new task, and it is to this task that we must speak.

Those of us who are aware that we are among the returnees, the recycled ones—those of us who perished in the Holocaust and have returned—are realizing that our job was not completed with our sacrifice; we must now perform the follow-up work. It is forty years and more since the Holocaust, and, just as the people of Israel spent forty years in the wilderness completing the Exodus from Mitzrayim, so have we now spent forty years in the wilderness struggling to come to terms with our trauma.

The survivors have been unable to come to terms with it; there is too much guilt in having survived. Why was *I* spared when so many others perished? Could I have saved my friend, my cousin, my parent, my child? Did I do enough to try to save them?

The children of the victims have been unable to come to terms with it; there is too much anger, too much pain. Why were *my* parents murdered? Why was *I* left alone? Why did they do this to *me*? Can we ever again trust anyone but ourselves?

Only one group can come to terms with the trauma; only one group can help the others to come to terms with it—the victims themselves, the victims ourselves—and it is for this purpose that we have returned. We have returned in order to see the Holocaust in a new light and in order to help others see it in that same new light. "Never again!" is the cry of so many, and it is our task to change humanity so that another Holocaust will not be needed.

What was the meaning of the Holocaust? What produced the Holocaust? What caused the Holocaust? The Talmud teaches us that the Holy Temple in Jerusalem was destroyed because of causeless hatred and that it will only be rebuilt through causeless love. The Holocaust, too, was a result of causeless hatred, and it can be redeemed only through causeless love.

In the Torah we read of the expulsion of Hagar and Ishmael from Abraham's camp (Bereshit 21). In all the events leading up to that expulsion—which, except for God's promise to Abraham that "the son of the bondwoman" would become a great nation, would have been, effectively, the murder of Hagar and Ishmael—Ishmael is never mentioned by name. He is "the lad" or "the son of the bondwoman," but never is he named. Indeed, although Hagar and Ishmael are Abraham's wife and son—for Sarah, despairing of ever having a child of her own, had given Hagar, her bondwoman, to Abraham as a *second wife* (Bereshit 16:3)—they are not called by those titles either. The first step in preparing for the murder of Hagar and Ishmael is to dehumanize them by denying their names and their positions. As they are reduced to classes rather than individuals, they become less human and easier to kill.

The great crime of the Holocaust was not the killing of fourteen million human beings, horrific though that mass murder was. Indeed, the murders were but the natural outcome of what came before. Nazism's great crime was not the murders but the separation. When people are separated into groups—us and them, fully human and less than human, good and bad, master and slave—it becomes easy for the dominant group to destroy the dominated group. After all, it is not as if it were the murder of human beings; it is just the elimination of an underclass.

When the Nazi ideology declared that Jews, Gypsies, Slavs, homosexuals, and others were less than fully human, and when the people under the Nazi's rule came to believe the great lie, it became easy to turn from separation to killing. And every time we make separations between and among peoples, we grant the Nazi ideology another victory!

When we view the Holocaust as solely a Jewish tragedy, we allow Nazism to win, for we thereby declare that the killings of the Gypsies, the Slavs, the homosexuals, and others are not worthy of our remembrance. When we say, "Let them remember their own, as we remember our own," then we act exactly as Nazism would have us act, for we then separate humanity into two classes: those whose tragedies we remember and those whose tragedies we forget.

When we blame "the Goyim" or even "the Germans" for the tragedy of the Holocaust, when we refuse to buy German products as a way of "punishing" the perpetrators of the Holocaust, we act in accordance with Nazi ideology. "Do not perceive those others as individuals," Nazism declared. "Put them into groups, put them into categories, deal with them as monolithic entities. After all, they are not really fully human. They are only 'the lad' and 'the son of the bondwoman.'"

In the first chapter of Bereshit we are told that God says, at the conclusion of each "day" of Creation, "It is good." There are two exceptions—the second "day," which does not receive the designation "good," and the sixth "day," which is called "very good." Why are these "days" different from the other "days"?

The second "day" is not called "good" because it is a day of separating, not a day of creating. On the second "day," the waters above the firmament were separated from the waters below the firmament, and this separation of waters from waters, even though it was ordained by God and even though it was necessary to the creative process, is sufficient to cause the designation "good" to be withheld from the second "day." How much more so, then, all our petty human separations!

At the end of the sixth "day," God looks at everything in Creation and finds it all to be "very good." It is only when God looks at all Creation in unity, Creation taken as a whole and with no separateness, that God says, "Very good."

If the Holocaust is to be redeemed—and it must be redeemed or it will recur with ever greater and greater intensity—we must transcend our separations. We must get over our feeling that all the world is against us. We must cease acting the role of Ishmael—"everyone's hand against us and our hand against everyone." We must learn that all human beings—*whoever they may be and whatever they may do*—are God's children, created in the image and after the Likeness of our Divine Parent, and therefore, are our brothers and sisters!

Perhaps the most difficult part of all this will be dealing with the memory of those who administered the Holocaust. How can we forgive those who actually took part? How can we deal with the Eichmanns, the Demjanjuks, and all the others?

A tale is told of two Buddhist monks. The order to which they belonged had a very strict rule which forbade a monk's touching a woman. As the two monks were walking through a forest, they came to a stream. Beside the stream was a woman, and she said to them, "O most holy monks, please hear my plea. I must return to my child, who is in our cabin some distance on the other side of this stream. I had come across the stream to gather some food, but the stream has now swollen, and I am not strong enough to get back across and bring food to my child. Can you help me?"

Upon hearing the woman's plea, one of the monks picked her up in his powerful arms, carried her across the stream, and set her down. Thanking him profusely, the woman went on her way, and the monks, too, continued on their way. After a while, the second monk said to the first, "My brother, you know as well as I do that the rule of our order forbids us to touch a woman. Why, then, did you carry that woman across the stream?"

"My brother," replied the first monk, "I picked her up, carried her across the stream, and put her down. Why are you still carrying her?"

Those of us who have returned are ready to lay the burden down. Those who survived must learn to do so as well, and so must the later generations. We cannot continue to carry the Holocaust with us, to cradle it in our arms as would an overly possessive parent, for doing so is the surest path to a new and still vaster Holocaust. But how do we recover from the pain, from the injury, from the trauma and anguish?

It has been suggested that the Holocaust may have been a *Korban*, an offering. Indeed, the very word by which we designate it—Holocaust—referred originally to the sacrifice which was wholly consumed on the Altar of the Holy Temple, the offering which was given wholly to God. It may very well be that it is precisely by perceiving the Holocaust as a *Korban*, that we will be able to deal with it and redeem it.

If the Holocaust was an offering, if it was a sacrifice to God, then all those who participated—the perpetrators as well as the victims—were carrying out their roles, their tasks, knowingly or not, for *Kiddush Hashem*, for the sanctification of the Divine

Name. The perpetrators were victims—of their own inhumanity, if one is unready to consider the cosmic interpretation—as much as were those who were murdered.

The time has come for us to cease being territorial about the Holocaust—"It's our tragedy, and no one else can share it"—and to begin to recognize that it was not exclusively our tragedy. Six million Jews were murdered, it is true. It is equally true that millions of Gypsies, Slavs, homosexuals, and other despised minorities were murdered. They perished with us in the death camps, and it is long since time for them to share our memories.

The tragedy of the Holocaust was as real for the other victims as it was for us, and, what is more, it was as real a tragedy for its perpetrators as for its victims. If one believes in *gilgul* (the kabbalistic term for reincarnation) in the traditional manner, then the perpetrators of the Holocaust must surely reap the consequences of their actions. They must pay in future lives for their actions in the Holocaust.

If one believes in a divine tribunal and an afterlife of reward and punishment, then those who carried out the Holocaust must, even more certainly, reap their punishment. Their tragedy is, then, the pain which they must suffer in the world to come, and that pain is far greater than the pain of their victims.

Finally, if one believes in a type of *gilgul* which sees each soul as growing in successive lives to become able eventually to be reunited with the Creator, then the suffering of the perpetrators of the Holocaust is their knowledge and their memory of the task they had to perform in the cosmic scheme of things.

The kabbalistic tradition speaks of the ten *sefirot*, the ten essences through which God performs the Creation. The tradition speaks of each *sefirah* as being contained within each of the others. We may extend this concept to understand that every human being is contained or reflected in every other human being. If there were those who perpetrated such a crime as the Holocaust, then that is a clear message from the *M'rachemet shel Olam* (the Merciful One of the World) to each one of us that we, personally, have not done enough.

When we transcend our possessiveness about the causeless hatred that resulted in the Holocaust, when we recognize that we and all humanity are one and that injury to any human being constitutes injury to all human beings, then, through causeless love, will we finally redeem the Holocaust. In so doing, we will erect a new Temple, one in which we can present offerings of our selves rather than sacrifices of blood.

Joel Ziff

Partzufim Faces of Light: On the Evolving Relationship with God A Process of Spiritual and Psychological Development

There is life after the impasse.
In the moment of darkness,
a craving for light
which inevitably and
inexorably
illumines that darkness,
a multi-faceted rainbow of light
 with many faces,
 faces with names,
 and faces yet to have names.

I speak of you, with words of praise,
 I honor your name with songs of love.

I speak of your glory, and I do not see you,
 I describe visions of you, and I know you not.

Through hands of your prophets, the mysteries of your servants,
 You have revealed images of your honor and glory.

Your power and your greatness,
 They described what is manifest in your acts.

They described images of you, but not your Essence,
 They found likeness of you in your works.

They imaged you in many visions,
    But you are one beneath all the images.

They saw you as old and as young,
    Your hair as grey with age, and black with youth.

Aged on the day of judgement,
    Youth in battle, like a warrior, fighting hand-to-hand.

Dew of Light upon your head,
    Your locks of hair, Darkness like the night.

I glorify you, you want me,
    You are for me a crown of beauty.

Your head, like pure fine gold,
    Upon your forehead inscribed your Holy Name.

Your glory shines upon me, and my glory upon you,
    You are close to me when I call you.

May my meditation be pleasing to you,
    For my soul longs for you.

Anim Zemirot
Shabbat morning liturgy

One must, however, take care not to understand this conversation with God . . . as something happening solely alongside or above the everyday. God's speech penetrates what happens in the life of each one of us, and all that happens in the world around us, biographical and historical, and makes it for you and me into instruction, message, demand. Happening upon happening, situation upon situation, are enabled and empowered by the personal speech of God to demand of the human person that he take his stand and make his decision. Often enough we think there is nothing to hear, but long before we have ourselves put wax in our ears.

The existence of mutuality between God and man cannot be

proved, just as God's existence cannot be proved. Yet he who dares
to speak of it, bears witness, and calls to witness him to whom he
speaks—whether that witness is now or in the future.—Martin
Buber[1]

━━━━━━━━

Sarah sits in the middle of the room, crouched over, with her
hands covering her head. Several times she repeats the words, "I
can't do it," each time with more feeling in her voice. Sarah is a
participant in a workshop integrating psychotherapeutic process
and spirituality. In the corner of the room, another workshop
participant stands on a chair, looking towards Sarah and saying
softly, "I'm here for you." He takes the role of God in this psycho-
drama, helping Sarah to externalize the experience of spiritual
dialogue. The rest of us in the group are touched by the power of
the drama, by the depth of feeling Sarah has taken the risk to
show us, by the paradox of a God who whispers, "I'm here" while
standing removed and far away. When did Sarah first conceive of
God in this way? Was the source in a child's reading of the Bible?
In the image of her rabbi exhorting his congregants? In a limited
capacity for warmth on the part of her parents?

Whatever the reason, she need not be limited by this face of
God. God is simply the word we use to inadequately describe that
presence in the universe which is all knowing, all seeing, all
powerful, and all merciful. God manifests in infinite forms.

Group members offer Sarah other possibilities, sharing their
perspectives with examples of God's response: a confrontational
God, saying "Wipe your tears! Get up! Go on with your life!"; a
God of reason saying, "What happened? Tell me how you feel";
and a variety of comforting images of God. Sarah feels most
attracted to the image of a God who embraces the scared little girl.

The person enacting God steps down off the chair, comes close
to Sarah as she sits on the floor, embraces her, and says "I'm here
for you!" Despite the artificiality of a staged exercise and the
awkwardness of the presence of a group of what once were

---

1. Martin Buber, *I and Thou* (New York: Charles Scribner's Sons, 1958),
136–137.

strangers, the little scared girl inside Sarah is moved. She begins to cry, tears of relief replacing the frozen withdrawal of fear.

Sarah's experience provides a graphic example of the potential for integrating spiritual and psychological development. Utilizing psychotherapy can make the spiritual realm accessible and connected to our lives while drawing upon the wealth of the spiritual tradition to empower the psychotherapeutic process. As we experience the archetypal and mythic level through ritual and through biblical images, we have an opportunity to reflect upon the personal meaning and connections. The purpose of this article is to examine the notion of a relationship with God through a psychological lens, using developmental theory as a tool for clarifying the various possibilities in that relationship. The psychological framework facilitates the integration of a relationship with God into the process of adult growth and development.

The Relationship with God: Problems and Possibilities

The presence of God is experienced in many ways, with many names. He is a God of many faces: the creator, the source of all life; an inexorable force in history who decrees that the children of Abraham shall be slaves in Egypt; the compassionate redeemer who hears the cries of the Israelites and performs miracles to free them from their servitude; the nurturing parent who sustains them with the Mannah in the desert; the firm parent who makes demands and expects compliance; the source of mercy who forgives lapses; the leader of a people who carry out the divine plan on earth.

The relationship with God and the dialogue of that relationship takes many forms: at a moment of connectedness with others, we may experience the oneness of life; atop a mountain, there may be a sense of awe for the infinity of creation; in vulnerability and neediness, a reaching out for help from a divine Parent; in anger and frustration, a struggle for power and control, or perhaps surrender to a force that overwhelms; in the search for direction, an experience of guidance; in the moment of creation, an experience of love-making with Essence.

How do we access that relationship? We can look to a variety of sources: the stories of our tradition as recorded in the Torah; the ritual practices and customs that punctuate our activities and create islands in time for reflection and renewal; the natural world, the complex ecology of life in this universe; the divine spark which dwells within each person, a spark we experience at moments of connectedness with others and with ourselves.

The religious practices and texts serve as vehicles for transmitting the variety of possibilities for relationship that have been experienced through the course of history, each generation receiving from the past, each generation adding unique contributions for the future. It is not always easy to access those possibilities. This living relationship with the source of life is a fragile one. We can barely conceive of the idea of a personal relationship with a transcendant Essence which is infinite, unnameable, and beyond any conception. If it is difficult to imagine such a relationship, think how much more challenging it is to experience this relationship, to speak to a God who speaks to us.

The depths of meaning and possibility are buried within language, images, and stories that may be alien to us and our experience. The images appropriate to a patriarchal, tribal society in the desert may not speak to us. For example, the image of God as the protecting shadow may have powerful associations only for one who dwells in a desert. Some of the images are embedded with sexist and hierarchical notions that we find oppressive. To compound the problem, our notion of God is based upon our life experience as well. Those notions may be based upon negative experiences of formal, institutional religion, of parental and other authority figures, or of cultural norms and prejudices.

The framework designed to liberate possibilities instead provokes resistance. The disconnection with the notion of an I-Thou relationship with the Source of Life is so deep that we may no longer even experience the loss. At best, we conclude that God is dead; more likely, we simply stop considering the value of an alive spiritual relationship. Religious practice is abandoned or becomes a mechanical and unnecessary appendage to our lives, an appendage we neither reject nor embrace. We are left without even a language for describing the spiritual experience. Words like "God" feel awkward and distant from our reality.

That deficit has serious implications for adult development. In childhood, we are bonded to and depend upon our parents. They serve as mediators between ourselves and the world, as protectors, and as nourishers. That bonding is an essential part of development. As adults, we need to extend the possibilities for support, nurturance, and guidance beyond the boundaries of a single human being. We need to look to other sources: within ourselves, from others, and in the world. We need to bond to the force of life itself. The name we give to that force is "God."

Carl Jung expressed this notion in his concept of the collective unconscious:

> . . . the individual psyche is not just a product of personal experience. It also has a pre-personal or transpersonal dimension which is manifested in universal patterns and images such as are found in all the world's religions and mythologies.[2]

By recognizing the reality of the collective unconscious as a reservoir of truth, we learn to listen to its communication to us. In this way, we afford ourselves an optimal degree of life and development. The collective unconscious speaks to us through symbols, stories, and metaphors. That understanding is continually refined and clarified as we discover new potentials and recognize deficiencies in our understanding. From this perspective, the relationship with God is a therapeutic relationship, which provides a rich archetypal pool of images, stories, and liturgy that nourish our understanding.

That pool has been enriched through the generations. The Bible provides us with recorded fragments of our ancestors' relationship with God; fragments that allow us to know the possibilities of that relationship. The mystics built upon this framework, utilizing the various names of God and the *Sefirot* (ten aspects of divinity) to define the various archetypal energies. Each is a *Partzuf* (a face) of God. Each manifests itself in a unique way when it is needed. In Chasidism, the mystical tradition was extended, emphasizing

2. Edward Effinger, *Ego and Archetype* (New York: Penguin, 1972), 3.

the idea of a personal relationship with God, an ongoing dialogue. Martin Buber popularized the concept of dialogue and the I-Thou relationship. The task remains to extend the idea of dialogue with God from an interesting theory to a practical therapeutic process.

Developmental Psychology and Spiritual Development

As we explore our relationship with the Source of Life, the perspective of developmental psychology offers a useful framework for clarifying and extending the possibilities. The process of growing up involves a series of stages. During each stage, we struggle with particular issues and concerns. What we learn provides a foundation and a reference point to which we refer when we encounter similar concerns later on in our lives. We internalize this learning in the form of an ego structure that influences how we respond to others and how others respond to us. It also affects how we integrate the various parts of ourselves.

Emily Ruppert, basing her approach on object relations theory, describes five stepping stones in the developmental process, each characterized by a particular style of relationship:

You ARE Me (Symbiosis)

You KNOW Me/I KNOW You (Awareness of Self/Other)

You OR Me/Me OR You (Individuation)

You FOR Me/Me FOR You (Support)

You WITH Me/Me WITH You (Cooperation: Following/Leading)

You AND Me (Collaboration)

You ARE Me

During the first months of life, the relationship between mother and infant is one of symbiosis, a merged identity, a fused relationship. There is no difference between self and other: perceptions, feelings, and needs are identical and complementary.

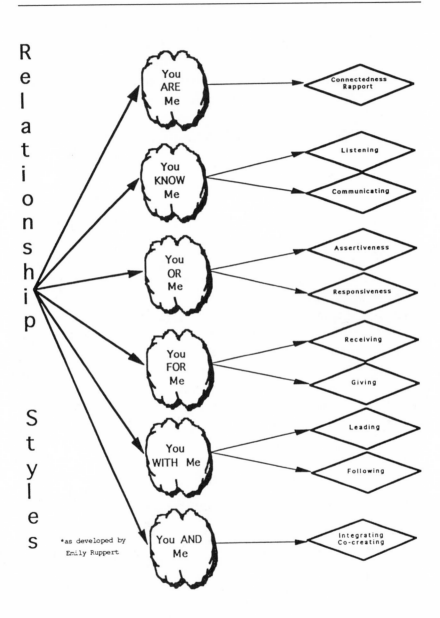

*as developed by
Emily Ruppert

The connection transcends language and understanding. It involves an intuitive experience of interdependency.

A strong symbiotic bond is essential for healthy development. The infant learns to trust the new world in which he/she lives. The safety and security of symbiosis provide a foundation which allows the infant to develop autonomy and independence. The experience of connectedness also establishes the basis for empathy with others; as we are accepted and responded to, we learn to accept and respond to others. The capacity to surrender to symbiosis is the archetype for later relationships, such as in the merger that occurs in an intimate sexual relationship, and the identification with the larger "we" of family, community, and planet.

An infant who does not receive the foundation needed— symbiotic bond—is likely to have severe problems. The child may never make contact with others, remaining autistic. Or, there may be a retreat from connection with the outside world in a psychotic reaction. If the symbiotic bond is somewhat impaired, if it is erratic or characterized by ambivalence (such as when an alcoholic parent is not dependable, or if a child was not really wanted), the child may grow into an adult who believes he/she has no right to exist or to have needs satisfied. In the same manner, the person may have an impaired capacity to perceive, acknowledge, and accept the basic needs of others and their connectedness to oneself.

As adults, recognition and acceptance are necessary when needs overwhelm us. If they are not supplied, we become depressed and withdrawn. Similarly, there are times when our acceptance and recognition of others' needs is vital. On the societal level, the problems of nuclear proliferation and hazardous wastes heighten awareness of the interdependence of all life.

There are times when we need to experience the oneness of all life, to experience a symbiotic connectedness in which separateness disappears. That experience reinforces a sense of trust in oneself, in others, and in our environment. It helps us to develop a perspective on the conflicts and difficulties which would otherwise overwhelm us. That perspective helps clarify our goals and ways to reach them.

That moment occurred before creation when there was only

the One. It occurred again when the Israelites stood at Sinai in the moment of revelation. It is to occur once more when the Messianic vision is fulfilled. The experience is replicated each week during the Sabbath and each year during the time of *Yom Kippur*.

The symbiotic bond, the experience of the connectedness of all life, is central to the mystical experience. It describes the moment in which a sense of separateness gives way to an identity composed of self and other and a feeling of having merged with the source of life. This experience of "at-one-ment" is associated with the name of God—*YHVH*—the unpronounceable name of God which is the root of the verb for being. This name, beyond conception and articulation, is pronounced simply as *HaShem* (The Name). This is the name which was spoken only on the day of "at-one-ment," *Yom Kippur*, by the high priest in the Holy of Holies. It is also associated with the kabbalistic name of God, *Ayin* (No-Thingness) which is also known as *Keter* (the crown), or *Ayn Sof* (Without End).

The surrender of separateness—a deliberate, therapeutic regression—enables us to experience a connectedness beyond words which transforms and heals us. The ritual practices and the liturgy of prayer create an opportunity to experience this surrender and then return to our lives with renewed clarity and commitment.

You KNOW Me/I KNOW You   You OR Me/Me OR You

The experience of symbiosis is a temporary one. The infant begins to experience differences in needs. The infant's cries may be ignored by a tired parent instead of responded to by a concerned one. A desire to bite by an infant who now has teeth and greater strength may generate anger in a mother who previously enjoyed nursing. The infant begins to differentiate inside and outside, self and other.

The result is a struggle in which the differences are sometimes irreconcilable, and a win-lose conflict is created in which the needs of one person in the relationship are not satisfied. The infant learns both in winning and in losing. Winning reinforces the sense of trust in one's essential power, in our ability to make our needs known and to obtain positive responses from others. Winning also helps us to discover that our power is not so destructive that it will destroy our opponent. The other survives in spite of the loss. Losing provides reinforcement of the other polarity. We discover that we are not annihilated even when another's power overwhelms us. In both cases, the struggle helps us learn more about ourselves, others, and our environment. "NO" lead to "know."

A successful experience of this struggle provides a foundation for those times throughout life in which there are differences between oneself and others. It is the source of knowing that we are sometimes different in our perceptions, perspectives, and needs. It is the source of trust in our ability to engage in struggle when that is necessary, of our ability to succeed in that struggle without obliterating the other, and the ability to fail without being obliterated.

There are a variety of difficulties that can occur at this stage of development. Sometimes the parent may deny his/her own needs. In this case, the infant never discovers that he/she is different than the parent. The child grows into an adult who does not realize that his/her own perceptions of reality and needs may be different from those of another person. Sometimes, the parent may totally reject the child's attempts to assert her/himself, creating a framework for adult life in which self-assertion and self-differentiation are associated with undue anxiety. Sometimes, the parent may be so overwhelmed by the child's power that the child develops into an adult who has an unrealistic view of his/her own power. It could be viewed as destructive, able to obliterate the other, or as omnipotent, able to get all wants satisfied. As adults, there are times when we need to be able to acknowledge that we are different than another person, that our needs may be conflicting, that there is a struggle that is necessary, and that we and the other person can survive, regardless of who wins and who loses.

The concept of struggle permeates the biblical stories. Abraham surrenders to the demands of a God who asks him to leave his home and later, to sacrifice his son. He ultimately discovers that the sacrifice is not a sacrifice, but merely a stage in the journey which ends with the fulfillment of a promise. Abraham confronts God when he challenges the decision to destroy the cities of Sedom and Amorah. Jacob battles with the angel, a battle that ends in impasse, a battle in which Jacob receives the new name, *Yisrael*, wrestler with God. The Israelites struggle with the God of the desert. And there is struggle and conflict for Job, who loses all his material goods, his health, and family when God tests his faith.

The archetypal essence of this stage is embodied in the kabbalistic myth of creation. The spiritual Essence contracts to create a possibility for separateness instead of oneness. It is embodied in the *Sefirah* (the archetypal energy) of *Gevurah* (God's greatness), which is associated with the quality of Judgement. It is also connected to the idea of *Yirah* (Awe-full-ness). It is this quality to which we refer in the blessing made on hearing of a death, *Baruch Dayan Emet* (Blessed is the True Judge).

As adults, we turn to those archetypal images at times when we feel alienated, isolated, and alone. We draw from that well to nourish the understanding of separateness as a legitimate experience in life. We use the archetypal images to remind ourselves of the need, at times, for separateness, for differentiation of self from other. We are then able to trust the value of a win-lose struggle and trust that there is value whether we win or lose, both for ourselves and for others. The spiritual perspective supports us especially as we face the most difficult confrontation, dealing with issues of death and dying.

The validation of that struggle allows us to stay in relationship with the Essence of Life even as we experience distance, skepticism, separateness, and conflict in the realm of spirit. For the mystic, the divine presence is everywhere. In the words of the Psalms, "Your kingdom is the kingdom of all worlds." (145:13) Anger with God, distance from spirit is a legitimate experience. One who distances from God and returns has attained a higher level than one who remains totally pure and righteous.

You FOR Me/Me FOR You

Each style of relationship—symbiosis and separateness—reflects an aspect of the human condition, and each style is inadequate in and of itself. As we mature, we explore possibilities for relationship which incorporate both perspectives, recognizing our interdependence as well as our independence.

The child discovers possibilities for receiving support. Building upon the symbiotic bond, he/she accepts his/her dependency, looks to the parent for help, and develops trust that help will be provided. Building upon the acceptance of separateness, the child learns to clarify needs, to communicate effectively, to gain some flexibility concerning how and when needs are met, and to develop skill in acknowledging what has been received.

The child also learns to acknowledge the symbiotic bond, to respond to needs of others while retaining autonomy, and to give support in ways he/she can, setting boundaries as needed, and accepting the acknowledgements that are given in return.

There are times, as adults, when we cannot function autonomously and need support. There are times when others need our support as well. The learning in early childhood provides a foundation for later life at times when similar styles of relationship are needed. When this foundation is weak or inadequate, a person will experience difficulty as an adult in acknowledging and responding to dependency needs in oneself and in others.

This style of relationship is expressed in the concept of God as a parent. In the biblical drama, that notion is embodied in the God of the desert, the God who provides a pillar of smoke and a pillar of fire to lead the Israelites through the desert, who provides the Mannah which sustains them, who promises and threatens, who encourages and sets limits, who makes demands, who expects standards to be followed, who wants to be praised in return for acts of loving kindness.

We turn to the archetypal image of God as parent at times when we need support. We can select from the wealth of images in the tradition to clarify the specific quality of parenting that we need at particular times: nurturance, limit setting, challenging, etc. We can also draw from the archetype to clarify the quality of parenting we are called on to provide, allowing ourselves to be a vessel for the expression of the divine parent on earth.

You WITH Me/Me WITH You

The tension between the symbiotic bond and the struggle for separation is further resolved in the discovery of possibilities for cooperation. As the child matures, she/he learns to relate to others not only from a position of dependency, but from a cooperative position as well. In a cooperative relationship, one person takes the role of leader, defining the content and the context, while the other person follows. Although there is a hierarchy in terms of power, both people are equal participants. The symbiotic identity is expressed in the mutual acceptance of their different roles.

The child needs to develop skills in both roles, learning to follow and to lead. As leader, the task is to define, direct, encourage, and supervise while staying responsive to feedback, suggestions, and constructive criticism. As follower, the task is to be responsive to the guidance from one's partner while providing needed feedback. As with preceding stages, the experiences of childhood provide the foundation for cooperative relationships in adult life. If the child fails to learn to follow or to lead, or if the child develops ineffective ways of responding, problems will result in relationships which require cooperative behavior.

The relationship with the source of life is often a cooperative relationship. God as parent who leads the children of Israel through the desert gives way to the image of God as king of the nation of Israel. Within the framework of mysticism, the image is of the Creator who looks to us to finish the task of creation according to the divine plan. The image of God as follower is also found in the Bible when Elijah takes the initiative, asking God to manifest the divine presence as the prophet struggles with the priests of Baal. Similarly, in the *Talmud*, when Rabbi Eliezer attempts to win an argument with his colleagues by appealing to supernatural signs, a voice from the heavens affirms the primacy of human leadership. God reveals the *Torah*, but follows us as we adapt it, interpret it, and elaborate on it.

There are times when it is helpful for us to clarify direction and focus in our lives by thinking of ourselves from the perspective of responsive followers who carry out the divine plan for creation. For the mystics, the cooperative relationship also exists in the other direction when we take the leadership role in our relationship with the Source of Life. Human beings are viewed as superior to angels insofar as they can exercise choice. In other words, they can take a leadership role in clarifying and manifesting the kingdom of God on earth, while angels can only carry out the plan as followers. It is we who create new names for God.

You AND Me

Although the cooperative style of relationship allows each person to be equal participants, there remains an inequality in power. That inequality finally resolves itself when the child develops skills of collaboration. In the collaborative style of relationship, each person is a separate individual with different needs, perceptions, and resources; yet, each works to resolve differences so that needs of both are respected and satisfied.

The collaborative style integrates the symbiotic bond and the individuated mode of relating. As in the individuated mode, each person is recognized as separate with differing needs, perceptions, and resources. As in the symbiotic mode, each validates and supports both oneself and the other. A win-win orientation towards conflict and problem solving replaces the win-lose mentality in the individuated mode, the need for one person to be dependent in the supportive mode, and the need for one person to have the power in the cooperative mode. Instead, conflicts are resolved in a relationship of equality, with equally valid perceptions and needs, with equal ability to solve problems, with equal right to make decisions, and with equal commitment to finding a mutually satisfying solution.

In learning to collaborate, the child needs to develop creativity in problem solving and flexibility in considering possibilities for meeting needs with a variety of solutions. Skills of all the preceding stages are needed as well: the ability to recognize the symbiotic connection, to clarify differences, to give and receive support, to follow and to lead. The collaborative style is a relationship of equality in participation and in power. It is the relationship of lovers, of co-creators, of mature, adult commitments.

The mature relationship with the Source of Life is also a collaborative relationship. It is the relationship described in the Song of Songs of King Solomon, the relationship with God as a relationship of lovers. From the perspective of mysticism, it is the concept of the spark of divinity found within each person, a spark which rejoins its source, a spark which contains a unique aspect of divinity, a spark which is both part of the one-ness and a separate, individuated existence.

We turn to that archetypal image at times when we need to

clarify or expand the possibilities for collaboration as we struggle with life issues, seeking to discover win-win resolutions for conflicts in our lives that appear to defy integration. We utilize the archetypes to challenge ourselves to expand our vision beyond the limits created by prior experience. We take responsibility for our part of the task of finishing creation by rejoining the sparks that are the aspects of divinity which appear to be in irreconcilable conflict in the world.

The Evolving God

The relationship with God is a living, intimate encounter with the Source of Life. It is a passionate relationship with moments of love and of anger, of security and of fear, of need and of appreciation, of joy and of sorrow. There are times of connectedness and times of distance, of giving and of receiving, of leading and of following, of creating together. Like other powerful relationships, it takes work. It is an ever-changing relationship in which each partner touches and transforms and, in return, is touched and transformed. In relationship with God, we open ourselves to possibilities for extending who we are and who we can be. The call to transcend who we are is heightened in the relationship with God, who, by definition, represents possibility and transcendance.

As adults, there are times when we need to access each of the styles of relationship. There are times when we painfully discover that what we have learned is insufficient, and we find that these developmental deficits limit our capacities to respond and impair our ability to cope with problems. The ensuing crises challenge us to develop new possibilities. At those times, the ability to access the archetypal images of spiritual relationship is a valuable resource.

Yehudit Goldfarb
Illustrations by Nancy Katz
and Maya Wallach

Hebrew Letters That Bring Forth Life Energy

It was about four-thirty on a morning, late in the spring of 1979 when Rabbi Zalman Schachter-Shalomi directed an eager but half-asleep group of Aquarian Minyanites to go outdoors, find a private "alone" space, and listen for a personal revelation as the night slowly turned into day. We had spent Shavuot night—the anniversary of the night before the revelation at Mount Sinai—sharing and studying together. Those of us who were still awake had just impersonated the ten *sefirot* (basic modes of God's creative power) on a living, moving "Tree of Life" (Figure 1). Reb Zalman had chosen me to play the position of *Binah* (Understanding) or "The Mother of All That Is Alive." I felt honored and shy, and as a mother of three in a group of mostly single adults, I was aware of its appropriateness. I remember little of what Zalman had us do as the *sefirot*, but I remember distinctly what my body felt like in the position of *Binah* in relation to the other people. I felt very far from the person who stood in the position of *Malkhut* (Sovereignty) at the lower end of the tree. My focus seemed to return again and again to the top of the tree, to *Keter* (Crown), and across from me to *Khokhmah* (Wisdom). I wanted the crown of inspiration to open to me, to reveal why I was here, in this world, at this time, as a woman, as a Jew, as a "Yehudit."

I welcomed Zalman's suggestion of going off by ourselves. The whole night had involved relating to others. I was eager to go outside. We were at a campsite in the Sierra foothills of California, where rolling meadows with occasional large oak trees give way

49

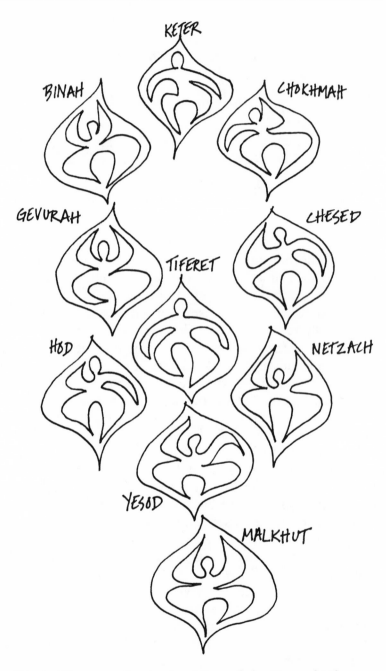

Fig. 1. The ten *sefirot* in the shape of the Tree of Life.

to pine forests. The air was crisp and refreshing, and although it was still dark, it was possible to locate the trail through the woods to the lower meadow by looking up at the sky and noting the thin strip where the treetops allowed the stars to shine through. How appropriate to follow the stars, I thought, for our campsite was named "Lodestar."

Walking carefully down the steep hill from the dining room where we had spent the night, I soon emerged into the open space of a meadow. But it was too open for the sense of privacy I sought, so I walked across it to the edge of the woods on the far side. Just at the point where the low bushes were changing to tall trees I found some large flat rocks to sit on. I made myself comfortable and looked back toward the east at the forest on the other side of the meadow. The dark outline of the trees against the only slightly less dark sky was barely discernible. And there I sat and listened, and listened and watched, and watched and wondered.

As the sky slowly began to lighten, the outline of the trees became more and more distinct. I began to see shapes that drew my heart out toward them with the beauty of their silhouettes. I found myself saying over and over again, "Hebrew letters, Hebrew letters." Tears started welling up in my eyes as I felt my deep love of Hebrew and the shapes of the letters. It wasn't so much the fact that the trees resembled Hebrew letters as my witnessing distinct shapes emerging from one blackness that struck me with wonder and excitement. Perhaps my playing *Binah*, the embodiment of understanding that comes from an awareness of distinctions, had heightened my sensitivity to the splendor of the newly emerging world. My body felt warmed by the variety of the ways in which trees interacted with sky, straight pines with curving oaks, gnarled apple trees with bristly thistle bushes. And each of these creations I knew could be named using Hebrew letters whose shapes and sounds would somehow capture its essence. I longed to know those Hebrew letters, to work with them in a way that transmitted to others the extraordinary sense of interconnectedness and aliveness I felt.

I resolved to take up Hebrew calligraphy. I imagined myself writing *ketubbot* (wedding contracts), certificates of circumcision, documents proclaiming the acquisition of a new name, letters to

God. But a year later, when I tried calligraphy and found that my body became tense whenever I wrote, and when I looked realistically at my life situation—one small child and another on the way—I gave up that dream. Even as I gave it up the call of the Hebrew letters took on a new form.

I remembered that when I first began to teach the twenty repetitive, integrative movements of *T'ai Chi Chih* in 1978 I had said to myself that in Temple times there must have been twenty-two Hebrew letter movements as healthy and integrative as *T'ai Chi*. *T'ai Chi* was the physical embodiment of the three Chinese philosophical traditions of Taoism, Confucianism, and Buddhism. Its origins could be traced to a mixture of sacred dance, martial arts, and health exercises. Similarly, it seemed logical to believe that the dances of the Temple in Jerusalem would be based on the *Alef-Beit*, since Jewish tradition teaches that it was through the power of the Hebrew letters that the world was created. Rabbi Lawrence Kushner had written in *The Book of Letters: A Mystical Alef-bait*: "The אוֹתִיּוֹת *OTIYOT [letters]* are more than just the signs of sounds. They are symbols whose shape and name, placement in the alphabet, and words they begin put them each at the center of a unique spiritual constellation. They are themselves holy. They are vessels carrying within the light of the Boundless One."[1]

I began to ask God, off and on whenever I would remember, to let me channel the twenty-two Hebrew letter movements that must have once been known. During the summer of 1979 I had participated in a "Dance of the Letters" with the women at Moshav Meor Modi'im in Israel. We had done movements and sounds while spelling out words of healing for a woman giving birth at the Moshav. I remembered the movements as being beautiful and flowing, but they did not focus on the actual shapes of the letters. I wanted movements that would bring the shapes to life and that would allow a mover to tap into the infinite energy stored in the very form of the *otiyot*.

I continued studying Jewish mysticism independently and with whatever teachers would pass through the Bay Area. And I continued to teach *T'ai Chi* along with supporting texts drawn

---

1. Lawrence Kushner, *The Book of Letters: A Mystical Alef-bait* (Woodstock, Vermont: Jewish Lights Publications, 1975), 17.

from Chinese philosophy. After several years of exclaiming to friends how I was repeatedly finding parallels between the Jewish and Chinese texts, I was finally challenged to design a class based on my insights. And so I began to teach a course comparing classical texts from Chinese philosophy and the Jewish mystical tradition. The more I studied, the more I held to my dream of discovering a Jewish movement form comparable to *T'ai Chi*. I found teachings supporting the centrality of the *Alef-Beit* for life itself. In his book *The Wisdom of the Hebrew Alphabet: The Sacred Letters as a Guide to Jewish Deed and Thought*, Rabbi Michael Munk quotes the Maggid of Mezritch, Rabbi Dov Ber: "It is known in Kabbalistic literature that the letters of the *Aleph-Beis* were created first of all. Thereafter, by use of the letters, the Holy One, Blessed be He, created all the worlds. This is the hidden meaning of the first phrase in the Torah, *'In the beginning God created* את*'*—that is, God's first act was to create the letters from א to ת.[2] Citing the *Sefer Yetzirah (The Book of Creation)*, reputed to have been written by the Patriarch Abraham, Munk explains that the twenty-two sacred letters are "profound, primal spiritual forces"[3] through which God articulates God's will in Creation. It therefore seemed logical that "personifying" the Hebrew letters in one's body might help to align one's will to God's will.

Another important focus in my life during the 1980s was helping my husband Reuven publish the illustrated Jewish literary magazine, *Agada*. Coincidentally, or perhaps not so coincidentally, Reuven had decided that the cover of each successive issue of the magazine would depict a letter of the *Alef-Beit*. He collected quotations about the letters and often chose teachings about particular letters to go on the inside front cover. One of the teachings he picked was the following excerpt from Rabbi Yitzchak Ginsburgh's book, *"I Am Asleep Yet My Heart Is Awake": A Chassidic Discourse:*

"The 'letters' of a Jew are the letters of Torah and *t'fila* (prayer). The Torah letters are the building blocks of the universe. Each of the

---

2. *Or Torah*, quoted in Michael Munk, *The Wisdom of the Hebrew Alphabet: The Sacred Letters as a Guide to Jewish Deed and Thought* (Brooklyn: Mesorah Publications, 1983), 19.
3. Munk 19.

twenty-two Hebrew letters is a channel connecting the Infinite with the finite. Each is a particular state of contradiction of spiritual light and life force. The shape of each letter represents its individual form of transformation of energy into matter. . . . Every letter which emerges in thought and speech is drawn from the inner essence of the intelligence and emotions of the soul."[4]

Rabbi Ginsburgh had gone on to explain that when the Torah letters are combined into words they become "houses" which "receive power to give life even to physical creatures," and for this reason "the inner life of every creature is its Hebrew name."[5]

According to Rabbi Ginsburgh, the letters of t'fila are "upward-bound channels that connect the soul to God," and ". . . by uttering the letters of Torah and t'fila, the Jew becomes a partner bound with God in the action of creation. While we are in exile, though, we say the words without being able to comprehend their creative power—just as in general we are insensitive to the continuous act of creation, the constant flow of the letters into all beings."[6] The exile to which Rabbi Ginsburgh refers is "the exile of the Jewish soul—the apparent loss of Jewish identity"[7] in modern times, which he likens to a "spiritual exile" in which the soul is asleep and the inner eyes are closed to reality. He notes that we are unable to see "our signs" (ototaynu)[8]—meaning both "signs" in the form of "the supernatural wonders of Divine Providence, which are hidden during exile in the guise of nature,"[9] and "signs" in the form of the letters of the alphabet, the letters of Torah and t'fila; we have lost touch with the innate sanctity of the letters and our lives. This teaching by Rabbi Ginsburgh helped me to see the potential for tikkun olam (repairing the world) in a movement form based on the shapes of the Hebrew letters: it might reawaken the sleeping soul, revitalize our bodies, realign

---

4. Yitzchak Ginsburgh, "I Am Asleep Yet My Heart Is Awake": A Chassidic Discourse (Jerusalem: Gal Einai Publications, 1984), 3, quoted on the inside cover of Agada 8 (1985).

5. Ginsburgh 4. See also R. Shneur Zalman of Liadi, Tanya, part 2, chapter 1 and 12.

6. Ginsburgh 4.

7. Ginsburgh 3.

8. See Psalms 74:9.

9. Ginsburgh 3.

and integrate our inner and outer worlds, restore a sense of sacredness to our speech and actions, and open a channel for conversing with God. By nourishing our Jewish identity in a holistic way, it might facilitate a return "home" for many exiled Jewish souls.

In November 1987, Reb Zalman was again the catalyst for my soul discovering its purpose in this lifetime, for he created a sacred space within which the channel opened for me to receive the movements I had dreamed of for so long. Over eight years after my hearing the call of the Hebrew letters at Lodestar, I attended the first Mystery School weekend at Fellowship Farm near Philadelphia. In preparation for the Mystery School I had spent the previous weekend writing my spiritual autobiography. Looking back at the patterns in my life and writing close to a hundred pages of my soul's story was both exhausting and deeply cleansing. I felt "caught up" and ready for the next step. Then, on Saturday night after Havdalah, I received my first *"ot adena"* (graceful letter).

In an exercise early in the evening Reb Zalman had us play the "rebbe" for each other, and I was profoundly moved by the experience. Now it was time to play, to sing, and to dance. Eve Ilsen sang song after song, some in Yiddish, some in Hebrew, some in Ladino. I found myself reaching up toward the ceiling at an angle, "grabbing a piece of the infinite" with my fingers, closing my fingertips together in a budlike gesture as I drew my wrist first back toward my forehead and then down to my shoulder, then reaching up again. After playing with this motion repetitively, first with one hand and then with the other, I realized that I was forming a *Yud* (Figure 2). I soon found myself pointing one toe toward the floor, a little forward and to the side, while I brought the backs of my hands together and allowed my fingertips to fold first inward and then upward in a somersaulting movement until they were stretched above my head pointing to the heavens. As I stepped forward and brought my hands down on the sides in a circular movement resembling a breaststroke, I realized with a flash of joy that I had just moved in and out of a *Lamed* (Figure 3). I repeated the movement over and over again, and when I found myself bending over slightly as I brought the backs of my hands together and then unfolding my body with an undulating roll as I reached upward, I was reminded of the full-flowing Yemenite step which I had learned from Margolit Oved many years before. At that time I had felt that the basic Yemenite undulation movement was the closest thing to *T'ai Chi* in Judaism because it integrated the body vertically. Soon the *Lamed* began to change and I started stepping forward fully onto one foot until the back toe of my other foot rolled over; at the same time I brought the backs of my hands together and let them unfold upward with an undulating roll until my wrists rested at my forehead with my thumbs together and my fingertips pointing forward so that they were above the toes of my forward foot. Now I was the *Gimel* (Figure 4). I rocked back, bringing my hands down by a path similar to the one through which they had traveled upward, and repeated the movements over and over again, first on one side, then on the other. I began to feel tingling in my fingertips as I often would when I did *T'ai Chi*. I got a little giddy. The letters were coming through!

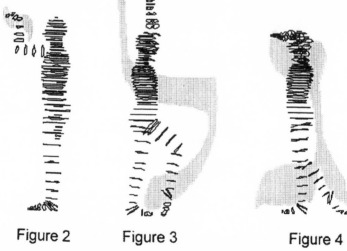

Figure 2   Figure 3   Figure 4

The *Alef* came next with a wonderful alternating pattern of extending outward in all directions and then coming back to a centered vertical alignment as I lowered my hands in front of my chest. I kept my hands crossed at the wrists with fingertips directed upward until they swept down and then outward again into the full expansion of the next *Alef* (Figure 5). Each time my hands came down in front of my body I felt as if I were returning to oneness from the place of multiplicity. My body posture reminded me of the numerical value of Alef as "one," which, in the kabbalistic tradition, often signified the "perfect unity" or "The Mysterious One, Incomparable, Unknown and Unknowable."[10] Each time my arms were outstretched and my head tilted in line with the upward extended arm, I was reminded that *Alef* also signifies "thousand." As I gazed under my arm, I experienced the sensation of looking down upon the multiple dimensions of a newly created world, as if I were the *Alef* that came before the *Bet* of *Bereshit*—"In the beginning. . . ." In fact, the next letter movement to come through me was the *Bet*. Then came the *Dalet*, as a turning movement that reminded me of Egyptian hieroglyphs (Figure 6).

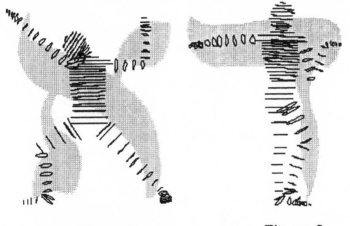

Figure 5   **Figure 6**

Six *otiyot* came through that night. Before I went to bed I wrote descriptions of them in my journal and then sat down to study the Torah portion for the next week. As I read the Hebrew I found that the letters forming each word wanted to tell their story to me. Each letter seemed to come with a phrase, or sometimes even a full sentence, to explain its connection to the next letter and to expand the meaning of the word as a whole. I became very

---

10. See Rabbi Jerry Winston's *Colors from the Zohar—Drawn from the Classic of Jewish Mysticism* (San Francisco: Barah Publishing, 1976), 16.

excited. I sensed I had tapped into a reservoir of understanding that would at once nourish and delight my soul for a long time.

The next step came as the result of an "act of God," declared so by United Airlines the next evening. I had left the retreat early Sunday afternoon to catch my return flight to Oakland from Newark Airport. I had heard that there were severe snowstorms in the Rockies, and, as I waited in line at the counter to check in for my flight, I heard that planes were not being allowed to fly out of Denver, the connecting city for my flight home. It looked as if I was going to have a long wait at the airport. Then, with only one person left in line in front of me, the clerk reported that management had declared the snowstorm an "act of God" and all passengers would be given accommodations at the nearby deluxe hotel until the morning. So there I was, with an entire evening to spend alone in a spacious hotel suite away from the pulls and tugs of my usual life at home.

I decided to ask for the other Hebrew letter movements. And each time I asked, I received a movement. What does a *Hay* feel like? And my body would move into the form of a *Hay* and out again, in again and out again, in repetitive, flowing movements, very similar to the twenty repetitive *T'ai Chi Chih* movements I had been teaching for over nine years. I soon had forms for all the letters, including the final letters. I wrote descriptions of each one as I learned it.

By the time I was finally on the plane home, I found myself flowing with words—English words. Poems and parables and little jewel-like insights began to flood my consciousness. I wrote during the entire flight back to the Bay Area. At the time, I called what I was writing: "Fragments of Yehudit's Scroll (for Zalman)— The Second Level of *T'ai Chi Chai* (Supreme Ultimate Life)." I considered the first level of "*T'ai Chi Chai*" or "The Dance of *Ruach HaHayyim*" to be the "rhythmic integration" of the Hebrew Letter Movements themselves. Ideally, the second level would be the verbalizing and sharing of the truths revealed by the first level. When I arrived home I felt as if I had opened a Pandora's Box of creativity that I was extremely reluctant to turn away from, but which the demands of my everyday life required I close, at least temporarily. I felt that I now knew why my soul had come into this body, why I had been given the opportunities and tests that I had. I also sensed that I needed to refine and strengthen my vessel still more, to let the Hebrew letter movements "cook" internally for a long period of time before I began systematically testing their energy flow so that I could share them with large numbers of people. For me they seemed to be gateways to infinite possibilities for learning and growth, but I wanted to be sure that they were also healthy channels for increasing awareness.

Reb Zalman was again to play a role, although somewhat indirectly, in bringing the Hebrew letter movements into the public realm. It was the call for proposals for the 1989 P'nai Or Kallah that pushed me to test each of the original letter movements and revise them as necessary, to give the movements a formal name—*Otiyot Khayyot* (Living Letters)—and to commit myself to a date for an introductory workshop. And it was Reb Zalman who helped me to expand the movements by asking, "Do you also have movements for the vowels, the *nikudot*?" Very shortly after he asked the question, the *nikudot* movements "came through." So by the 1989 Kallah I had an entire form of independent, flowing repetitive movements for all the block Hebrew letter shapes and for the *nikudot*. I had begun to play with word dances formed by moving my body in and out of consecutive shapes. Sometimes I moved silently. Sometimes I sounded the letters as I moved in and out of their shapes. Sometimes I sounded out entire words as I spelled them with my body. When I added the *nikudot* to my word-spellings, I experienced deep resonances as I extended my breath while I sounded and moved at the same time.

In August 1991 I was to complete a circle on the spiral I had started in June 1979. At the Joys of Jewishing Summer Encampment I was honored by my community as an *Eshet Hazon* (Woman of Vision) and given the name "*Ot Adena*." The ceremony planned by the community to so honor me took place at Lodestar, in the meadow between the rocks where I had sat that Shavuot morning long ago and by the trees whose silhouettes had called out to me so clearly, "Hebrew letters, Hebrew letters." The rocks on which I had sat turned out to be no ordinary rocks. They had deep bowl-shaped cavities, for the native peoples of the area had used them for centuries to grind their grain. I had settled myself in an ancient kitchen and awakened to an ancient dream.

When Rabbi Abraham Abulafia wrote in *Otzar Eden HaGanuz* about the power of the Hebrew letters, he cited a reference from

Isaiah which referred to "the letters that will come" (Isaiah 44:7).[11]
I do not know if I was taught or if I just imagined that this passage
was the basis of the teaching that just before the time of *Meshiach*
(the Messiah) the Hebrew letters would come to center stage
again in a new and vibrant form. With the publication of Rabbi
Aryeh Kaplan's translation and commentary on the *Sefer Yetzirah:
The Book of Creation*,[12] Rabbi Yitzchak Ginsburgh's *The Hebrew
Letters: Channels of Creative Consciousness*,[13] and Matityahu Glazerson's *Letters of Fire: Mystical Insights into the Hebrew Language*,[14] the
incredible depth and power of the Hebrew letters were being
recognized by an ever-increasing number of people. Abulafia had
seen the letters as providing "the closest way to truly know
God,"[15] a "key to open the fifty gates of wisdom,"[16] a channel for
"the divine influx, which could bring [a person's] mind from
potential to action."[17] My experience with practicing, sharing, and
teaching the Hebrew letter movements—*Otiyot Khayyot Meviot
Khayyut* (Living Letters Bringing Forth Life Energy) as I now call
them—has given me hope that Isaiah's dream of a Messianic time
of peace can actually become a reality. In the peacefulness and the
sense of balance and centeredness which the Hebrew letter
movements bring to many people I see an integrated path for
healing and renewal of both body and soul. The movements have
also provided many students with a point of renewed connection
to their Jewish roots and their personal spiritual task. For example,
one student wrote to me that, after doing the repetitive Hebrew
letter movements for the letters in his name and then creating a
word dance with those letters, he had experienced a profound
new understanding of his Hebrew name and how it fitted the life

---

11. See Rabbi Aryeh Kaplan's *Meditation and Kabbalah* (York Beach, Maine:
Samuel Weiser, 1982), 85.
12. Kaplan, *Sefer Yetzirah: The Book of Creation* (York Beach, Maine: Samuel
Weiser, 1990).
13. Ginsburgh, *The Hebrew Letters: Channels of Creative Consciousness* (Jerusalem: Gal Einai Publications, 1990). Also published in Northvale, New Jersey, by
Jason Aronson, as *The Alef-Beit: Jewish Thought Revealed Through the Hebrew Letters*
(1991).
14. Matityahu Glazerson, *Letters of Fire: Mystical Insights into the Hebrew
Language*, trans. S. Fuchs (Spring Valley, New York: Feldheim Publishers, 1991).
15. Kaplan, *Meditation* 84.
16. Kaplan, *Meditation* 85.
17. Kaplan, *Meditation* 85.

path he had chosen: "Through your *otiyot* you helped me do some healing work with my name and my legacy. The movements gave me a physical signature of an identity that I began to discover at the Kallah . . . Yehudit, the process of doing your movements of the letters gave me a physical knowledge of the significance of the person inside me to whom I was finally opening up. It was like an initiation, a sealing of my legacy, my identity into my very physicality."

The Hebrew letter movements have taken on a life of their own. New variations come through periodically. A friend of mine, Henry Ezekiel Adams, who is a master martial artist and healer, worked with me to uncover what we call *Ruach HaLev:* the Internal Art and Heart of Fire Dancing, a kabbalistic meditation/ healing/martial art founded by Henry and based on *Netivot Etz Chayyim* (Hidden Paths of the Tree of Life) and the *Netivot Alef-Beit* (Mysterious Paths of the Hebrew Letters). *Ruach HaLev* includes interactive drills and sensitivity drills, as well as applications of a variety of Hebrew letter movement forms in a martial arts context. It extends also to healing meditations based on the Hebrew letters. Henry continues to channel the primal energies of the letters in new forms and to find healing applications for them.

Meanwhile I have been experimenting with integrating the Hebrew letter movements into the prayer service. For example, on the High Holy Days for 5754 (1993), I led the congregation in the repetitive movements for the letters of the Divine Name as transitions between the various parts of the service. In order to focus our *kavannah* (intentionality) toward unification and wholeness, each time we moved in and out of the shapes of the letters we also chanted *"L'Shaym Yehud Kud'sha B'rikh Hu U'sh'khintay"* (For the sake of the unification of the Holy Blessed One and the Presence of the One). We did the lower *Hay* before the prayers concerning the body, the *Vav* before the songs of thanks and praise, the upper *Hay* before the *Bar'khu*, and the *Yud* before the *Amidah*. Then we combined in a consecutive sequence the movements for *Yud, Hay, Vav, Hay* in a Name Dance before the Torah reading. On Rosh Hashanah, as preparation for the *shofar* blowing, I led the congregation through the movements and sounds of the *nikudot* in the kabbalistic order corresponding to the *sefirot* from *Keter* to *Malkhut*. The response to the movements within the context of the service was extremely heartening.

As I continue to experience with my friends and students the combination of playfulness and creativity, of balance, and integration of body, heart, mind, and spirit which the Hebrew letter movements inspire, I am reminded of the words of the prophet Ezekiel when he was given a vision of the revitalization of the dry bones of the house of Israel (Ezekiel 36:37–37:17):[18]

> God said to me, "Son of *Adam*, can these bones live?" I answered, "O God, Lord, You know."
> Again God said to me, "Prophesy over these bones. Say to them: O dry bones, hear God's word. This is what God the Lord says to these bones: Behold, I will cause breath [*ruach*] to enter you, and you will live. I will lay sinews on you, cause flesh to come upon you, cover you with skin, and put breath [*ruach*] in you, and you will live; and you will know that I am God."[19]
> . . . Then God said to me, "Son of *Adam*, these bones are the entire house of *Yisra'el*. Behold, they say, 'Our bones are dried, our hope is lost, and we are cut off.' Therefore prophesy and say to them, This is what God the Lord says: Behold, O my people, I will open your graves, and cause you to come up out of your graves, and bring you into the land of *Yisra'el* . . . I will put My spirit [*Ruchi*] within you, and you will live; I will place you in your own land; then you will know that I God have spoken it, and done it, says God."[20]

I see in these verses a vision of the period of history through which I have lived. After the Holocaust the world witnessed the rising of God's people from the graves of Eastern Europe and their return to their own land. I now hope to do my part in bringing the Breath of God back into the Body Yisra'el, for, after all, I was once told that my name, Yehudit יְהוּדִית, signifies "one who channels God's Name (*Yud Hay Vav Hay*[21]) through the door of this world (*Dalet*) until the end of time, the time of *Meshiach* (*Tav*)."[22]

---

18. Translation adapted from Kaplan's *The Living Torah: The Five Books of Moses and the Haftarot* (Brooklyn: Maznaim Publishing, 1981), 1299–1303.
19. Ezekiel 37:3–6.
20. Ezekiel 37:11–14.
21. The two parts of the final *Hay* are divided into a *Dalet* and *Yud*.
22. Rabbi Shlomo Carlebach, November 1981.

References

Agada 8 (1985): inside cover.

Ginsburgh, Yitzchak. *The Hebrew Letters: Channels of Creative Consciousness.* Jerusalem: Gal Einai Publications, 1990. [Also published in Northvale, New Jersey, by Jason Aronson (1991) as *The Alef-Beit: Jewish Thought Revealed Through the Hebrew Letters.*]

―――. *"I Am Asleep Yet My Heart Is Awake": A Chassidic Discourse.* Jerusalem: Gal Einai Publications, 1984.

Glazerson, Matityahu. *Letters of Fire: Mystical Insights into the Hebrew Language.* Trans. S. Fuchs. Spring Valley, New York: Feldheim Publishers, 1991.

Kaplan, Aryeh. *The Living Torah: The Five Books of Moses and the Haftarot.* Brooklyn: Maznaim Publishing, 1981.

―――. *Meditation and Kabbalah.* York Beach, Maine: Samuel Weiser, 1982.

―――. *Sefer Yetzirah: The Book of Creation.* York Beach, Maine: Samuel Weiser, 1990.

Kushner, Lawrence. *The Book of Letters: A Mystical Alef-bait.* Woodstock, Vermont: Jewish Lights Publications, 1975.

Munk, Michael. *The Wisdom of the Hebrew Alphabet: The Sacred Letters as a Guide to Jewish Deed and Thought.* Brooklyn: Mesorah Publications, 1983.

Winston, Jerry. *Colors from the Zohar—Drawn from the Classic of Jewish Mysticism.* San Francisco: Barah Publishing, 1976.

===

Shohama Wiener

Connecting God's Names and My Name: A Spiritual Journey

God appears to each of us in the way we need to be reached, teaches a Midrash on the burning bush. When God spoke to Moses, it was with the voice of his father, so he would not be frightened. Later, when Moses asked God for a name (Ex. 3:14), he was told *Ehyeh asher Ehyeh,* a name filled with alternate meanings: "I am that which I am," or "I am that which I will be," a name that connotes "being" without any descriptive limitations. The Bible, siddur, and rabbinic literature contain many names for God, each reflecting a different aspect or attribute of divinity experienced by spiritual seekers. These names have been used as vehicles for comfort and growth, with the understanding that beyond all these names there is only One who is named.

For me, the equally important question has been "Who is the I?" What is the name or what are the names God has for me? What spiritual significance do these names have? As we are *b'tzelem Elohim* (in the image of God), we too are filled with complex ever-evolving meanings.

This sacred search for a spiritual name is aptly described by Julius Lester.

> . . . while on retreat at the Trappist monastery in Spencer, Massachusetts, one of the monks told me, "When you know the name by which God knows you, you will know who you are."
>
> I searched for that name with the passion of one seeking the Eternal Beloved. I called myself Father, Writer, Teacher, but God did not answer.
>
> Now I know the name by which God calls me. I am Yaakov Daniel ben Avraham v'Sarah.

65

I have become who I am. I am who I always ways. I am no
longer deceived by the black face which stares at me from the
mirror.
I am a Jew.[1]

Like Lester, I was drawn to search for the deeper name, the
name that would call forth those aspects of my soul waiting to be
birthed. Before I knew of the work that psychologists were doing
in synthesizing psychological and spiritual processes, I experienced the need to explore the relationship between a self yearning
to grow and a Spirit calling forth the growth. The place of
interface was the name. My name. God's name.

What follows, then, is a very personal essay on the major
changes that have appeared in my more than half a century of life,
changes in the way I address God, and in the "I" who addresses
God. I sense the widespread hunger today for personal spiritual
experience and hope that my willingness to reveal aspects of my
journey will encourage others to search and to share. It is in our
searching and our sharing that we truly meet the One.

"Dear God. You who have created me, nurtured me and guided
me. You who have been with me in the garden of childhood, the
wilderness of adolescence and young adulthood, and the promised land of maturity, how shall I speak of You and Your Name?"

The answer comes. "There is only one way to speak of The
Name, and that is with the clear truth of the now. With the best
vision, the most open heart, and highest courage I can summon."

When I was a child, I talked to God with simplicity. In English. My
name then was Charlotte. Although I knew the blessings, for me
they were not a connection to God, only a conduit for my
Judaism. But God was the one I could ask for help, especially with
tests. God's name was "God."

Somewhere around the age of twelve I became conscious that
there was something amiss in praying, "Dear God, let me get a
100 on my test tomorrow." I began to think in universal terms,
and the likelihood of a God who listened at all seemed doubtful.

---

1. Julius Lester, *Lovesong* (New York: Henry Holt, 1988), 1.

From that point until my mid-thirties, I hovered between atheist and agnostic. This attitude was reinforced by my studies at Wellesley and Harvard in the early 1960s, the "God is dead" era.

As I look back, I regret that my prayer book did not offer choices like *makor hahayim* (Source of Life) or *hey ha'olamim* (Life of all the worlds). I think I could have accepted a universal principle, a source of life and energy as a working definition for God, and that this would have kept me from feeling so alienated from Judaism.

However, I did not have any religious role models at this period. God's name was for me an anthropological relic, used seriously only by primitive-minded believers. In the few times a year that I dutifully attended services, I read the prayer book by skipping over all the names of God. It seemed better to be an honest agnostic than a hypocritical believer. Honesty may generally be the best policy, but in my case it only led to frustration. It was particularly troubling when my children asked to attend religious school, and my daughters would sit up in bed talking to the one whom they called God. Most problematic of all, they chose to prepare for Bat Mitzvah, and I faced the position of being a fraud in front of the Ark, mouthing words of prayer I could not claim as my own.

This all changed on the first day of Sukkot, 1978, when once again, I spoke to God. It was an experiment born of great personal pain and longing. I wasn't sure there was a God, so the conversation ran something like this. "Dear God. I don't know if You exist as a listening being, but if You do, and You let me know You are listening, I promise that I will listen back, and act upon that listening." Following this, I went to morning services, and read the prayers as they were written, speaking God's names each time they appeared.

By the end of the service, I knew I had been heard. All my senses had shifted, my heart was aroused, and it was as if the sanctuary had been redecorated in living color. I left that morning with an inner commitment to study for an adult Bat Mitzvah. During my course of study I contemplated the varied names of divinity in the prayer book and Bible. Each one had its significance, and its power to take me into exciting and mysterious worlds.

The strongest name for me, however, was *Elohey Avraham*, God of Abraham. I felt that, like Abraham, I had been called to leave my father's house and go on a journey, destination unknown (Gen. 12:1). This God of Abraham was an enormous source of love, compelling me to search out the breadth and depth of Jewish tradition, and moving me to a path of service.

At times I sensed this God sending energy that felt both physically passionate and male. It was not from an old man on a throne with a white beard, but a man of charm and virility, more like the midrashic handsome young man with dark curls whom the maidens saw as their rescuer from the straits of Egypt, or the lover in *Shir HaShirim*, the Song of Songs. I was experiencing immanent, divine male energy in connection with prayer, Torah, and Shabbat.

My friends and relatives wondered about my sanity, but I knew that I had found a reality too powerful and too enticing to be ignored. As I delved deeper in my study of Hebrew, it became clear to me I needed to speak with this God as my God, and that I needed a Hebrew name to make the fullest connection.

I tried taking the Yiddish name I had been given at birth, Shulamis, and making it Hebrew, Shulamit. For six months I tried. It wasn't working. I didn't feel like Shulamit and I was losing my ability to pray. I felt intuitively that I needed a name that would let me draw in more strength and wisdom.

I thought of Avram who became Avraham, of Sarai who became Sarah, and of Hoshea who became Yehoshua, each one receiving a new name for a new mission in life. I prayed for guidance. It came through the vessel of a Hebrew dictionary. Having decided that I needed to keep a connection to the grandfather for whom I was named, Shlomo, I systematically began looking at all the words beginning with the letter *shin*, the first letter of Shlomo.

When I came to *shin-hey-mem*, I stopped. Every variant seemed to reach out and speak to me. The letters stood for *Shlomo Hamelekh*, Shlomo the King, and for *Shir Hama'alot*, the Psalms of Ascent, my favorite group of psalms. These letters also spelled the word, *shoham*. *Shoham*, the sacred mother-stone, was an onyx stone worn by the High Priest on his shoulders with the names of the tribes inscribed on it. It seemed like more than coincidence that onyx was my favorite stone.

When I meditated on the name *shoham* I could feel my self expand in response to its sounds. Further research revealed kabbalistic meanings which resonated for me in an awesome way. Here was a name I could spend a lifetime trying to become worthy of, a name that would draw forth from God those qualities I most sought to receive and impart—love, wisdom, holiness, and peace. All that remained to make the name perfect for me was to add the letter *hey* at the end, making it sound more feminine, and emulating our forebears who added to their names a letter of God's name.

For the next seven years, praying in the synagogue was a joyous adventure, and while I encountered various struggles with aspects of traditional theology and practice, I found nourishment in the prayer books of all the streams of Judaism. The masculine tone of the siddurim served me well, as I needed to draw in male strength to enter the world of rabbinic leadership. This balance changed dramatically in the mid-1980s as I began to read about and experience the contributions of Jewish feminism.

God now appeared to me in a new form. The change was announced by a vision of Miriam that I experienced while meditating in my Sukkah in 1987. Miriam replaced Abraham as my main ancestor guide, and *Mayim Hayyim* (Living Waters) became my new name for God's presence.

I found myself moved to explore intensively the worlds of meditation and healing, and desirous of spending more time with nature and creative rituals, and less with the synagogue and Jewish texts. I had connected with Shekhinah, the female aspect of Divine energy that is both "out there" (the Matrona, consort of the *Ha Kadosh Baruch Hu*), and "in here" (the Indwelling Presence). Shekhinah was both creative life-force and heartbeat of every part of the universe. My spiritual center had moved, and I had to move with it.

Once again, the prayer book had become problematic, a stumbling block to my relationship with God. I realized the problem was not with God, or with names of God in the Torah, but with the names chosen by the people who standardized the prayer book. Jewish prayer books refer to *Yud-hey-vav-hey* as Adonai, which means "my Lord." Adonai is a very limiting substitution for *Yud-hey-vav-hey*, because it implies maleness and a God who rules through domination. The word Adonai makes me uncomfortable unless I become absorbed in the musical elements of davening, which take me to a place beyond words.

Yud-hey-vav-hey, the four letter name of God, is more accurately rendered as *Hashem* (The Name). *Hashem* was and continues to be a name I relate to with love and warmth. According to one line of kabbalistic interpretation, the *yud* and *vav* represent maleness, the two *hey*'s represent femaleness, the first pair (*yud-hey*) God's transcendence, and the second pair (*vav-hey*) God's immanence. The letters also represent God as perceived through actions, feelings, thought, and being. This name, The Name, includes all God's names. When I daven by myself, I pronounce *Yud-hey-vav-hey* as Hashem.

My problems with the liturgy were present even in feminist services. It wasn't any easier to say *"Brukhah At Shekhinah"* (blessed are you, Shekhinah). A female goddess? I was raised to shudder at the thought. Yet I have seen her frequently the past few years in my meditations and visions. Her presence comes both from on-high and from very near. She is beautiful, immensely loving, and serene. I know she is the counterpart to the male energy I encountered in prior years, and because of her, I have finally begun to feel pride and enjoyment in singing praises to Shekhinah.

Many of my colleagues are upset with the use of feminine God language because they think it implies duality, and not the One that Judaism affirms. This is not my problem. Jewish mysticism has long recognized the male and female elements of the Godhead, and the need to unite them. *L'shem kudsha brikh'hu u'shekhintey* (For the sake of the unification of the Holy One Blessed be He and His Shekhinah) is a kabbalistic phrase said before many prayers and blessings.

The struggle I had and still have is that I believe strongly in the importance of *k'lal Yisrael*, in keeping the Jewish people together as one large family. It is meaningful to me that wherever I go in the world, I can join in prayer with my family. I can follow the siddur. There are times when it is comforting to say the same words my ancestors have said for thousands of years. Moreover, there are times when a name I have rejected or ignored comes alive for me with new meaning. For the sake of Jewish continuity, the next generation must know the traditional words, and have the opportunity to encounter the spiritual heritage of our past. On the other hand, my soul cries out for change and for balancing the hierarchical, male names for God that predominate in traditional texts.

In the last couple of years I have felt a shift, a new name for God. I see it as shimmering white light. I hear it as *Noga*, Bright One. I feel it as Love. Bright One does not have a gender, but does have a heart, reminding me of the Talmudic expression, *rahmana liba ba-ey*, the compassionate one seeks the heart. Bright One is transcendent and fills me with awe, but also with joy. I can merge with Bright One, and return as myself with a new radiance. I no longer want to wear much black onyx, and I seek out the colors of the rainbow. The journey continues, and I trust in the One who guides it.

Simcha Paull Raphael

The Dance of Rainbow Colors

Gather around my friends. Listen closely to these words of an ancient and contemporary Hasidic tale, an archival remnant of the no-longer-esoteric tradition. I'll tell you this story, exactly as I first heard it.

The Vision

It was a mid-autumn morning, many years ago. The young and spirited Reb Zalman was sitting on his meditation stool, contemplating the infinite mysteries of Creation. Concentrating deeply upon the stillness of eternity, over and over he pondered the burning question, "How did God create light?"

All of a sudden, in a flash from nowhere, an image burst forth—a rainbow-colored *talis* with seven stripes on each side. It danced in radiant light, moving, flowing colors of the spectrum, from ultraviolet to infrared. A technicolor dreamcoat, with *tzitzis*, glimmering in the mind's eye.

Reb Zalman's entire being was absorbed into the meditation, contemplating, "How did God create light?" Once again an answer resounded from the infinite depths. "God wrapped Herself in a Rainbow *Talis* of Light and it began to shine." In creating light God created humanity and the rainbow aura of the soul, touching and being touched by God.

In another room of the house where Reb Zalman was meditating, voices could be heard. A baby cried and the telephone rang. As quickly as it has appeared, the vision receded. Reb Zalman completed his *davvenen* and hurriedly donned his overalls in preparation for the day's work. But with this vision was seeded the *B'nai Or*[1] *talis*.

The Search

Reb Zalman felt a burning determination to find a concrete form for the radiating image of his vision. Soon he was wandering the alleys and streets of Brooklyn in search of a talismaker. He visited many, but nowhere could he find a willing weaver who would spin rainbow colors on a loom. At the Munkatcher Talis Factory, a pious old Hasid responded with indignance. "A rainbow-colored *talis*?" he asked. "What is this you want, a Purim *talis*? Is this a new sect or something? We don't want to have anything to do with it."

There was no rainbow talis to be found in Brooklyn. Rejected but unrelenting, Reb Zalman resolved to search elsewhere for the *talis* of his inner vision, the *B'nai Or Talis* of the Children of Light.

To Ville de Montreal, in La Bella Province of Quebec, he went, to lead a Shabbos workshop—a *Gigeleh*—at Hillel House. There he knew a man, his last hope, a Jew named Chazin, a *yiddische talis-makher*. "A rainbow *talis*? No!" He too refused without a second thought. No rainbow *talis*.

The Original Five

Almost in despair, Reb Zalman frantically looked through the yellow pages for *vetements religieux* (manufacturers of religious vestments). "Karen Bilow Vetements religieux," he found the name, instantly dialing a telephone number. After a succinct conversation, and a favorable response on the other end, he ran into the street, hailing the first passing taxicab, and immediately went to visit the place.

With controlled enthusiasm Reb Zalman showed the people a

---

1. B'nai Or has since had its name changed to P'nai Or.

model rainbow *talis*. He explained the colors, the size, the *tzitzis*. They agreed to weave five rainbow *taleysim* on the very same looms used to manufacture the garb for Catholic Church sacraments.

Legend has it that Reb Zalman kept but one *talis* of the original five, distributing the remaining four to very special, holy *neshomos*.

The "Talisarium"

A few months later the time drew near for Reb Zalman to go to summer camp. "Religious Environmentalists" at Camp Ramah was the job description. In preparation for two months of activities, the young Lubavitcher raced through the garment district of Manhattan to various manufacturers. He gathered remnants from them, any cloth with stripes and colors.

At the camp, Reb Zalman set up a *talis* manufacturing area—a "talisarium." With his big hands and loving touch, the skilled furrier's son taught the campers to use the rented sewing machine to sew their own beautiful, multicolored *talleysim* of all designs. The "talisarium" was the inaugural do-it-yourself, *Havurah*-style *talis*-making venture.

Walking the Rainbow

Years passed—over two decades. There were many *shabbosim* and *yom tovim*, many *talmidim* and congregations, many *neshomos* who danced the ecstasy of the Rainbow. With his *streimel* and big beard, swinging, balancing between heaven and earth, Reb Zalman prayed, danced, and walked the Rainbow across North America, teaching, sharing, loving, caring, laughing, and holy-making.

Eventually a *talis* company in Israel began manufacturing the *B'nai Or talis*, imported into the United States for local consumption. Over the years, the rainbow-colored *talis* has become a familiar sight, elegantly worn by many at *B'nai Or* retreats, and in

Havurot and Minyanim. From Berkeley to Boston, Mount Shasta to Poughkeepsie, Philadelphia to Toronto, from the cities of Europe to the holy city of Jerusalem, it covers *huppahs*. It adorns *hassan/kallah* (groom/bride), men and women rabbis, young and old. The *B'nai Or* rainbow *talis* functions as a prayer shawl—a Robe of Light—in which to wrap the Self for prayer, meditation, healing, and devotion.

Recognizing the Unfamiliar Rainbow

Still, for many Jewish individuals and communities, the *B'nai Or talis* is often an unknown and unfamiliar sight. Given the total number of *talleysim* in use today, a rainbow-colored prayer shawl is an uncommon artifact in innumerable religious environments. Seen for the first time, it is conspicuous, sometimes awesome, frightening or threatening, but it arouses both curiosity and interest.

But whether it is a familiar personal friend or a rare obscurity, there is no soul that cannot recognize the majestic beauty of the *B'nai Or talis*. Wherever it is worn, it evokes a sense of aesthetic holiness and radiates a mystical quality of rainbow light.

The Story Is Retold in Montreal

Recently a woman walked into Rodal's Bookstore in Montreal and inquired about talleysim. She had heard of, had seen, wanted to purchase . . . "I'm not sure what it looks like, but you don't seem to have it here . . . a rainbow colored *talis*." "Sorry, we don't have a rainbow *talis*," sighed the aging Mrs. Rodal, the wife of the learned man people called Rabbi "Roidell."

Perusing the bookshelves, one of Reb Zalman's Hasidim overheard the conversation. He walked over to the two women as they stood leaning over a pile of talleysim. "Rainbow *talis*! Yeah, there is a rainbow talis!" he almost startled them. "It's called the *B'nai Or talis*." Hurriedly he explained about Reb Zalman . . .

Rabbi Schachter from Winnipeg . . . Karen Bilow . . . here in Montreal . . . now manufactured and distributed by Talitnia. Not everybody knows about the *B'nai Or talis*, this is true. But Mrs. Rodal said she was going to order some soon.

The lady who had inquired said she'd come back again sometime in the future. The young Hasid, running off to an appointment, paid for two books with a credit card and left.

Rainbow Rebirth

Not everybody knows about the *B'nai Or talis*, but for many folks it represents a symbol of renaissance, a rebirth of Jewish life and *neshomeh*, a phoenix rising from the ashes of Auschwitz becoming a "re-Jewvinated" Judaism with depth, richness, and multicultural diversity. It is a symbol that has grown out of the *B'nai Or* social organism, extending across the globe wherever Jews pray and celebrate. The rainbow *talis* has become a living symbol embodying hope, holiness, and light for all who aspire to live a creative, revitalized, spirtualized Jewish lifestyle in today's global culture.

The Story Goes On

The story of the *B'nai Or talis* is still being told. But this brief ancient contemporary Hasidic tale, of the no-longer-esoteric tradition has its ending, its *piece de resistance*. Once, many, many years after the rainbow meditation vision, aging and tiring Reb Zalman traveled across the northeastern states for yet another *gigeleh*. The *Zayde* of *Havurah* movement, the Professor of Davenology, and *B'nai Or* Rebbe was at a conference to share Torah and song with other *neshomos*, other holy seekers. There was Reb Zalman teaching the crowds to dance. Drinking and dancing and jumping off mountains like Reb Israel, visiting many worlds like Reb Zalman of Liadi, and learning to fly like Reb Nachman, there was Reb Zalman Shalomi teaching the crowds to dance, to walk rainbows.

A young man walked up to the Rebbe to say hello, to ask a question. He too was wearing a rainbow *talis*, identical to the one he had seen swaying from side to side in devotional fervor. "Where did you get your rainbow *talis*?," he asked. "I also have one. Yours is just like mine."

"*Barukh Hashem*," Reb Zalman smiled lovingly. "Yeah, I also have a rainbow *talis*. *Barukh Hashem* . . ." He paused. "We're both wrapped in the Rebbono shel Olam's Robe of Light."

The *davvenen* resumed. Reb Zalman, with his new friend in close step, once again walked the rainbow. The vision had come full circle. Here was the waving spectrum of colors; the technicolor dreamcoat was radiating light in front of his eyes, dancing the dance of the rainbow. There was the shining light that God had created, embodied in a hitherto unknown young man who had never before heard of Reb Zalman, of *B'nai Or*. There he stood, covered by the radiant *B'nai Or talis*. There was the shining robe of the rainbow light—the shining light that God had created.

At that moment Reb Zalman saw the fulfillment of his vision. He understood that wherever they would meet anywhere on the planet, at any time, his Hasidim would always be able to recognize each other by the *talis* they wear, the Rainbow *Talis* of the Children of Light.

Bernard DeKoven

Serious and Silly Find God

One of Reb Zalman's gifts to us is the inclusion of giggles and
zaniness in our spiritual work. Another is the awareness that there
are different roles played out in our inner dramas, which can bring
us insight if used consciously. This brief piece by Bernard DeKoven
illustrates both the serious and the silly.

Of all the players on my inner playground, Serious and Silly are
the best known. They've played together for years. They understand each other intimately. They can play the most complicated
games you can imagine. And, from time to time, they can really
play beautifully together.

There's one particular game that they can never play particularly well; yet, they play it almost all the time, and seem to really
enjoy it. It's a variation of hide-and-seek and peek-a-boo and
achieving enlightenment.

Typically, Silly suggests the game. Serious always wants to be
Seeker. This, actually, is a good arrangement. Serious is an expert
at keeping rules and being fair and defining what's off limits. Silly,
on the other hand, is remarkably good at being the Hider.

Next they decide on home base. The inner playground is full of
potential home bases and hiding places, from Toe to Tongue,
Throat to Lung. Silly usually picks the Nose.

Silly will play Hider, and Serious, as we already predicted, will
play Seeker. Serious focuses all attention on being the breather,
the nostril, the sensor of the air. And then begins to count
(backwards, by primes, from 97).

Silly is supposed to be hiding by the time Serious reaches zero.
Despite years of practice, Serious just can't ignore Silly for the

whole count. So, as usual, Serious has to start over again several times before Silly is really ready to hide.

Finally, Serious completes the count. At last, the moment of truth. Serious, in a blink of the inner eye, reaches the unavoidable conclusion that Silly is definitely hiding.

At this point, the game almost always breaks down. It's just too much for both of them. For Silly, hiding is fun, but only for a little while. And for Serious, just the thought of being all alone, leaving home base without Silly . . . it's almost too frightening. Even Serious doesn't want to have to be *that* serious.

Fortunately, both Serious and Silly have had a lifetime to play. All it takes to get Silly out of hiding is someone to say "Allee allee oxen free."

I don't know why they keep on playing hide-and-seek. Tag is a much better game for both of them. They'd never have to be apart. And, together, they could even find other players to play with. I tried to ask them once, when I thought they were between games. And they started running after me, yelling "You're *IT*."

Russell Fox

Is Telling the Story Enough?

A Hasidic master tells:

> When there was a need for divine intercession, the master would go to a secret spot in the woods, build a special fire, recite words of prayer containing the mystical names of God, and the prayer would be answered. His disciples did not know where the secret place was, but he could build the fire and recite the words, and that was sufficient. His disciple, my teacher, did not know how to build the fire, but he could recite the words, and that was enough. As for me, I can only tell the story, and that is enough to have the prayers answered.

The year is 1994. It is a windy October afternoon on the upper West Side of Manhattan. I am seated at a table in the library of the Society for the Advancement of Judaism, together with fifteen of my fellow students at the Academy for Jewish Religion, the seminary where I am beginning my third year of studies toward rabbinic ordination. My kippah is firmly on my head, and my pen and paper are out to take notes. The class, which is about to begin, is called *Keruv* (bringing-close) or Outreach, and will be taught by several different teachers. This week's teacher is to be Rabbi Shlomo Carlebach.

Uncharacteristically, he arrives on time, with his trademark vest and guitar, and his assistant, Rabbi Sam Intrator. He greets people, sits down at the head of the table, tunes up his guitar while the Dean of our school formally introduces the visiting lecturer. The visiting lecturer dives right into a niggun. Yes, I had heard this niggun before. I closed my eyes, rocked with the tune, and let it take me back, back to another place and time . . .

It was 1987 and the place was Amsterdam. I had recently

moved to this Dutch city from a Buddhist meditation community on the coast of the Netherlands. I wanted to participate in a new chavurah that Reb Zalman urged us to form after a weekend workshop in Jewish spirituality that he had given in Amsterdam that spring. I was twenty-four and had just spent a year meditating and living close to nature. Therefore convinced that I could do anything, I took over a small organic macrobiotic restaurant on the Haarlemmerdijk, a funky, down-at-heels street of stores just outside the city's center. What did I know? I thought I knew how to cook, and like Siddharta in Hermann Hesse's book, I believed that I could think, I could wait, and I could fast. I hired a bunch of foreign hippies and anarchists who lived in houseboats or squatted in houses to help run the place, and I was in business.

Was business good? Well, *baruch Hashem*, there was always food on the table. A friend of mine and a fellow member of the chavurah said that she knew a singing rebbe who could come and perform at the restaurant. Mind you, I had grown up Reform Jewish and the whole thing had turned me off. What did I know? "A singing rabbi?" I replied, "That's nice, we've been looking for musicians. Maybe with some music, more people will come to eat. Sure, ask him to come, do a little concert." For a while nothing happened. I continued to stir stir-fries and roll out whole-wheat pie crusts. Each week she called me back, telling me more and more about how holy and spiritual this Shlomo What's-his-name (I could never remember—Callenbach? Carlstad?) was supposed to be. It left me cold. I was very drawn to things Jewish but still skeptical as to whether there was actually anything spiritual there. Finally I got a call directly from Israel from his right-hand man there, Rabbi Yehoshua Witt. "Russell," he said, "the holy rebbe wants to come to Amsterdam. He hasn't been there in years. If he can sing at your place, it would be the highest. Can you do it, brother?" I looked out at my restaurant, all seven tables and ten by thirty-five feet of it, and without blinking, said yes. "Good," said brother Yehoshua, "The rebbe is coming to Amsterdam in ten days. Put out the publicity."

Ten days! Like one possessed I raced to put the word out. I did not have time to meditate. But, as we all know, when you are working on a good thing, help always shows up. Two days later, two intense Israelis with caps like the one my zaide used to wear, appeared in my restaurant. Meron and Aharon knew Shlomo and they wanted to see what kind of a place this was. Before he even set foot in my establishment Meron slapped the side of my doorway and cried out, "Oy, what is dis? De rebbe is gonna play in some goyisch house where der is no mezuzah?" I felt like I had gotten pulled over by a traffic cop—in a country where I didn't speak the language. "You have a mezuzah to put on de door?" What did I know? Meron sized me up. "What's your name?" "Russell," I reply. Meron roared, "I can't talk to you if you use some goyische name. What's your Hebrew name?" I remembered Sunday school. I remembered feeling bored and ridiculous. "Yerachmiel," I somehow got through my teeth. I *detest* my Hebrew name. "Look, Yerachmiel, it's a mitzvah." I must have looked pretty blank by then. To be honest, I wasn't sure what a mezuzah was, but I wasn't about to reveal my ignorance. "Okay, so you don't have, I get you." Amid arranging sound systems and tickets they returned the next day. Aharon was the good cop. He motioned me over to the door. He had a little yellowed roll of parchment wrapped in plastic in his hand. "You have some tape? You can put de *mezuzah* on your door. I show you how." His eyes burned at me even more intensely. "This is what you say: You say *baruch* . . . and *atah* . . . and de name of de God . . . and *elokeinu* . . . and *melech* . . ." I felt befuddled and unnerved. Why such intensity over a little roll of parchment?

Several people called about the concert, wanting to know if I was under rabbinical supervision. I refrained from retorting that we were under Divine Grace, if that were sufficient. After all, my restaurant was vegetarian, so what was there not to be kosher about, I said testily to myself. Do they think somebody sneaks into my kitchen at night and laces everything with lard? It felt patently unfair. After all, I was in the business of purveying wholesome meals, not satisfying somebody's rabbinical hangups.

The evening before the ever-more-momentous concert, Rabbi Yehoshua Witt himself came to the restaurant. He had come all the way from Israel. Amsterdam was important, he said, Amsterdam was a very high place. He wanted to be there when the rebbe played Amsterdam. I looked at his black hat and fringes and declined to ask if I could serve him dinner. Good Heavens! What had I gotten myself into? All I wanted was a singing rabbi and a little music for the atmosphere, so people would come eat wholesome meals! Instead I get mezuzahs and rabbinical supervision and holy brothers and a portent of something earth-shattering. My ambivalent Jewish self was on overload as I climbed up into my loft above the restaurant that night. Meditation did not help.

The morning of the concert I woke up sick with the flu. I couldn't do anything. I still don't know how it all got done. People came and went—it was all a blur. The afternoon wore on, and my head was pounding. People asked questions, somehow I gave them answers, I don't even remember what. It gets dark early in Amsterdam in January, even before dinnertime. I sat in a corner, exhausted. The door was opened. Someone took tickets. Aharon said, "There's enough room for everyone who wants to come. You'll see. When the rebbe is here, it is like the Beit Hamikdash. There was always enough room for everyone to stand in the Beit Hamikdash." I thought to myself that the Beit Hamikdash probably had more than seven tables. The hour of the concert arrived. The rebbe did not. No one seemed to mind. The place was filled with Jews: Jews from my chavurah, Jewish hippies, Orthodox Jews, Israelis, American Jews, Dutch Jews. And they were all happy and having a good time—in my restaurant. Some of them were even eating wholesome organic meals.

A half hour after showtime Shlomo arrived. Dressed in what I would come to recognize as his trademark white shirt and black vest, and his gray hair down to his collar. He greeted everyone close to him with a hug; he seemed to know a lot of people there. What was this secret fellowship, I wondered. Without theatrics he stepped up to the microphone at the makeshift podium. He took up his guitar and started singing, an old sweet haunting melody with Hebrew words I could not make out. The room was electrified. Yehoshua joined him on a second guitar. People clapped hands. He stopped. He told a story about a banker and money and how it is so important not to give up hope. He spoke easily, matter-of-factly, as if he were talking to a friend. High Holiday services at my childhood Reform temple were never like this. Shlomo talked about how it was so important to help another Jew. Open your hearts, he would say, open your hearts. Every Jew is so precious.

He struck up another melody. It was too much—too much intensity, too much holy fire. I couldn't take any more. I started crying, quietly, sitting on the bar at the back of my restaurant. *Yes*, I thought, I understand why this means so much to them. *Yes*, I thought, it can be this good to be a Jew. *Yes*, a heart can contain so much joy and so much yearning (yearning for something I never knew I was lacking) and not break. *Yes*, these were my people.

The concert rolled on. Somehow people got up and danced, even though the room was packed solid. Somehow heaven seemed so close. Toward the end, Shlomo said, "I want to thank Reb Russell for inviting us here and opening his holy restaurant to us." All eyes looked in my direction. I was speechless; the gratitude was mine (just how much I would realize only later). Shlomo played his last song, and told his last story of the evening. Everyone had become brothers and sisters, if only for a moment. Feeling pounds lighter, I hugged Shlomo good-bye and cleaned up with my crew. Even after the rebbe left, the air was still electric.

Six months later, he came back to play at my restaurant. This time I knew why. Again he moved hearts and touched souls as only he could. Half a year after that, I was asked if Reb Shlomo could come again. Sadly, I had given up the restaurant. It had lost a lot of money. Some rented hall was found for him to play. It wasn't the same. Who knows? Perhaps the only reason I had had the restaurant was so that Reb Shlomo could have a place to play in Amsterdam. What did I know?

I open my eyes, coming back to the here and now. I think of the long journey I have taken from reluctant Jew to would-be rabbi. Shlomo puts down his guitar and speaks to the assembled students. He looks tired. "First of all" he says, "I want to tell you, I hate the word outreach. I especially hate the term *professional* outreach. Like a man is a professional husband, or you're a professional mother, or God," he pauses and rolls his eyes, "is a *professional* God?" Everyone laughs. This sets the tone for the entire talk. How to be a rabbi with soul. How to bring people close. Everyone takes notes. He finishes with another niggun. Everyone thanks him. "Oh," says Shlomo, "I see I am on the calendar to be back here next week, but I can't make it. I'll be out of town. Is two weeks from now okay? Then I can give you some more Torah on how to make holiness in people's lives. So in two weeks, God willing." He hugs people good-bye and he leaves.

"God willing." We use that phrase so easily, not stopping to think about what it means. God was not willing, this time. Ten days later, Reb Shlomo died of a heart attack while getting on yet another plane to yet another destination.

A fire is gone from the world. A man who inspired and brought lost souls closer, and warmed chilled spirits, has given his last Torah. A man who made Yiddischkeit come alive, and brought his own flavor of Jewish renewal to the world, now lives only in our memories and in our stories.

This is the history: Reb Zalman and Reb Shlomo go back a long way. They were both boys in prewar Vienna. They both came to America after the war, and studied together whenever Reb Shlomo would come by the Lubavitch yeshiva where Reb Zalman was a student. They were each sent out by the Lubavitcher Rebbe of that time to bring and teach yiddischkeit to the world, and both went beyond the realm of traditional hasidism to reach out to people whom no one else could reach. They were colleague rebbes, kindred souls, and lifelong friends. Reb Zalman and Reb Shlomo were like brothers. Perhaps they complemented each other—if Reb Zalman is the midwife to the Children of Light, the B'nei/P'nai Or, Reb Shlomo was the kindler of the holy fire. Oy, such a cold world we are left with. What do I know? If I don't know how to light the fire, and if I don't know the right words to say, is telling the story enough?

Karen Barth and Samuel Barth

Four Worlds and the Mission of Our Lives

The Checkbook Stubs of our Lives

Our tradition teaches that each of us will one day come to the final *din vecheshbon* (judgment and reckoning). How will we be judged on that day? One could say that the real values to which we subscribe can be measured by the way in which we spend our money, and when we come to be judged, our checkbook stubs (and credit card summaries) will be part of the testimony called. In this age of power breakfasts and one-minute management, perhaps the pages of our planning calendars—the very hours of our days—will also be called upon to testify about us. How have we used our time in this life? If, as the great rebbes have taught, we have a mission and a purpose in this life, have we fulfilled the mission? Have we been able to bring our attention and energy to those tasks which are truly important, or have we been caught up with trivialities. If (God willing) we are granted seventy or eighty years, or even one hundred and twenty, how will we account for our days?

There is the well-known story of the management consultant who met a group wandering in the forest. She was able to help them devise far more efficient strategies for clearing a path, moving the group forward, and taking care of daily needs. After a few days she asked about their destination, only to receive the response, "We don't know—we're lost!" We can be lost at the deepest level, while appearing to make good progress in the more visible world.

The kaballistic model of four worlds—Being, Knowing, Feeling and Doing—gives a framework against which we can check the flow and direction of our lives.[1] We offer here an introduction to the deep work that can be attempted with this background. We look forward to expanding upon this work in the future in the light of responses from those who walk a part of this path with us.

Purpose: The World of Atzilut (Ultimate Emanation)

Please, O God have mercy upon me that I should not live a life of futility. May I always reflect upon myself, "What am I doing in this world?"

(Personal Prayer of Rabbi Nachman of Bratslav)

The World of *Atzilut* is the highest place, approaching, even partaking of, the unspeakable, unknowable realms of the Divine. In this realm we are conscious of our inadequacy, of the vast chasm that separates us from the source of our lives. In this place, standing albeit momentarily against an absolute standard, we can reflect on the true purpose of our lives.

AN EXERCISE: Imagine (may it not come for many years) the time of your death and the things that will be said of you. What should they be? For what deeds, traits, relationships, teachings, skills, do you hope to be remembered? What does God want of you in this life? What three things (no more) are most important to you?

Write down (and write you must) the mission of your life, as you see it now. In the realm of strategic planning this is the setting of the mission. In the light of this mission we will develop our concrete vision for the near future, our plans to execute the vision, and look for the tools that will help us on the way.

---

1. For this understanding of the four worlds we are indebted to Reb Zalman.

Plan- and Vision-making:
The World of Beriah (Creation)

This is the world of conscious creation. Here, the intellect holds sway and rationality comes to cloak with substance the inchoate sense of purpose we find in the realm of *atzilut*. In this realm we are conscious of our strengths and weaknesses, of the demands on our time, our responsibilities to family and to *tikkun olam*, the repair and support of the world. We must weigh choices in the balance, but the balance is already defined from our work in *atzilut*, and we cannot forget the purpose to which we are called, the driving mission that we have discerned for our lives.

AN EXERCISE: List five goals for the medium-term future of your life (something between three and seven years from now). How do they relate to your mission?

List the five major achievements or results of your life over the past three to seven years. How do they relate to your mission?

Is there harmonizing work to be done between the worlds of *Atzilut* and *Beriah*? If so, try to identify goals that will meet your immediate needs and be harmonious with your life purpose. Or perhaps some change of direction is called for.

Vision-making is setting the medium-term goals for your life in a way that moves towards the fulfillment of your life mission. There will be tasks for the coming year, and for years after that. These goals are good to review each year at Rosh Hashanah (Jewish New Year). Components of a vision for the coming year(s) might include commencing/completing a formal process of learning, finding a partner in life, making a disciplined commitment to spiritual practice, taking responsibility for transforming a personal flaw or failing, helping some person or group of people sustain themselves with greater dignity/security in the world, being elected to public office—President of the United States or local council—and many other possibilities.

AN EXERCISE: Review the vision you have developed for yourself. Is it realistic? Is it achievable? How will you begin to move forward? What must you achieve this month, this year? Begin to set a plan into place.

Making Change Happen: The World of Yetzirah (Formation)

'These words that I command you this day shall lie upon your heart' (Deut. 6:7). The Kotzker Rebbe teaches that even if the words lie *only* on the surface of the heart, this too is of value, because at some time there will be a tiny opening into the heart, and then the words will be absorbed.

U'tshuvah u'tfillah u'tzdakah ma'avirin et roa hagzerah True inner turning, prayer and good deeds can transform the harsh decree.
(High Holy day Liturgy)

There are many battles to be fought to actualize our purpose in this life, and the field of battle can lie deep within us. The world of *yetzirah* is the place of emotional formation, where we hone the inner fires that will drive our plans and deeds in the outer world. Our tradition offers us two great models: *teshuvah* (turning or repentance) and *kavvanah* (focus, concentration, or intention). These tools can help us in the process of inner change.

AN EXERCISE: Consider tasks and goals that you have set for yourself in the past. Have they been achieved? If not, what has been the main impediment?

In light of this exercise, there may be preparatory work to do. The Talmud teaches that *kavvanah* does not necessarily come easily, and offers the parable of the woodchopper who spends the first half-day of employment sharpening the ax. He is considered to have earned well the day's wage.

How can you prepare yourself to succeed in the vision you have now developed for yourself? Are there individuals who can be of help to you among your family, friends, and colleagues? Can you share the execution of your plans with others? Are there classes in prayer, in communication skills, in time management? Is this a time in your life when the self-discovery found in therapy will be necessary?

Efficiency in Action: The World of Assiyah (Action)

Rabbi Tarfon says, 'The day is short, and the work is great and the laborers are sluggish, and the wages or high, and the Master of the house is insistent.'

(Sayings of the Fathers 2:20)

The world of Assiyah is where inspiration, plans, and emotional energy turn into action. This is the place where many people fail. After thinking through your priorities and preparing yourself emotionally to change, you may find that you are stuck in old, inefficient habits. You may find yourself subject to "the tyranny of the urgent" where things that are urgent, but not very important, almost always win out over the things that are truly important in your life. You may find yourself scattering your energies across too many different tasks and finding it hard to complete them. You may find yourself wasting time or simply procrastinating.

To overcome these challenges, the technologies of "time management" as developed in the business world can be very helpful. This technology includes the use of computers and automation, but it also involves the development of a set of skills in managing your calendar, eliminating time wasters, using deadlines constructively, learning to say "no," managing interruptions, organizing your paperwork, etc. There is an extensive body of literature on these skills.

AN EXERCISE: As you begin to implement your new life plan, keep a two-week log of how you are spending your time. Think about the important time categories in your life and write them across the top of a page. Then put the hours of the day down the left-hand side. Make fourteen copies and fill out one for each day. At the end of the two weeks, total up the time spent in each category. How does this compare with your priorities and your plans? What is getting in the way? What can you do about it? Repeat this exercise every few months until you obtain a result that is consistent with your mission and your goals.

Conclusions

"And God said to Adam, Where are you?" (Genesis 3:6)

Our journey through the four worlds shows us the potentials and pitfalls that can await us at many different levels. In so many areas of our lives we have the opportunity to be inspired by the strength and empowerment that come from a full integration of our energies: of our intellect and emotions, of our deepest dreams and our successful actions. This is the unity that is stressed in mystical and philosophical tracts within our tradition.

This is the power we can find if we are able to bring this process to bear upon the planning we do for our lives. In the words of Psalm 90, attributed to Moses, "Teach us to number our days— that we may find wisdom in our heart/mind." It is only when we develop a consciousness about how we are spending our days that we truly begin to live a life of wisdom.

PART II

Fiery Words,
Bright Visions:
Renewing Our Texts

Jack Riemer

David, Bathsheba, Nathan, and Woody Allen

The David-Bathsheba story, as it is usually called, is one of my favorite chapters in the Bible. Most of us are familiar with it, either from Sunday school or from the movies. I think it is a fascinating story, and so I want to study it with you four times in this essay: once as it appears in the Bible, once as it is understood in the rabbinic literature, once as it appears in contemporary Israeli fiction and once as it appears in American life in our time. Do you remember the Japanese play *Rashomon*, in which the same story is told from four different points of view, and each time you find that you have to reconsider how you understand the story? This is the way I want to study this chapter. Each time we examine it I want you to think about these two questions: according to each version of the story, who is the hero? and who is the villain? I think the answers to these two questions change with every retelling.

1. The Biblical Tale

The story appears in chapters eleven and twelve of the second book of Samuel and really marks the midpoint of the life of David. Up until this point, David is the darling of the Bible. Everyone loves David. God loves him, the people love him, and Michal, the daughter of Saul, loves him so much that she rescues him from her own father. Jonathan, the son of Saul loves him so much that he warns him and helps him escape from the anger of his father. Everyone loves David, but I am not sure that David loves anyone. When Saul and Jonathan are in trouble, when they are going to

95

war against the Philistines, David arrives too late to be of any help to them. He writes an eloquent elegy lamenting the loss of Jonathan, but he arrives too late to save him. Michal, the daughter of Saul, saves him from her father and he runs off into the desert. He is lonely there, so he marries once and then again, and then again, and then again. And he never writes to her, not even once. It is only years later, when it is politically advantageous for him to do so, that he takes her back again. But by then they have little in common, and the marriage is empty and meaningless for them both. Davis is *the loved one*—that is what his name means in Hebrew—and at least until this point, everything goes well for him; the people love him, God loves him, he is a victorious warrior, a great lover, a sweet psalmist. Then, in this chapter, he faces a turning point. From here on, his lie is one of heartache, defeat, and distress.

> 1. And it came to pass, at the season of the year when kings go out to war, *vayishlach*, that David *sent* [emphasis mine] Joab and the soldiers and all Israel, and they destroyed and Ammonites and besieged Rabbah. But David *yoshev*, David stayed in Jerusalem.

Is there an implied criticism in this verse? David won the hearts of his people because he led them into battle; he went before them. But now David is a middle-aged king, and so he sits at home and sends the soldiers off to fight.

There is irony here. The story starts out with the soldiers lying in the trenches and David sitting at home. It will end with David lying on the ground in grief and distress.

The key word which appears in almost every sentence is the word *vayishlach*. David is the king so he sends commands and makes things happen. At least it seems so in the beginning. In the end, God will send and David's situation will change.

> 2. And it came to pass at evening time that David got up from his nap and went for a stroll on the roof, and from the roof he saw a woman bathing and the woman was very beautiful.

Again, there is implied criticism here: The soldiers are fighting while David is taking an afternoon nap?

Roofs were flat so the king strolls on them, and he happens to notice a beautiful woman bathing. There is no suggestion in the text that she was deliberately flaunting her beauty. She has probably simply forgotten to draw the shade.

> 3. *Vayishlach*, And David sent to *inquire* about the woman (to find out who she was. And he was told: Is this not Bathsheba, the daughter of Eliam, the wife of Uriah the Hittite?

What is "is this not Bathsheba" supposed to mean? Is this someone whom David is supposed to know or once knew? And notice that the Bible calls her the wife of Uriah the *Hittite*. Would David have slept with her had she been a native's wife instead of a foreigner's wife?

> 4. *Vayishlach*, And David sent messengers and they took her and brought her to him, and he slept with her, and she had been purified from her menstrual period, and she went back to her house.

"They took her" does not mean that they dragged her by force. They simply told her the king would like to see her. Was this a passionate reunion or a one night stand, a genuine love affair or a casual encounter? The text does not say.

Why does the text tell us that she had been purified after her menstrual period? The text is not concerned with the laws of menstrual purity but with the question of establishing paternity. If her husband is away in the army and she has had her menstrual period since he left, then it will not be possible to claim that the child is his.

> 5. The woman conceived: *vayishlach*, and now she sends a message to David: "I'm pregnant!"

What more did she write? Was there a relationship between them? Was she frightened? The text skips quickly over all these details. It is not really the David-Bathsheba story but the David-Nathan or the David-God story. In the whole story Bathsheba only speaks this one time and just these few words.

Why is her pregnancy a problem? In almost all of the countries of the ancient world, the king can take whatever or whomever he wants. Only in Israel is there this strange and radical idea that the law applies to the king, too. Only in Israel is it a problem if the king commits adultery. But that is the way it is in this land, so David has to do something quickly to avert a scandal.

> 6. *Vayishlach*, David sends a message to Joab, his nephew, the commander of the army saying: *shlach*, send me Uriah the Hittite. And Joab sends Uriah to David.

Notice that David calls him "the Hittite" but Joab calls him simply "Uriah." The general knows no distinctions between his soldiers. To him Uriah is simply a soldier. He does not care where he comes from. This is part of the military ethic.

> 7. Uriah came to David, and David asked him how Judah was and how the soldiers were and how the battle was progressing.

David pretends that this is why he has called Uriah back, so that he can get a report on how things are at the front.

> 8. David said to Uriah: Go down to your house and wash your feet. And Uriah departed out of the palace, and there followed him a gift of food from the king.

"Wash your feet" may be a euphemism for making love. What David is thinking is that if Uriah spends a night at home and afterwards a child is born, no one will be able to prove whose child it is.

A gift of food arrives at their home, courtesy of the king, and this is how Bathsheba finds out that her husband is in town. Were she and Uriah getting along? Or was there already trouble before David arrived on the scene? We cannot say for sure, but often when a third party breaks up a marriage, the relationship was already in trouble. Here Uriah makes no effort to contact his wife and tell her that he is in town. We wonder why.

> 9. Uriah slept at the door of the palace, together with all the servants of his king and did not go down to his house.

The point of telling us that he slept with the king's servants is so
we will know that there are no witnesses who can prove he did
not go home and sleep with his wife.

> 10. And when they told David: "Uriah did not go down to his
> house," David said to Uriah: "Have you not come from a long
> journey? Why did you not go down to your house?"

David has his spies follow Uriah to see whether he goes home or
not. When he gets the report he summons him and asks for an
explanation.

> 11. Uriah said to David: "The Ark, and Israel and Judah, are all
> living in tents, and my master Joab, and the servants of the Lord are
> encamped on the open field; how can I go home and eat and drink
> and sleep with my wife? I swear (by that which is the holiest thing
> in the world to me) by your life, how can I do such a thing?"

Does Uriah know? It is possible. Walls have ears and rumors travel.
Perhaps gossip reached him in the army and perhaps he is only
playing with David. Or perhaps he is sincere. Perhaps he is truly
patriotic and cannot let himself have any pleasure while his
buddies in the army are suffering. But David is desperate when he
hears this speech.

> 12 and 13. David said to Uriah: "Why don't you stay in town one
> more day and then I will let you go. And Uriah stayed in Jerusalem
> another day . . . And David called him to dinner and plied him
> with food and with drink and tried to get him drunk, and when the
> meal was over Uriah went and slept with the other soldiers of the
> king, and did not go back to his home.

David tries to weaken the resolve of Uriah by plying him with
food and drink. But in the immortal words of one of the great
theologians of our time, W.C. Fields, "You can't cheat an honest
man." Uriah eats and drinks with the king and then goes back to
sleep with the other soldiers, again creating witnesses to his
whereabouts. And now David is really desperate.

> 14 and 15. And it came to pass in the morning that David wrote a
> letter to Joab, *vayishlach*, and he sent it with him to Uriah. And he

said in the letter: "Please put Uriah in the forefront of the battle, and then retreat from him so that he is smitten and dies."

David is asking Joab to commit the ultimate act of betrayal. Armies are built on a promise of loyalty. Soldiers obey—that is the meaning of the salute—And they do so trusting that their commanding officers will be loyal to them. David is asking Joab to betray one of his own soldiers. If he does, David will be forevermore beholden to Joab, but in his desperation David has no choice.

Does Uriah open the letter on the way? We don't know.

> 16 and 17. And it came to pass, when Joab kept watch upon the city, that he assigned Uriah unto the place here he knew that valiant men were. And the men of the city came out and fought with *Joab*. And there fell some of the people, and Uriah the Hittite died also.

There is something strange about this verse. It is as if Joab started to carry out David's request, and put Uriah where he knew there would be heavy fighting, and then couldn't go through with it. Perhaps it went against the grain of his military ethic. And so, at the last moment he pulled Uriah out, and that is why the text says that when the enemy attacked they fought with—not Uriah, whose name we expect to find here—but Joab.

And yet Uriah does die in the battle. Did he somehow maneuver himself back into the fray when Joab was not looking?

> 18 to 25. Joab sends a messenger back to David and tells him what to say very carefully. He tells him to report that there were heavy casualties and that they foolishly drew too close to the enemy's wall from which archers could rain arrows down upon them. And he tells the messenger to mention that Uriah was one of those that fell in the battle. And when he gets the message, just as Joab had expected, David is not upset. He sends best wishes back to Joab and to the army and wishes them more success the next time.

> 26. And when the wife of Uriah heard that Uriah her husband was dead she mourned for him.

This can be read one of two ways. It can mean that she *really* mourned for him or else it can mean that she went through the motions of mourning for him. Did she know what David had done? Did she ask? Did she care? We do not know.

> 28. When the mourning period was past, *vayishlach*, David sent for her and took her into his home, and married her. And she gave birth to a child. But what David had done was evil in the sight of the Lord.

It looks like mission accomplished. David has averted a scandal. When the child is born no one will be able to prove anything. The birth may be seven months from the time of the wedding or eight months or one, and no one will be able to say a thing. It looks like everything has gone as David wanted it to, *but* what David had done is evil in the sight of the Lord and so . . .

> 1. *Vayishlach Adonay et Natan*, God sends the prophet Nathan to David.

Up until now David has been sending. *Now God sends*. He sends the prophet Nathan to confront David. And the prophet does so, not directly, but by means of a parable that he tells the king. He says:

> There were two men who lived in the same city; one was rich and the other was poor. 2. The rich man had many flocks and herds. The poor man had nothing but one little lamb whom he loved, whom he had bought, had raised from infancy; that grew up together with him and his children; that ate of his food and drank from his cup and slept in his bed; that was like a child to him. 4. And there came a visitor to the rich man, and he took pity on his own flock and took the poor man's lamb instead and served it to the stranger that came to him. 5. David's anger was kindled against the man; and he said to Nathan: "As the Lord lives, the man who did this deserves to die!" And Nathan said to David: *"THOU ART THE MAN!"*

David is caught up in the story and he becomes furious at this dreadful deed. Uriah swore by the holiest thing in his life which was David; and David swears by the holiest thing in his life which is God.

And then come those two ringing words of accusation: *Atah Ha'ish*! (You are the man). And Nathan goes on to call David a murderer, an adulterer, a traitor. He asks David in the name of God, "How could you have done such a thing? God loved you and God gave you so much and He would have given you even more. How could you betray God this way?"

13. And David answers: *Chatati La'Adonay* (I have sinned against the Lord).

This line, even more than the ringing words of Nathan, is the real climax of the story. In every country of the ancient world, in most of the countries of the medieval world, and in many of the countries of the modern world, if you called the ruler a murderer and an adulterer and a traitor, *no insurance company would give you a policy*. It is to the eternal credit of King David that he responds the way he does. Instead of saying "off with your head" he says the hardest words there are for any ruler to pronounce, "I have sinned against the Lord."

He says these words but how do we know that he means them? Lots of people come to the synagogue on Yom Kippur and mouth the words of the confessional, tapping their breasts politely as they do, but they don't really mean them. How do we know that David is sincere when he says these words?

In chapter five of the second book of Samuel, there is a list of all the children who were born to David in Jerusalem: Shammua, Shobab, *Nathan* and Solomon. Hardly anyone in the Bible is named after someone else. We don't have two people named Isaiah or two people named Jeremaiah or two people named Moses. But David names his child Nathan, as a *walking reminder* of the person who shook him and shocked him and shamed him and broke his pride. The *fact* that he names his son Nathan is proof that David is sincere when he says, "I have sinned."

There is much more to the biblical story. The child, born ill, hovers between life and death in a coma for a week and then dies. And there is the effect of that child's illness on David and Bathsheba and on David's relationship to God, but let us stop the biblical story here and ask two questions. According to this biblical account, who is the hero of the story? and who is the villain of the story?

I think we would have to say that Nathan is the hero and David is the villain. Now let us tell the same story through the eyes of the Sages of the Talmud.

2. The Talmudic Version of the Tale

As a rule, the Sages are honest in how they portray the biblical characters. They paint them warts and all. When Abraham sins, they say so. When Moses sins, they say so. But there is one exception to this rule. They whitewash David. "Whoever says that David sinned errs." They claim that whoever went out to serve in the army of David would write his wife a bill of divorcement before he left so that she would not be left in limbo if he were to be missing in action.

That comment is a little farfetched. It is a historical anachronism to think of Uriah the Hittite writing a bill of divorcement for his wife before he goes off to war. If that were the custom, then why is the prophet Nathan so upset and why does David himself say, "I have sinned"?

Why do the Sages whitewash David and deny his sin, a favor they do not do for any other biblical figure? The answer is that David represented the one bit of hope that this battered bereaved people still had to hold on to. The Temple was gone. Jewish sovereignty was gone. The Romans ruled the land. And therefore, three times each day the Sages ordained that we pray in the Amidah for the coming of the day when the Son of David will rule once again. Each time a Haftarah is recited in the synagogue they ordained that we conclude with a blessing that "On his throne may strangers sit no longer." David's return was the one hope they had to cling to in the midst of darkness, and so they did for David what they did for no other biblical figure—they denied his sin. If you understand the story through rabbinic glasses there is *no hero* and there is *no villain* because *nothing bad happened.*

3. In Israeli Fiction

In the mid-sixties an Israeli novelist named Moshe Shamir wrote a novel called *The Poor Man's Lamb* which promptly climbed to the top of the best-seller list and stayed there for many months. It is a fictionalized retelling of the story of David and Bathsheba, told through the eyes of Uriah.

Shamir creates his characters with great imagination. Starting from that phrase in the story, *Halo zot?* (Is that not Bathsheba?) he suggests that this was not a casual one night thing, but that David and Bathsheba had known each other years before. When David was in the wilderness fleeing from Saul, he and Bathsheba met and fell in love. But her father would not let her marry this man, on whose head the king had put a price. On the rebound she married Uriah. But years later, when they met again, Shamir suggests that the old love came back to life.

And then Shamir imagines that Uriah suspects the affair, that he hears rumors even before he is summoned back to Jerusalem. And this is why he does not go home but instead sleeps in the barracks, in the presence of the other soldiers. And then, Shamir imagines, on the way back to the army, Uriah opens the letter that David sent through him to Joab. At first, his reaction is fury, "My wife has done this to me? My king has done this to me?" He is ready to run away back to his own people, the Hittites. But then he reconsiders. After all, she *is* his wife and he loves her, and David is his commander and friend for many years. So he seals the letter back up and delivers it to Joab. Later, when Joab pulls him out of the sector where there is heavy fighting and takes his place, he maneuvers to get himself back into another place where there is heavy fighting so that he can get himself killed, thereby saving his wife and his king from disgrace. As Shamir retells the story, Uriah's death is not a plot of David's but an act of noble suicide.

Before Uriah returns to the camp and his impending death in battle, Shamir imagines that he sends off the true story to his kinsmen, the Hittites. He has it buried in a jar and put into one of the caves at Qumran. Who knows, he thinks to himself, someday a shepherd boy may wander into that area and throw a stone into one of those caves and find the jar and open it and read the manuscript. And who knows? Someday that manuscript may even be translated into Hebrew and if it is, then the Hebrews of the future may learn from it how their ancestors once treated a Hittite. On that wistful note the novel ends.

Why did the book sell so well in Israel? What nerve did it touch in so many Israelis? I think they bought it in such great numbers because it spoke to them, not about the Hittites of old, but about the Arabs of their own time. For two thousand years we Jews have been in favor of minority rights because we were a minority. Now for the first time in many centuries we are a majority, and we must deal with the question of how we will treat the minorities in our midst. When Shamir turned Uriah into the hero, when he makes the tale into a story of minority rights, and when he claims that Uriah was treated badly because he was a Hittite, he spoke directly to the spiritual concerns of the people of Israel.

There is a sad footnote to the story. When Shamir wrote this novel he was obviously quite dovish, quite sympathetic to Arab rights. Years later he wrote another book *My Life with Ishmael* in which he expresses a much more hawkish mood. He begins that book by saying that he is named after his uncle who was killed by the Arabs in 1929, and that his uncle was named after his uncle who was killed by the Arabs in 1885. And so it goes, he feels; there is no end in sight. It is sad that one who had such high hopes and such ethical ideals has become so weary and so despairing over the possibility of peace.

Notice that one character is missing in Shamir's version of the story. From the few lines in the Bible he has created a Bathsheba of flesh and blood. He creates a David and a Uriah that are credible. One character he leaves completely out of the story— Nathan the prophet.

Why does he leave Nathan out? Because to deal with Nathan is to deal with God. Nathan is simply the voice of God. Shamir is a secularist. He believes deeply in ethics and yet, he does not believe in God. He believes in *mitzvot* (commandments) but not in a *Metzaveh* (Commander).

Can there be ethics without religion, commandments without a commander? That is the question that Nathan's absence from the story raises. It is one that Israelis and Jews everywhere are struggling with.

4. *The Story's Echoes in America*

I think it would be fair to say that Richard Nixon was not one of America's most pious presidents, and yet, he introduced a custom of worship that no previous president had ever done. By the end of his administration he cold hardly appear in public without being jeered because of Vietnam and Watergate. So, since he could not leave the White House to go to church, he had services each week in the White House. He invited a different minister, representing a different denomination, to conduct the services each week.

One of the people invited was a rabbi. He is a very great rabbi and I do not mean to be disrespectful of him, but he gave a dreadful sermon. It contained one paragraph that was so obsequious, so ingratiating, that it offended everyone. He was speaking of how we never fully grasp the significance of events while they are going on. The Egyptians did not realize the full meaning of the Exodus of the Israelites. The people at the time of Cyrus did not comprehend the full significance of his declaration permitting the Jews to return to their land. And then he said:

> I hope that it is not presumptuous of me, a guest of the President of the United States, to pray that the future historian looking back on our generation, may say, as I have said of Lincoln, that in a period of great trial and great tribulations, the finger of God pointed to Richard Milhous Nixon, giving him the vision and the wisdom to save the world and civilization, and also to open the way for our country to realize the good that the twentieth century offers mankind.

Ugh! What an embarrassing sentence that is! How could he possibly have said that? I think I know how. When he got up to speak, the image of his father, who was born in Czarist Russia, must have been before him.

His father never dreamed that he could ever see the Czar, much less speak in his presence, much less chastise and criticize him. And so, the rabbi chose not to rock the boat or spoil the party. It was enough, his father would have said, that his son was invited to speak at the White House. He should not spoil the celebration by being rude.

Eartha Kitt chose to do differently. When she was invited to sing at the White House, she spoiled the party. She said to the President, "Mr. President, stop the bombing!" As a result, her career was ruined, and the FBI harassed her for years. This rabbi, rightly or wrongly, chose to do differently. He chose to speak words of over-generous praise, so as not to offend.

The sermons given at the White House by those ministers were published in book form. Then a counter book was published by Stephen Rose, with the engaging title *Sermons NOT Preached at the White House*. The two books were reviewed together in the *New York Times*. And the reviewer compared them this way: "The first book has elegance and grace. The sermons in them show erudition and manners. There is only one thing missing in them. The *Voice of Nathan* is not there." (emphasis mine.)

Here is a second story about Nathan and American politics: Some years ago, Congress established a new medal, one of the most prestigious that anyone in this country can be given, and one of the provisions of the law is that the medal must be presented by the President of the United States. The first recipient of the medal was Elie Wiesel and the event was scheduled many weeks in advance.

Then came one of those incredible coincidences that no novelist could have ever dreamed up. Three days before the presentation was scheduled to take place, the Bitburg controversy broke out in the press! The President was going to visit Germany and the German government had arranged his itinerary. One of the stops was going to be at a military cemetery, in which S.S. men were buried.

What to do? Reagan could not graciously withdraw without offending his German hosts. The Germans held firm and insisted that the itinerary could not be changed. There was an uproar of protest from Jews and other people who were deeply offended at the idea of the President of the United States paying tribute to

Nazis. Frantic negotiations went back and forth between the camp of Elie Wiesel and officials at the White House. At one point Mr. Wiesel threatened to withdraw from the ceremonies. At another point the president did too. No compromise could be worked out in time, and the ceremony went through. The President came and presented the medal. Elie Wiesel thanked him graciously, and then, on world television, in front of hundreds of reporters and broadcasters, he turned to the president and said, "Mr. President, that is not your place! You belong with the victims, not with the killers!"

It was a dramatic scene and the papers were full of editorials the next day praising Elie Wiesel for his courage. One newspaper writer put it best, "The voice of Nathan, bottled up for centuries in books that were studied for centuries in villages like Sighet, exploded in Washington today." It is a memorable line, for it expresses the great wonder of this ancient story that still has power to speak, that centuries later it can still serve as a model for the prophetic task—to speak truth to power.

But there is one more nuance of the story that has been generally overlooked. Why did President Reagan come to the ceremony, knowing full well that he would be rebuked on world television? Why did he not excuse himself, citing the pressures of presidential responsibilities, and send someone else in his place? Or why did he not present the medal and then leave, instead of staying and being publicly photographed by the cameras while being publicly rebuked?

I can't prove it, but I have a hunch that this willingness to stay and be chastised was an act of morality that should not be underestimated. And if that is so, then it opens up yet another perspective on the biblical story and the identity of the real hero.

No one knows the name of the author of this tale and no one can say for sure when it was edited or when it entered the book of Samuel. But this much we can say for sure: Whenever it was written and whenever it was redacted, it was done in the time when a descendant of the House of David was on the throne. There was never any other kind of king in Judah, for Judah lived by the tradition that only a descendant of the House of David was eligible to be king. (There were never any revolutions in the land, since it didn't pay to overthrow the king if you were ineligible to take his place.) Whoever that king from the House of David was, he allowed this story about the great sin of his ancestor to be told, to be recorded, and to be included in the book of Samuel! He chose not to censor it and not to execute its author, just as Ronald Reagan chose to stay and endure public rebuke. For this, he deserves our respect. Who are the heroes of the biblical tale? The one who had the courage to tell it and the king who had the graciousness to allow it to be told.

5. And Now Woody Allen

We must make one last stop on our journey with this tale. Woody Allen is not known for having great respect for Judaism or for religion in general. *Zelig* and *Annie Hall* and his other films have been criticized for making fun of Jewish values. But his film *Crimes and Misdemeanors* may be an exception.

Noam Zion, a Bible scholar who lives in Israel, suggested to me that the film could be studied as a Midrash on the David-Bathsheba story by drawing a few parallels between the ancient and modern stories: First, Judah is the central character in the film, and David comes from the tribe of Judah. Second, the protagonist becomes involved in an adulterous relationship and wants to kill the woman in order to avoid scandal, just as David did. Third, he has to beg a favor, not from his nephew as David did, but from his brother, someone to whom he dislikes being beholden, just as in the David story. And last, he is obsessed with being found out and afterwards, he is plagued with guilt.

Judah is an ophthalmologist, and he turns to his patient, the rabbi, in search of answers to his guilt and fear. He keeps pressing the rabbi to tell him whether God knows and whether God sees everything that happens here on earth. If God does not know or see, then murder is not such a terrible thing, then it is not a crime, but a misdemeanor. Judah gets no clear answer to his question but, as the movie ends, we see a striking contrast between the rabbi and the eye doctor: In the last scene the rabbi, despite his nearly total physical blindness, is dancing at his daughter's wedding, dancing to the song *I'll Be Seeing You in All the Old*

Familiar Places. Judah, standing on the sidelines, envies the rabbi. The rabbi knows something, has something, that he doesn't know or have. The rabbi is able to dance despite the darkness, while he is not.

That last poignant image of the blind rabbi dancing at his daughter's wedding is very powerful. In the words of one reviewer, the rabbi is "like a match flickering bravely in the midst of howling darkness, casting a pure flame." The rabbi is envied by the doctor for he can see what the eye doctor cannot see. He can see with the eyes of faith.

Isn't it surprising that Woody Allen, whose films have generally otherwise been so flip, nihilistic, and ultimately cynical about life, should have made a movie that hints of more to life than we can see, that suggests that there is a way in which those who do good get some spiritual strength that is denied to those who do evil?

We have followed the wandering of this biblical tale from Jerusalem, where it takes place, to Babylon, where it is read in a totally different way, back to modern Israel, where it speaks to a whole new situation. From there we traveled to Washington where it came alive in a whole new setting and spoke to truth and power again. We then followed it to Hollywood, where it was retold in a new way and with a new focus.

Who can say where or when this story will reappear and what it will mean in the future? In the meantime, we can only marvel at how this ancient tale continues to speak to so many people in so many places with its eternal message.

Moshe ben Asher and Khulda bat Sarah

To Know the Queen

A story within a story, this piece grapples with the tension and connections between the desire to experience holiness, and the need to live a life of holiness.

I am the Lord, I have called you in righteousness,
I have taken you by the hand and kept you;
I have given you as a covenant to the people,
  a light to the nations,
    to open the eyes that are blind,
  to bring out the prisoners from the dungeon,
    from the prison those who sit in darkness.
                          —Isaiah 42:6–7

He sat in the shadow of the wall. High in the cell a small window shed a square of the morning light on the floor below. He looked away from it . . . he had not seen the light. He sat facing the wall. Neither did he see the wall.

Most of the time he could look at nothing but his hands. "I thought I knew these hands," he murmured, as if they had a life of their own. "I thought I could trust these hands."

He repeated to himself the details of the killing, but there was no solace in them. By now they formed a sort of chant, beginning with the turn of the key in the lock. He had been drunk when he loaded the truck that morning. He remembered fumbling with the key. He remembered again the point of the actual killing, the precise moment that he imagined separated life from death, the moment when her body hit the truck. No—it was the truck hitting her, or maybe it was the moment when she had been thrown clear of the truck. At the instant of recollection his whole body shook. But it was not enough. It was never enough.

He listened to his heartbeat at this point, thinking, as always, that *his* heart was still beating. There was no way out. "If I were to take my own life . . . ," he thought to himself. But that would be another killing, and perhaps more guilt. And so the chant went on, for almost a year now.

Except for the visits of the rabbi, he was alone. Actually he was angry with the rabbi, who had counseled him to "live in God through prayer and the mitzvot. Keep the Sabbath here," the rabbi would say.

Whenever the rabbi visited, he would grasp him impatiently by the hand, demanding, "Tell me the secret! I want to know the secret!"

"Which secret?" the rabbi always asked him.

"You know what I mean," he cried, angry that the rabbi should not know by now what was in his heart—the path to the Divine, the Way Out!—which seemed to him to be bursting from his body.

Finally the rabbi told him this tale.

Once there was a merchant who had become impoverished. What he wanted, more than anything, was to know the Queen. She was known to be compassionate and righteous, and he felt that if he could only be near her, if he could but be in the company of her righteousness and her wealth, he would be happy.

He sought out the wisest man in his village, and asked, "How can I come to know the Queen?"

"Why do you want to know the Queen?" asked the wise man. "Do you want the Queen's power and wealth for yourself?"

"No," the peddler replied. "All I want is to be in her company—to sit at her right hand."

"What will become of your family?" the wise one asked.

"My children are grown and my wife dead. Who else is there for me to live for?"

"And who will serve your customers?" the wise one queried.

"My customers," he replied, incredulous at the older one's concern. "Of what importance am I to them? They will be served by others. What I want is to be near the Queen. What must I do?"

Now it happened that in his village this merchant was famous for his ability to manipulate and remember long lists of numbers, and it was also known that he had always treated his customers fairly. But he did not realize the importance of these things, so he thought himself of little worth.

"Very well," said the wise man, who was frequently consulted by the Queen about her problems.

That very day the Sovereign came to learn of the poor peddler who could count, and she quickly realized that he could be valuable to her. For in the Queen's court there was much miscounting, even by the court's most respected members. So she had him brought to the palace to sit at her right hand, to keep track of all the royal counting.

Thus the peddler became a peer. He sat near the Queen, and he was cloaked in velvet robes. He occupied a great chair, although, of course, not as great as the Queen's.

At first he felt almost ecstatic to be in the Queen's presence. She was fair and she was good, just as he had heard. But as time passed he began to understand that it was not only the fairness of the Queen, but the fairness of the law as well that made her subjects whole in their petitioning, and he became preoccupied with that. It seemed to him that the law could hold the meaning of his life. Suddenly he remembered the wise one's question about who would serve his customers. In his preoccupation he began to make mistakes in counting. This angered the Queen.

She demanded to know the cause of the counting errors. "Are you so bored and preoccupied that you can't keep your mind on your counting?"

"No," he replied. He explained his fascination with the reasons the Queen used in granting or denying the petitions. "It's only that I want to know why."

In fact, in his own heart he knew that it was more than that. What he really wanted was to bring the Queen's righteous rule to the people in his own village, and he knew he would have to leave the Queen to do that. He begged her to release him from service and allow him to return to his village, family, and friends.

The Queen thought a long time before she answered. "First you begged to be in our company, and now you beg not to be in our company . . . ? The benefits we granted you are paid for by a lifetime of service. However," she added, "We can see you will serve us better among the people."

"So, you may leave the palace, but only on these three conditions: First, you must *live* the law that you have learned here. Second, you must always use your freedom to demand justice for yourself and all others. And third, you must never again seek to be in constant company with us. In these ways you can fulfill your obligation to us."

The peddler left the palace that very hour, with no more possessions than he had come with, yet not impoverished. Arriving in his village before nightfall, he was welcomed by his friends and neighbors as an intimate of the Queen. They asked him when he would return to the palace, and they showered him with requests and petitions that they wanted him to make to the Queen on their behalf.

"I am not going back," he answered. "The Queen has given us freedom and the law, and these are what we need for a good life."

Barbara E. Breitman

Mi Dor L'Dor:
An Intergenerational Midrash
on the Akedah

The midrashic process has enabled Jews to maintain a dialogue with ancient texts generation after generation, infusing old stories with the perspectives, insights, and imaginations of people of the contemporary era. Just as in dream worlds, so it is in the world of midrash: time is neither linear nor historic. In dreams, images from childhood can co-exist with images and people the dreamer encountered just yesterday. In midrash, biblical characters can speak the words of contemporary Jews and even play out their struggles. Characters who had no voice in ancient texts can suddenly break their silences and speak in modern idioms. Through midrash, Torah continues to unfold like a timeless and eternal dream, as Jews of every generation bring new associations and understanding to ancient myths.

By introducing many previously assimilated, often alienated American Jews to the history and concept of midrash, Zalman gave us a creative means for entering the age-old dialogue between Jew and text, for creating a relationship with tradition. In recent decades, many Jewish women (some influenced by Zalman's teachings) have used the midrashic process to provide new interpretations of biblical stories and to fill in silences in the text so we can finally "hear" women of the Bible and Talmud whose words and thoughts were never recorded. This is one way the consciousness of contemporary Jewish women are becoming a part of the evolving text of the Jewish people.

The biblical story of the binding of Isaac (Gen. 22:12) has inspired countless midrashim over the centuries. Remarkably, each generation seems to find more to say about this well-worn tale. In his recent book *God was in this Place and I, i did not know it* Rabbi Lawrence Kushner proposes "that the key to decoding the binding of Isaac legend, or, as it is known in Hebrew, the Akedah, is concealed back in the strange relationship Abraham, our father, had with Terah, his father." Kushner himself, seems to have been moved to this insight by reading Joel Rosenberg's poem "God of Abraham, God of Isaac" in which Rosenberg has Isaac say after the Akedah: "(His voice now changed into a man's); 'But tell me, Abba, you have left your father's house. And will I do the same, and will my child?'"

As a psychotherapist, my own thinking was sparked by the insights of these two contemporary poets, because they were looking at intergenerational family legacies to uncover Abraham's psychological motivation in the story of the Akedah. As I combined family system's theory with a perspective on the gender dynamics of intimate family relationships under condi-tions of patriarchy, the text yielded yet another midrash, linked conceptually to Kushner's and Rosenberg's. While what follows is not a midrash that fills in the voices of the matriarchs, it is one which explores some of the gender dynamics of family life under patriarchy.

The First Generation:
Creating a Legacy of Cut-offs

Jewish legend, as is well known, has expanded on the biblical *lech l'cha* "Go forth from your land, from the place of your birth, from the house of your father" (Gen. 12:1) with the famous midrash about Abraham and his father Terah's idol shop. According to the midrash, Terah ran an idol boutique in the land of Ur. One day, Terah left his son Abe in charge of the store, and the rebellious son spent the day smashing all the idols. When he was done, Abe placed the hatchet in the hand of the biggest one. Terah returned to find his inventory destroyed and yelled at his son in great distress, "What have you done? Why have you destroyed all my idols?"

Calmly, Abe replied, "I did not destroy them. I cooked a delicious dinner for them, but they all fought for the food. Then that big one took the hatchet and smashed all the others!"

Terah became enraged. "How can you tell me such lies? Do these idols have any soul in them? I made them all myself. They are just dumb wood and stone."

"So why do you worship them, old man?" screamed Abe as he smashed the last idol and ran away from home, never to be seen or heard from by his parents again (Gen. 11:31).

From the perspective of a family therapist, what occurred between Terah and Abe is known as a "cut-off." Unable to resolve a conflict in family relationships through compromise, negotiation, or the toleration of differences, the child "cuts off" completely from the parent. Often this happens when parents are extremely overpowering or controlling, insistent that their child do what they say, believe as they believe, sacrifice their own point of view. The child can wind up feeling that the only way to have a mind of one's own, a life of one's own, is to break completely from parents. The problem is that cut-offs can have serious consequences.

Not having learned how to resolve family conflict while maintaining the relationship, not being able to experience a healthful differentiation of self from the family of origin, the child, as an adult, can pass on the pattern of cut-offs to the next generation. Another consequence is the adult child, cut-off from intimacy and connection with their family of origin, can cling tenaciously to *their* own children. Because they feel so traumatized by their earlier experience of separation and loss, they unconsciously recreate the stifling enmeshment of their own childhood.

Abe cuts-off from his father to follow his dream. Strong-willed and driven, he believes he is destined to be the father of a great nation. He believes God has chosen him for a sacred mission. Abe has staked his life on it. He's left home, parents, and everything familiar. But there is one serious hitch. His wife is infertile! What a blow to a man obsessed with becoming the father of a great nation! His beautiful Sarah, the wife who was willing to follow him to the ends of the earth, cannot bear the children he needs to make his name great.

Unable to abandon his mission, Abe longs to find a way to sire this great nation. After much soul-searching and heartwrenching decision making—similar to what people go through who decide to enlist the services of a surrogate—Sarah offers for Abe to have a child with her maidservant, Hagar. The economically distressed, much lower class, and probably darker skinned Hagar agrees to bear Abe and Sarah a child.

But as we know, surrogacy arrangements often result in bitter disputes between the biological mother and the adoptive parents. In our ancestral family, this battle could not be resolved in the courts. The women are left to struggle it out between themselves. In the patriarchal context of biblical times, when women's primary value seemed to derive from their capacity to bear children, Sarah and Hagar are pitted against each other around issues of fertility. Sarah wants desperately to be the mother of the new nation. She knows she will be lowered in Abe's esteem if she cannot produce children and she is afraid the surrogate mother will replace her in Abe's affections. The lower-class oppressed servant, elevated in her master's eyes after the birth of Ishmael, sees an opportunity to improve the conditions of her life and go gain some recognition for herself. After the conception of her son, she begins to maneuver for status in the family and starts to look down on Sarah: "He cohabited with Hagar and she conceived; and when she saw that she had conceived, her mistress was lowered in her esteem. And Sarah said to Abram, 'the wrong done me is your fault! I myself put my maid in your bosom; now that she sees that she is pregnant, I am lowered in her esteem. The Lord decide between you and me!'" (Gen. 16:4–6). Abe and Sarah's marriage becomes increasingly strained and tense. Abe even insults Sarah by trying to pass her off as his sister to King Abimelech (Gen. 20). Sarah grows more and more lonely and dejected.

Even in her old age, Sarah cannot let go of the hope of bearing Abe's children and regaining her previous stature in the family. Abe finds the idea laughable. "Abraham threw himself on his face and laughed, as he said to himself, 'Can a child be born to a man a hundred years old, or can Sarah bear a child at ninety'?" (Gen.

17:17). He overhears Sarah crying, and imagines she too is laughing (Gen. 18:12–15). And then, like a miracle, long after Sarah has already gone into menopause, she conceives and gives birth to a son in her old age. The tensions between Sarah and Hagar intensify after the birth of Isaac, as the two women vie for what little power they might have in the family. Picking up on his mother's hostility toward her mistress, Ishmael starts to taunt and torment the baby Isaac.

Returned to her status as female head of household, Sarah insists that Abraham send Hagar and Ishmael away. "Sarah saw the son whom Hagar the Egyptian had borne to Abraham playing. She said to Abraham, 'Cast out that slave-woman and her son, for the son of that slave shall not share in the inheritance with my son Isaac.' The matter distressed Abraham greatly, for it concerned a son of his." (Gen. 21:9–11). Abraham, understandably, is appalled by the idea. But he never learned how to resolve a family conflict without ending the relationship, so he can find no other alternative. Though he is tormented by the idea of abandoning a son, Abraham also feels guilty for the way he has treated Sarah since Ishmael's birth. Caught between the two women, with a history of cut-offs in his family of origin, Abraham sees no possibility for mediation. Unable to explore the possibilities of sisterhood under conditions of racial, class, and gender oppression, the women know only how to hate one another. And so Abraham sends Hagar and Ishmael off into the desert, repeating the pattern of cut-offs between father and son. The relationship between the women remains an open wound.

The Sacrifice

After casting out Hagar and Ishmael, Abraham is tormented by grief and guilt. He has sacrificed everything for his dream—this idea of a new God and a new nation. Perhaps he has lost too much. He has abandoned his father and mother. He has abandoned the land of his birth. He has rejected everything he was taught to believe. Now he has even abandoned his own flesh and blood—his firstborn son—to wander in the wilderness.

"What if all of this has been for nought?" Such terrifying thoughts plague Abraham at night. "What if my son Isaac does to me what I, Abraham, did to my father, Terah? What if Isaac abandons my God as I abandoned the gods of Terah? What if Isaac sees how I have abandoned my first son, and decides he owes no allegiance to such a father?" Abraham becomes a deeply troubled, tormented, and desperate man.

He resolves that he must ensure Isaac's loyalty to his religion, ensure that Isaac will believe in the one God of heaven and earth. He must prevent Isaac from ever cutting him off, from ever abandoning the faith of *his* father. Abraham decides Isaac must have an experience so profound, so terrifying, and make such a powerful impact, he could never possibly imagine casting off Abraham or his religion.

Abraham wakes up startled from a nightmare early one morning. He shakes Isaac out of bed while the boy is still sleepy and bleary eyed. Father and son set off on a journey into the grey morning with two servants and all that is needed for a burnt offering, except the sheep. They walk for two days. On the third day, Abraham tells the two servants to wait behind. He piles Isaac with wood and they continue their trek to the top of the mountain. When they arrive at the peak, Abraham constructs an altar, as Isaac watches, paralyzed by terror, knowing there is no sheep for the sacrifice. Finally, Abraham commands his son to make himself ready. He binds Isaac to the altar.

As Isaac lies trembling, Abraham raises the knife over his head. "I would sooner slay you here on this altar than watch you abandon me, abandon our faith," Abraham's voice is booming. "Isaac, do you understand? You must *never* do to me what I did to my father. You must promise. You must swear on your life! I would rather kill you here on this mountain as a Sacrifice to the Lord than let you live long enough to see you abandon me, our people, and our God!"

Terrified, Isaac swears loyalty. He promises always to follow in his father's footsteps. He promises ever after to sacrifice his soul to his father's will and to believe in the one God of heaven and earth.

Convinced and finally relieved, Abraham spies a ram caught by its horns in the bushes. He interprets this as a sign from God to trust Isaac and spare his life. "So Abraham went and took the ram and offered it up as a burnt offering in place of his son" (Gen. 22:13). Watching the lifeblood of the ram vanish in smoke, Isaac is terrified and speechless.

The Legacy of Cut-offs Continues: Jacob and Esau

Abraham has won his son's loyalty at the price of breaking his spirit. Isaac, cannot speak for many decades. From the day of the Akedah until his encounter with King Abimelech many years later, the text records nothing of Isaac's words—only his actions. Isaac shows little interest in marriage. Unlike his father who journeyed with his young wife far from home, and unlike his future son who will work for fourteen years to marry the wife of his dreams, Isaac shows little interest in finding a marriage partner. He clings to his mother's side after the traumatic experience with his father on the mountain. Sarah, after learning what her deranged husband has done to her beloved son, tries to protect Isaac from further abuse by keeping him close to her. Not until his mother dies is Isaac even willing to be introduced to a potential spouse.

When Isaac is forty years old, Abraham sends his servants to find an appropriate wife for his son, and to keep things all in the family, he instructs them to look only amongst his kinsmen. Isaac agrees to marry his cousin, Rebekah, according to his father's wishes. A fragile child/man, traumatized by paternal abuse and infantilized by an anxious mother, Isaac clings to his new wife for comfort after his mother's death: "Isaac then brought her into the tent of his mother Sarah, and he took Rebekah as his wife. Isaac loved her, and thus found comfort after his mother's death" (Gen. 24:67).

Unfortunately, Isaac is emotionally incapable of developing an adult, intimate relationship with a woman. He cannot allow any woman to replace his mother in his affections, and he feels locked into being the "child" in relation to his wife. He is also starving for the male companionship that was ripped away from him when Abraham became abusive and no longer offered a safe context for a father-son connection. Instead of enjoying time with Rebekah, Isaac prefers to go hunting with his son Esau, far from home, and hang out with the guys in bars and hunting lodges. With the "macho," rough-and-tumble Esau, Isaac tries to recapture the wild, boyish fun of youth that was so abruptly wrenched away from him.

Eventually Rebekah despairs of having a close, warm marriage. Instead, she turns to her younger son Jacob for companionship, relying on him to assuage her loneliness. Over time the family divides into unwholesome coalitions: Isaac favors Esau and rejects Jacob for being a "mama's boy," reminding him of his own disowned, hated self. Rebekah sides with Jacob against her husband. Over many years this unhealthy pattern persists and becomes rigidly embedded in the family: "When the boys grew up, Esau became a skillful hunter, a man of the outdoors; but Jacob was a mild man who stayed in camp. Isaac favored Esau because he had a taste for game; but Rebekah favored Jacob" (Gen. 25:27–28).

Finally, when Isaac is aged and blind, his scorned and embittered wife conspires with her precious son Jacob to outwit the failing old man and in her mind, rebalance the scales. Rebekah coaches Jacob to trick Isaac into giving the patriarchal blessing to him, her favorite, instead of Esau. Isaac's beloved Esau is cheated out of his rightful inheritance as the older son. And so Rebekah pays Isaac back for wasting her youth in a loveless, distant union, formed only to appease the father who has threatened his life. With the treacherous deed accomplished, the intergenerational pattern of cut-offs repeats. Jacob is forced to flee for his life from the enraged Esau and sees his father again only on the old man's deathbed.

A wanderer like his grandfather Abraham, Jacob sets forth on a journey of his own. It is a journey with its own twists and turns, in which his mother's brother creates the first of several opportunities for Jacob to make restitution for his treachery: Uncle Leban tricks his nephew into marrying his older daughter Leah, before he can earn the right to wed the younger and beloved Rachel. Leah bears six sons and a daughter, Dinah. Rachel, who has fertility problems, gives birth to only two sons, and only one survives, her precious Joseph. Rachel and Leah's maidservants give birth to four more sons. The conflict between the mothers leads to conflict among the children and competition for Jacob's attention. The stage is set for the sibling rivalries of the next generation.

Mending a Torn Tapestry: Joseph and His Brothers

As the only son born from a union of love in three generations, and loved by both father and mother, Joseph emerges as the special child, the one capable of healing the intergenerational pattern of cut-offs, unholy alliances, and betrayals. But first, Joseph needs to undergo a transformation from being the pampered, narcissistic, privileged son born to and raised by his father's favorite wife, to being the leader of a nation and healer of wounds.

As a young boy, Joseph knows his father loves him best of all his sons (Gen. 37:3–4), and he comports himself like a privileged character. His brothers grow to hate and envy him and eventually conspire to kill him, preparing to carry the legacy of cut-offs to its ultimate deadly conclusion. Joseph's story becomes the story of the one who finally integrates the shadow, the dark side of the family's legacy. His journey is a journey, literally, through the depths.

First, Joseph is thrown by his brothers into the pit, and stripped of all status and protection. Then he is sold into slavery and goes down to Egypt. Finally, after his encounter with Potiphar's wife, he is locked away for years in the dungeon. Throughout this time, Joseph dreams. He descends into the dark night of the soul. When he emerges, he is a man of great vision, a man with an integrated consciousness, able to face both good and evil in himself and others, able to lead and plan for the future. He has found meaning and purpose in his suffering and in his triumphs.

It is this transformed Joseph to whom the brothers finally

appeal for help. It is this Joseph who saves his brothers and their families. It is this Joseph who finally heals the family, by forgiving even those who have injured him, and by bringing the cut-off brothers, and father and son back into relationship. In healing these cut-off relationships and mending the torn and tattered tapestry of connection, Joseph discerns the movement and presence of a purpose larger than their human deeds: "I am your brother Joseph, he whom you sold into Egypt. Now, do not be distressed or reproach yourselves because you sold me hither; it was to save life that God sent me ahead of you . . . God has sent me ahead of you to ensure your survival on earth, and to save your lives in an extraordinary deliverance. So it was not you who sent me here, but God . . ." (Gen. 45:4ff).

The first book of the Torah thus comes to an end, as the first family of Israel heals the generations of wounds first inflicted by Abraham's initial break with his father and the gods of the past. In this light, the Akedah emerges as a turning point in the history of the family, the point in the intergenerational transmission process at which it was decided whether the God of Abraham would ultimately become the God of Isaac, and the God of Jacob.

Epilogue

The Torah tells us painfully little about the God of Sarah, the God of Rebekah, the God of Rachel and Leah. Interestingly, we actually hear somewhat more about the God of Hagar. The relationships between the women are not worked through or resolved in the text as are the relationships between the men. It remains the work of the contemporary descendants of these women to find ways to bridge distances and create understanding so we and future generations do not have to sacrifice ourselves, our sons, or our daughters to perpetuate our faith.

From Masa Ashlaya, attributed to Moshe ben Yitzhaq HaPardesan
(MS. private collection)
Translated and annotated by Marc Bregman

"Opening a Verse"

According to a traditional view of Judaism, at age forty men who are well-versed in Jewish law and traditions and are solid house-holders as well, may begin the study of Zohar, the premier text of Jewish mysticism. One of the Jewish Renewal movement's largest contributions to the public is the offering of the opportunity to study and experience the mystical side of Judaism.

This text records a mystical, meditative journey connected with the study of the Zohar. Meditating on the shapes of Hebrew letters is one traditional way Jews have accessed mystical experience.

Today was a very special day in the Yeshivah of Rabbi Pinhas of Koretz. For many years he had been teaching his inner circle of disciples. Now they had all matured and become grown men— the youngest having already passed the age of forty. Today was the day they had all been waiting for—the day that Reb Pinhas was to begin teaching them the holiest of the Holy Books, the Zohar, The Book of Light.

The Rabbi looked lovingly at his disciples. "Today, my students, we shall see with a new and different Light, for today you may enter the world of the Zohar."

Reb Pinhas began:

In the beginning of the Zohar we find the expression, "Rabbi Shimon *patah*." Now you all know from our previous study of the sacred books, that this expression is found often in the Midrash. And there we have learned that it means simply that such and such a Sage began his discourse with such and such a verse. But here, in the Zohar, it means something quite different. Here it means that Rabbi Shimon bar Yohai actually opened the verse.

The disciples looked puzzled. How is it possible to "open" a verse?!

Rabbi Pinhas explained:

> As Hasidim, you have learned that when you pray, each of you must put all his strength into the words he utters, moving from letter to letter, until he is no longer aware of what surrounds him. So too with learning Torah. Let each of you begin with a verse, putting all your strength into the words you utter.

The youngest disciple of Rabbi Pinhas, the silent and serious scholar Moshe ben Yitzhaq, closed his eyes tightly. With a flash of light his mind was filled with words of Torah, *Petah devarekha yair*[1] (The opening of your words shall give light). With all his strength he uttered the first letter of the first word. The letter *Peh* appeared to him as an open mouth filled with a strange brilliance. Like a moth attracted to the light, Moshe entered into the open mouth of the letter *Peh*. As in a dream he walked slowly on, gazing in wonder at the curving inner wall of the letter. Like a man wandering in a maze, he groped onward into this blinding light that seemed to deepen the darkness as it grew more brilliant. Passing beyond the circular pillar in the center of the letter, he peered into what he sensed was an open space. He felt he had arrived at a place that was somehow strangely familiar. He had reached the Holy Land and had entered an orchard—the Bet Midrash of Rabbi Shimon bar Yohai. And it was Rabbi Shimon himself who was speaking, "Budding blossoms have appeared in the land . . ."[2] As Rabbi Shimon spoke, it seemed as if blossoms actually bloomed and gave off a fascinating fragrance. Like a bee

---

1. Psalms 119:130
2. Song of Songs 2:12

lured by overpowering instinct, Moshe flew down to the flower. Drinking in the nectar, slowly he followed the curving inner wall of the flower down to the stem, down to the stem, down to the root, deeper and deeper, darker and darker . . . "Budding blossoms" refers to the Work of Creation, as it is written: "in the beginning God created the heaven and the earth. And the earth was without form, and void; and darkness was upon the face of the deep. And the Spirit of God hovered over the face of the waters. And God said: Let there be light. And there was Light . . ."[3]

When Moshe opened his eyes, he found himself gazing into the eyes of this teacher. The eyes of Reb Pinhas seemed to give off a strange light, as he gazed back into the eyes of his disciple, for Rabbi Pinhas saw and knew that this disciple had indeed entered the Zohar. He had felt its Darkness, but he had also seen its Light. And now Moshe ben Yitzhaq HaPardesan also knew what it meant to "open a verse."

---

3. Genesis 1:1–3

Edward Hoffman

The Kabbalah:
Doorway to the Mind

For millenia, adepts of the Kabbalah—the mystical offshoot of Judaism—have intimately addressed the nature of human consciousness and our relation to the divine. Key Kabbalistic texts have for more than fifteen hundred years dealt with such intriguing topics as dreams, meditation, altered states of awareness, the mind-body relationship, awakening intuition and "prophetic" qualities, and attaining spiritual ecstasy.

Yet Jewish mystics have always emphasized the importance of the seemingly more mundane—but perhaps, even more challenging—task of creating a pathway to the Holy One through the very midst of everyday life and the myriad distractions that surround us.

It was the early Hasidic movement that really brought the esoteric wisdom of the Kabbalah into the crucial sphere of daily existence for all who were receptive. Founded by the charismatic, lay Jewish preacher and faith healer known as the "Baal Shem Tov" (Bearer of the Good Name), this movement arose with astonishing speed in the latter half of the eighteenth century in Eastern Europe. The Baal Shem Tov preached that joy and bodily vigor are methods by which even the least schooled in formal spiritual practice can come closer to the deity. To his more erudite disciples, he also taught highly abstruse, meditative techniques involving unification of the Hebrew letters through complex visualizations. Interestingly, though, the Baal Shem Tov also instituted the practice of spiritual counseling between *rebbe* (spiritual master) and Hasid as a pivotal feature of the Hasidic way.

What form did such spiritual counseling take? And how does it relate to us at the end of the twentieth century? Especially with the new, emerging paradigm in Western psychology—with its humanistic and transpersonal perspective—Kabbalistic and Hasidic ideas and practices seem highly pertinent today. Indeed, a growing number of health care professionals—in fields now encompassing psychiatry and nursing, psychology and counseling—are utilizing classic Kabbalistic methods to help others achieve greater inner harmony and direction in life.

For central to this ancient system of knowledge is the notion that we are each cloaked in physical form in order for our soul to carry out a unique mission for the Almighty. The better able we are to recognize—and then conduct—our specific mission on this earth, the more joyful and fulfilled our lives become. Jewish mystics have long taught that the lack of a sense of purpose or direction is a sure sign that we have somehow lost our way and need guidance to remember our personal *tikkun* (sphere of rectification/redemption) for our present existence.

Early Hasidic leaders like Rabbi Nachman of Bratslav (great-grandson of the Baal Shem Tov) utilized many different techniques to promote inner growth in their numerous followers. Such techniques were highly individualized in nature, and always designed to aid a particular man or woman in a particular period in his or her life, within the larger boundaries of historical period and surrounding culture. Of course, some rebbes were renowned for practicing one or another form of spiritual counseling; such masterful "specialists" came to be known far and wide in the Hasidic world and Hasidim would journey many days for their annual spiritual counseling session.

The specific techniques of the rebbes included dream-analysis, imaginal work, mental shock, storytelling, and directed advice—often suggesting that the Hasid go to an unfamiliar town and "there you will find an answer to your problem." Oracular methods were also employed at times; these included Torah (Bible) divination and "soul-reading" through the rebbe's trance state. Recognizing acutely that each person dwells in a living social network that strongly affects his or her day-to-day life, the Hasidic founders made intense use of social forms of therapy or counseling to initiate momentum for growth in the Hasid seeking change within.

In my own practice as a psychologist, I have found the Kabbalistic emphasis on storytelling and on training the Higher Will to be quite effective in helping people to find their pathway to divine purpose. For centuries, too, Jewish mystics have prized the right use of imagination as a tremendously powerful force that can guide us through the vicissitudes of life. I therefore incorporate meditative techniques developing the Higher Will as well as the imagination, often adapting passages from age-old Kabbalistic works for this goal. Above all, the Kabbalah provides me with a comprehensive framework for placing a person's problems or challenges within a broader spiritual perspective.

The inspiring words of the thirteenth-century *Zohar* (Book of Splendor) say it well: "When the whole of man had been duly shaped with all its members, God associated Himself with him and put a holy soul into him . . . so that he might attain his full perfection. Hence, while the holy soul is still within man's body, it is incumbent upon him to multiply the image of the King in the world."

"There is in this an esoteric thought involved," the *Zohar* adds, "namely, that just as the celestial stream flows on forever without ceasing, so man must see that his own river shall not cease in the world."

The City of the Just

A Meditative Exercise

One of the most compelling and inspiring concepts within Judaism is that of the "City of the Just." Throughout millenia of Jewish folklore and mystical commentary, this notion has held a lofty position. Both the Midrash and Kabbalistic literature have incorporated the concept of a dazzling, heavenly realm where the most noble and righteous souls all mingle and dwell among one another. In the "City of the Just," the highest qualities within us are completely actualized. Likewise, the *yezer hara* (evil inclination) with which we are so familiar in everyday life has been utterly vanquished, or perhaps made totally unnecessary. At times, this theme has related to that of the "Jerusalem on high," which we are told has served as a model for what our earth Jerusalem will one day come to be like. Indeed, in the days of the Redemption, all cities and all places will mirror the radiance of this celestial City.

In keeping with traditional Jewish visionary thought, the image of the "City of the Just"—a region where only the righteous exist—is not regarded as merely a philosophical abstraction or a distant societal goal. Rather, this motif is seen to provide real sustenance for our own inner being—particularly our *neshamah*—that ceaselessly longs for greater spiritual experience in this mundane world. Kabbalists have for centuries stressed the importance of developing our higher imagination in this regard.

In this exercise, you are going on a journey—beyond this realm—to the "City of the Just" in paradise. Its inhabitants know of your plans to travel there—and indeed welcome your presence as a valued visitor. Your goal? To experience the reality of the "City of the Just" as thoroughly as possible—and to make use of your experience in your day-to-day, earthly existence.

Conduct your usual preliminaries. It may be helpful to make yourself as comfortable and relaxed as possible. With eyes gently closed for a couple of minutes, observe your breath quietly as it enters and then leaves your body.

Now, feel your inner self soar upward, transcending entirely the mundane world. Feel yourself ascending the rungs of the Heavenly Ladder and passing through many layers of clouds. As you traverse past the last cloud barrier, you now see in the distance the shimmering vista of the legendary "City of the Just."

Feel yourself fly towards its image and fully stop right in front of it. To aid in the power of your journey, the scene has acquired the reality of land and solidity before you. Enter the Gates of Righteousness now—and feel their splendor around you. Their presence marks the transition between your daily realm and this higher one.

As you pass through the holy Gates, you can begin to see the brilliance of the "City of the Just"—its homes and streets, its houses of study and worship. A dazzling light permeates everything you observe. The strains of wondrous music may also be heard in the background. Go into the first dwelling place next to you—it is a house of study meant for travelers such as yourself.

In it you may see some of the righteous deeply involved in mystical inquiry concerning the innermost secrets of Torah.

When you feel ready, continue your journey outside in the "City of the Just." As you sit within a courtyard garden, gently close your eyes and feel the radiance and nearness of the *Shekhinah* (Divine Presence). According to the Midrash, its splendor is ten thousand times brighter than the sun, but in your transcendent form you feel only its exalting strength upon your entire being.

When you feel prepared, return along the same path to the Gates of Righteousness. Thank the inhabitants of the "City of the Just" for allowing your visit—and then feel yourself descending through the cloud layers, back to your room. Merge with your normal being. Know that whenever you wish, you may embark on this higher journey—and that it will revitalize your sense of identity and purpose on earth.

After completing the first part of this exercise, you are now ready for its second aspect. This part will involve making use of your visionary experience to better carry out your personal *tikkun* (rectification) in the everyday world. Reflect briefly upon how you felt during your brief sojourn in the "City of the Just" and then answer the following questions:

First, how does this celestial City differ from the earthly locale in which you live? Be as specific as possible in identifying these differences.

Second, in what ways does your present abode—involving people as well as objects—resemble the "City of the Just"? Once again, be as specific as you possibly can.

Finally, what currently lies within your sphere of *tikkun* to help build the "City of the Just"—the worldwide "Jerusalem on high"—in your own locale on this planet? What specific actions await your involvement to bring about the mirroring of "above and below"?

Eve Penner Ilsen

Of Shekhina: The Creation

The title of the five-day gathering at which I received this inspiration was *Gaia Within and Without: The Kabbalah of Creation*. It formed the first half of the 1991 Wisdom School, an intensely collaborative project through which Reb Zalman and I intended nothing less than *real* transformation of us all, in the service of our planet.

As part of our preparation, we had been studying the beginning of *The Zohar*, both in the original Aramaic and in Danny Matt's translation, late one night.

I awakened the following morning in the midst of a remarkable, inarticulate experience of being vast, empty space, receptivity, and yearning. It finally emerged as a "singing-back" to the original description of tzimtzum, the self-contraction of the light of the Infinite One to make room for creation. After all, *The Zohar* follows the story of creation from the point of view of the primal, essential, contracted point—the Divine sperm, as it were. But what of the experience of creation from the point of view of all that primal potential, the vacated space?

The thoughts and words surged up during the end of the experience, with a keen sense of the inadequacy of language to express the reality. It was shocking, shaking, intense. It welled up from the place of unknown knowing.

> *"When the King conceived ordaining*
>   *He engraved engravings in the luster on high . . ."*[1]

When the hidden One conceived of conceiving
She was,   —in her absolute unity—

---

1. Daniel C. Matt, *The Zohar: The Book of Enlightenment* (Ramsey, NJ: The Paulist Press, 1983), 49.

So whole,
So total,
The great emptiness,
So full and filled with her own *is*-ness
That nothing could come to be.

And so, although
Invisible and no-thing,

She drew together her essence
Squeezing through
intensifying,
con-centr-ating
contracted, a

           point.

A point which, taking no space
(for there was not yet space)
WAS all intensity, all energy.
              Utter intensity
              Utmost contraction
              Pulsating straining to BURST FORTH
And She remained, VOID,
In Her empty vastness of utter possibility,
              While so intensely did her
              Bursting-forth energy
              Collect
              Contracting into so intense a
              Point
That it seemed as if separate, and other, and unto itself.

And in her absolute vastness she yearned

And yearned for her emptiness to be pierced
For all the secrets of her infinite possibilities
To be discovered and exploded into being.
And this longing void was
All there was,

Before time or space were,
Before was any thing.

And the great longing
of the most Concealed of the Concealed—
This concentrated point, at its greatest intensity
LEAPED in a blinding flash
That was neither white nor black nor red nor green nor any color
   at all.

Neal Rose

Fragments of Hasidic Spirituality

Jewish Renewal has also been called Neo-Hasidism. Reb Zalman's philosophy is rooted in Chabad Hasidism, and Jewish Renewal is very much informed by Hasidism in its approach to prayer, study, and celebration. Neal Rose describes here his sojourn, as both a student and a participant-observer, into the world of Lubavitch Hasidism, and reveals the fragments or sparks he has carried from that world into Jewish Renewal and his congregational work.

In Search of Reb Nachman's Flame

In the late summer of 1970 we set sail for Eretz Yisrael. The study of Buber's presentation of Nachman was high on the agenda. I carried with me two collections of Bratzlaver sources on the Holy Land as well as a small book that reported on Nachman's short pilgrimage to Israel in the nineteenth century. Yet for all my study and reading about Nachman, I had never spent any time among his contemporary followers. My entire sense of Bratzlaver spirituality was based on literary sources. What I did know about modern-day Bratzlav was that its yeshiva in Jerusalem's ultra-orthodox Mea Shearim was the unofficial center for the several thousand Bratzlaver faithful throughout the world. Most intriguing of all was that even after his death, Bratzlavers still looked to Nachman as their rebbe. Most of his followers felt that this was the Master's plan since, prior to his death, he comforted the bereaved Hasidim by telling them that his "flame" would also be with them. Ever since, they have followed the light cast by the "flame." This dedication to the man's guiding presence, while making perfect sense to the in-group, has led sarcastic outsiders to refer to them as "the dead Hasidim." For the followers, the "flame" manifests itself through Nachman's writings, so to study these teachings is to be in direct contact with the Master. He can also be invoked during prayer to serve as an intermediary between the worshipper and the higher worlds. In the pre-Holocaust era, Bratzlavers regularly journeyed to the Ukrainian city of Uman in order to pray, study, and celebrate at the Master's grave. It was at this shrine that many felt closest to the Master's spirit.

While there are occasional pilgrimages to the Uman shrine these days, the center of gravity has shifted to the Jerusalem Yeshiva and Nachman's chair, which sits in the building's main room. During the Holocaust Nachman's chair, or zaddik-throne, was smuggled out of Europe in pieces and rebuilt in Israel. It is a symbolic representation of Nachman's presence. All who are connected in any way to the Bratzlaver teaching, be they true believers or simply interested outsiders, relate to the chair in this way. Bratzlaver publications often have photographs of Nachman's gravesite and the chair.

Shortly after my arrival, I went in search of the chair and, more importantly, the warmth and power of the "flame" it stands for. I entered the synagogue and almost immediately saw the chair on the right side of the eastern wall. As I approached, a young student dressed in Jerusalemite garb was bowing reverently before the empty chair. I waited as he respectfully walked four steps backward so as not to turn his back on the Rebbe. I sensed the chair's numinosity in the Hasid's movements.

In the early 1980s, the chair was completely reconstructed by a Jerusalem carpenter, Catriel Sugarman, and his co-workers. The masterful restoration reveals some of the beauty of holiness that believers have sensed for many years. On the evening of the restored chair's unveiling, guests came from all walks of life: artists, poets, theatre people, and curiosity seekers. A band played Bratzlaver and other Hasidic music as people milled around the "new chair." At around ten in the evening a delegation of Bratzlaver faithful appeared. After viewing the new chair, they raised it up and began dancing, and eventually danced their way out of the party and headed for the Yeshiva—the physical representation of the ruling presence of Nachman was returned to its rightful place.

The most astonishing aspect of the Bratzlaver lifestyle is the devotion to and dependence on the spirit of Reb Nachman in the day-to-day happenings. Many, if not all, followers tell stories about people who have gotten across the narrow bridge of human existence with the help of Reb Nachman. There are literally hundreds of testimonial-type tales that relate the ways in which Hasidim believe God, through Nachman, has helped them. The most gripping story I know is that of the now-aged Hasid who, in the midst of his youthful spiritual struggles, "accidentally" came across what turned out to be the discarded copy of a Bratzlaver tract. Since the title page was missing, the young man did not know the book's author but found the spiritual style and method very helpful. Only after protracted use of the book's spiritual exercises did he find out who had composed the book.

Once it became known that the young man was a Bratzlaver, he was openly discriminated against and labelled a "dead Hasid," but the shunning he was subjected to did not discourage him from his spiritual practices. In the midst of all this turmoil, he faced a spiritual crisis and had no one to turn to. Dejected and anxious, he returned to his room, only to find a handwritten note telling him what he needed to do. He claimed the note was from Nachman. Today, many years later, the now-aged Hasid still has the note and does not question its origin.

As I spent more time in the Bratzlaver community I became aware of the various leaders who head up subgroupings of the small sect. I attended their classes and soon noted their different styles of interpreting Nachman's writings. After many of these sessions there was an opportunity for fellowship. I enjoyed talking most to the older Hasidim, especially those who had been in Uman at the Rebbe's grave prior to the war. They told not only of the celebration "at the Rebbe's," but also related many miracle tales about pilgrims who came to the burial site and the many blessings bestowed on them and their family members. There were also the fearful stories of Stalinist persecutions. The wonder stories of Uman had begun prompting younger followers to attempt a pilgrimage to the Uman shrine despite the obstacles created by the Soviets. The returnees told of hazards encountered by the pilgrims and described how they witnessed the saving power of God at the zaddik's shrine. Typical are the many stories of childless couples who, after the husband's return from Uman, were blessed with children. In all of these stories, Nachman is depicted as the zaddik-intermediary through whom the blessing had flowed, not as a passive channel but as an active advocate on behalf of "his people."

Bratzlavers, while today occupying an established place in the life of Mea Shearim, are still regarded as a bit strange by the other groups of Hasidim, not only because they have a "dead rebbe" but because of certain unusual practices. For example, it is quite common for these Hasidim to wake at the end of the night and join fellow members in some secluded spot where they individually talk out loud to God. As they walk in a large circle some speak softly, others yell out loud. This exercise is known as a "dialogue between a person and his Maker." The strong emotionality of these private meditations is also indicative of Bratzlaver synagogue services; there is often screaming, yelling, and clapping of hands, and sometimes even crying in the midst of public prayer. Throughout, God is addressed in Yiddish as "father" or "sweet father." Not only are the late-night dialogues with God highly personalized, but public prayer also has a quality of warmth and directness.

Hasid of a Hasid

Very early in the process, I became a regular at the home of Reb Gedalya Keinig, one of the leaders of the Bratzlaver subgroups. One evening each week, he gave a class in Bratzlaver Hasidism to a group whose size and makeup varied. We all sat in his livingroom/bedroom area with copies of the text in front of us as he read in Hebrew and translated in Yiddish. The materials studied were Nachman homilies or discourses whose starting points were biblical verses or quotations from sacred literature. The subject matter and themes varied but I began to develop a general idea of how Nachman saw the world and the nature of human existence. The world is the creation of an infinite God who, at times, seems very close to people and their lives, but at other times, man experiences the vastness of creation as a lonely creature. He feels at sea in what appears to be an absurd world without justice, wisdom, or kindness. While God ultimately rules the world there are many unclean and downright evil forces that appear to stand between man and God. This state of affairs could create in people a sense of helplessness and despair had God not provided links with Him through Torah, worship, command-ments, and the zaddik. Bratzlaver Hasidim, therefore, seeks to help people overcome all the obstacles that apparently stand between man and God by providing the spiritual tools of the zaddik, prayer, singing, dancing, storytelling, and communal support.

Groups like the one centered around Reb Gedalya acted as such a communal support. Reb Gedalya, while making no claims of being a rebbe, constantly received people in need of spiritual or material direction. Often he counselled these people based on the wisdom acquired from living a full life as a child, teacher, husband, father, and friend. At other times he advised people by quoting directly from Bratzlaver literature. There were times, however, when he sent people to others for help, to rabbis, doctors, or lawyers. The more I became involved, the clearer it became to me that Reb Gedalya's group saw itself as an island in a sea of worldliness. Within the confines of the spiritual island was the warmth, the beauty, and the power of *kedushah*, holiness. However, there was a need for the group and its leader to remind members of their faith and support them in the face of a very alluring world. Hence, much is done by the membership to assist their brethren and their families on all levels of life.

In addition to regular classes and private meetings with people, Reb Gedalya had two projects to which he dedicated his life: the rebuilding of a spiritual center in the Galillean city of Safed and the annual Rosh Hashana celebration in the nearby village of Meron. In his very gentle way, Reb Gedalya encouraged me to participate in all of these, and I soon became a "regular" marginal member of the group. I came to see myself not as a Bratzlaver, but as a student of Reb Gedalya. After a while I referred to myself as "a Hasid of a Hasid."

Reb Gedalya always talked to me about the group's events as if I were a longtime member. So in the summer of 1971, when I began hearing about the preparations for Rosh Hashana with Reb Shimon, I quickly realized he was referring to Rabbi Shimon bar Yochai, the early Talmudic mystic who is buried in Meron. The discussion around the table increased as we got closer to the High Holidays. Then "suddenly" I decided to attend. When I asked about details like room and board and even costs, Reb Gedalya replied that "at Reb Shimon's we would be blessed with abundance." Despite the growing number of activities by the nucleus of organizers, Reb Gedalya continued to speak of the entire process as the doing of Reb Shimon.

Several hours before the New Year we arrived in Meron. The celebration began with a preliminary immersion in the *mikvah*, the ritual pool. The pool and its bathhouse were built for a small number of people, but somehow it accommodated the several hundred men who were present. Prayer began shortly before dark and dinner followed. While the physical accommodations left a lot to be desired, there were no major incidents of anger or hostility when things literally got tight. For example, when we did not have enough cups, we simply shared, with children usually getting preference.

Prayers began early. In fact, I was awakened by the shouts of a Hasid in the next room counting his blessings. The synagogue services started around six in the morning and continued until two in the afternoon. As the heat of the day increased, the atmosphere in the crowded synagogue became more dreamlike, and I found myself in a kind of mystic dream state in which the profane world and its sense of time was unknown. Somehow it seemed that one set of prayers gave way to another, and time took on a plastic, fluid, unreal quality. I felt as if the two-day holiday would go on forever.

By late afternoon of the second and last day the mood had changed somewhat. I entered the synagogue to find a group of men doing a circle dance and singing in Yiddish, over and over, "Let the entire year be filled with joy." I joined in as the chanting grew stronger and the singing took on a wishful pleading quality. It suddenly struck me that this was a ritual of termination, one that was attempting to bring the mana of the mythic realm into the world of the profane. Our dancing, then, was quite literally a winding down.

The Galillean sky was full of stars when we packed into the buses for the return to Jerusalem. Shortly after we began, my young son began crying bitterly; he had developed a painful earache. Quickly the word passed around the bus that a little boy needed something for his hurting ear. First there came a glass of Coke and finally from the front of the bus an unknown Hasid sent us half a pain killer, the amount he normally gave his children. From somewhere in my mind I heard a Yiddish proverb, *"Zu gut und zu leit,"* meaning that the ideal of human life is doing justice both to God and man, living in both the religious and humanistic dimensions equally. The bus trip typified the entire holiday experience.

We finally reached Jerusalem around midnight. The quiet of the holy city covered us. It was hard to leave Reb Gedalya, so we walked toward his house. Once inside he served us tea. Each time I tried to say goodnight he asked me to have at least one more glass. After a while we lapsed into silence—Reb Gedalya was a master of silence. Several cups later I left with great difficulty.

The Spirituality of the Land

Nachman is often spoken of by modern historians as a "pre-modern Zionist," meaning that the strong emphasis on Israel in his theological thinking and preaching seems to foreshadow modern Zionism. In fact, there is much in his homilies about Israel as the spiritual center of Judaism, and poetically it is seen as the heart of the universe. Zion however is never only a metaphor, but a real place that is never easily settled; rather it must be conquered daily from the grips of the demonic forces standing as obstacles to proper settlement.

Reb Gedalya also saw living in the Holy Land as vital to Jewish spirituality. When students came to share the hardships of living in Israel, Reb Gedalya, no matter what material or spiritual remedy he advised, always saw the problem as the Rebbe did: as yet another spiritual obstacle to overcome in conquering the Land. This consciousness of the Land plays a central role in the reality of Bratzlavers in a way that is quite unique in the Hasidic world both in Israel and the Diaspora. In part, this explains why the majority of the faithful live in Israel, and those small numbers of non-residents visit frequently and dream of eventually settling on the holy soil.

This unique Bratzlaver approach to living in Israel is best exemplified in Reb Gedalya's long and often frustrating struggle to build the spiritual center in Safed. Each time an especially difficult problem arose it was immediately seen as part of the spiritual battle to conquer the Land, as another obstacle created by "the dark side," as something to be accepted and foretold in the Rebbe's teachings. Sometimes the problem was met head on. Other times it just required patient waiting. Yet no matter how slow the process was, Reb Gedalya reminded his co-workers that the Rebbe says "not to despair," especially when it comes to matters related to "the conquest of the Land."

Reb Gedalya's lifelong goal of establishing a Bratzlaver center in Safed often consumed him. In fact, only twice in his entire life did Reb Gedalya leave Israel. Both times he reluctantly went abroad in order to raise money for the project. The first trip in the mid-1970s seemed to have weakened him. The second trip in the early summer of 1980 drew the life force out of him. Ironically, he who so loved the Holy Land died on foreign soil far from family and friends. The disciple who accompanied him described the death scene. It sounded strangely like the last moments of Reb Nachman's earthly life.

The Teacher Within

Within hours of the return of Reb Gedalya's body to the Land, he was buried on the Mount of Olives. At first, it seemed to me that my discipleship—being a "Hasid to a Hasid"—had come to an end. Over the intervening years I have come to see Reb Gedalya as part of what has often been called "the teacher within." Recently, I attended a seminar conducted under the direction of the Journal Workshop House which, among other things, attempts to develop in the participants the realization that each of us has a teacher within. As I prepared for this exercise, I began to see the figure of Reb Gedalya. First I saw his dark, piercing eyes, and then I experienced a flashback to the midnight funeral procession when we escorted him to his burial site on the Mount of Olives. The following "dialogue" emerged. It has become the memorial that I had wanted to write for many years but could not.

I came and sat at your *tish* (table). At times we were few. At times we were many. We squeezed into your dining room, which also was living room and bedroom. Size made no difference. The teaching, the study was done with the same intense quiet fire of *hitlahavut*.

At the study table there were all sorts of people. Their differences often melded together in the light of your burning eyes. When necessary, the language of teaching changed from Yiddish to Hebrew. Ultimately you returned to Jerusalemite Yiddish. When visitors came, there was always time for introductions, welcoming words, and hot tea in clear glasses. At times you would answer their questions by simply opening one of Reb Nachman's books and reading verbatim—it seemed as if the two of you had become one.

You read and translated Reb Nachman's words. Occasionally the text was punctuated with a comment, a sigh, even a smile. There were times that you seemed to be a medium through which the dead Reb Nachman spoke. Questions, when raised, were answered respectfully and patiently. Then, when finished, you would return to the music of the text.

In the afterglow of Shabbat we gathered at the *tish* to lovingly take leave of the Queen of Days. We read her Nachman's stories of longing love of Her, the Shehinah-Bride, and sang Her love ballads to the beat of your silken hands on an old drum that resounded with joy.

We study the Rebbe's *Torah of the Void*; the Rebbe warns us not to speculate about Existence before Creation. The book closes; the conversation lapses into silence. Embarrassed, pained with self-consciousness, I try to beat back silence with stumbling, ill-shaped words, meaningless questions until insight strikes my thickened tongue. You are the master of silence. We are sitting at the Gate of Silence, the primordial staff of Creation, the ground from which the Ten Words of Creation grow.

Your hands were the instruments of prayer, often speaking

words of *kavvanah*, quieting strange thoughts. I came and stood beside your praying body; your *talit* wrapped me in prayerful light. The closer I came, the brighter I shone; the further away, the fainter my prayer-lamp. So I returned to your field to have my seeds of contemplation nurtured by you, the master of devotion.

I came fearing that my hatred would consume me. You listened and absorbed my pain. Then you began asking penetrating questions. Finally you asked me to imagine the hated person in the palm of my hand. "Would you," you asked, "destroy or allow him to live?" Your face relaxed and a gentle smile appeared as I said, "Let him live." The exercise, you told me, indicated that my hatred would dissipate and not devour me. I left feeling lighter and more alive. You healed and I was healed.

There was the time I came to you angered by my childish behavior. I described in great seriousness my ridiculous antics. And you began laughing and I quickly joined in. Your gentle humor washed away my anger. The curative power of laughter restored my humanity.

I can see you politely listening to me and denying any credit for curing, enlightening. But let me go on. Otherwise I will never feel I've returned any of your *hesed*, love.

There was the day I brought you an old woman who was in pain because she believed that her neighbor, the witch, had cursed her. Again you ask healing questions. "Does your husband pray each day? Does he wear a kosher *talit katan*? Is the *mezzuzah* on the door whole, kosher?" She went home to check, assured that if all these things were proper, she and her household would be safe and protected against the evil eye. When she left I voiced my skepticism indirectly: "Do you believe things work that way?" You replied, "I don't know, but she believed it." The patient reported back that all was well and her pain was gone.

When we first met, you had never travelled outside of the Holy Land and seldom left earthly Jerusalem. Nonetheless, there were myriad magical journeys I made with you to hidden dimensions of the mythic universe.

Above all, you wanted to restore the holy magic to the city of Safed. Painstakingly you and your people prayed and raised money, building the dream, step by step. Regularly you gathered us up, and like the students of the Besht, we travelled to old Safed. We arrived at a partially rebuilt structure. There we prayed at the graves of the holy souls in the Safed cemetery. Through you I came to feel that I was visiting the eternal presence of the Holy Ari and sitting at the blessed table of Rabbi Joseph Karo.

We returned to the sight of the dream. As the sun set you opened Reb Nachman's book of tales and began reading the story of the lost princess. Each time her suitor failed to rescue her your voice became sadder until tears finally rolled from your eyes. We saw and wept with you. A group of grown men weeping for a lost fairy princess? No, you were teaching us to cry for the *Shehinah*, the Holy Spirit in exile. Her pain became our pain. For the moment, we had been transported to the original time of the telling. I still weep for the lost princess. You taught us to cry real tears for God's pain.

I still walk behind you as your slow, steady, aristocratic gait carried you to the mitzvah of honoring—mother clothed in Shabbat finery and wearing a crown of foxtails, a son carries Purim foods to his aged mother. She, before whom the boy, now a grandfather, rises with *derekh eretz* (respect).

The lamenting wail of the phone called me to our last earthly pilgrimage. Through the deep silence of the night sea, sixty young men escorted you to the holy place. We cried, "Who would voice the Rebbe's Torah? Whose hands guide us on life's narrow bridge?" Then I heard you: *"borukh dayen emes* (blessed be the true Judge)." In silent anger I answered, "Amen."

Howard Schwartz

The Quest for the Lost Princess: Transition and Change in Jewish Lore

It is said that Rabbi Isaac Luria had great mystical powers. By looking at a man's forehead he could read the history of his soul. He could overhear the angels and knew the language of the birds. He could point out a stone in a wall and reveal whose soul was trapped in it. So too was he able to divine the future, and he always knew from Yom Kippur who among his disciples was destined to live or die. This knowledge he rarely disclosed, but once, when he learned there was a way to avert the decree, he made an exception. Summoning Rabbi Abraham Beruchim, he said: "Know that a heavenly voice has gone forth to announce that this will be your last year among us—unless you do what is necessary to abolish the decree."

"What must I do?" asked Rabbi Abraham.

"Know, then," said the Ari, "that your only hope is to go to the Wailing Wall in Jerusalem and there pray with all your heart before God. And if you are deemed worthy you will have a vision of the *Shekhinah*, the Divine Presence. That will mean that the decree has been averted and your name will be inscribed in the Book of Life after all."

Rabbi Abraham thanked the Ari with all his heart and left to prepare for the journey. First he shut himself in his house for three days and nights, wearing sackcloth and ashes, and fasted the whole time. Then, although he could have gone by wagon or by donkey, he chose to walk to Jerusalem. And by the time Rabbi Abraham reached Jerusalem, he felt as if he were floating, as if his soul had ascended from his body. And when he reached the Wailing Wall, the last remnant of Solomon's Temple, Rabbi Abraham had a vision there. Out of the wall came an old woman, dressed in black, deep in mourning. And Rabbi Abraham suddenly realized how deep was the grief of the *Shekhinah* over the destruction of the Temple and the scattering of her children, Israel, all over the world. And he became possessed of a grief as deep as the ocean, far greater than he had ever known. It was the grief of a mother who has lost a child; the grief of Hannah, after losing her seven sons; the grief of the Bride over the suffering of her children scattered to every corner of the earth.

At that moment Rabbi Abraham fell to the ground in a faint, and he had a vision. In the vision he saw the *Shekhinah* once more, but this time he saw her dressed in her robe woven out of light, more magnificent than the setting sun, and her joyful countenance was revealed. Waves of light arose from her face, an aura that seemed to reach out and surround him, as if he were cradled in the arms of the Sabbath Queen. "Do not grieve so, my son Abraham," she said. "Know that my exile will come to an end, and my inheritance will not go to waste. And for you, my son, there shall be a great many blessings."

Just then Rabbi Abraham's soul returned to him from its journey on high. He awoke refreshed, as if he had shed years of grief, and he was filled with hope.

When Rabbi Abraham returned to Safed he was a new man, and when the Ari saw him, he said at once: "I can see that you have been found worthy to see the *Shekhinah*, and you can rest assured that you will live for another twenty-two years. Know that each year will be the blessing of another letter of the alphabet, for the light of the Divine Presence shines forth through every letter. And you, who have stood face-to-face with the *Shekhinah*, will recognize that light in every letter of your word."

So it was that Rabbi Abraham did live for another twenty-two years, years filled with abundance. And all who saw him recognized the aura that shone from his face, for the light of the Divine Presence always reflected from his eyes.[1]

This tale, "A Vision at the Wailing Wall," derives from the city of Safed in the sixteenth century. It is one of a cycle of tales about the great Jewish mystic Rabbi Isaac Luria. The Ari perceives that one

---

1. *Shivhei ha-Ari*, edited by Shlomo Meinsterl (Jerusalem: 1905).

of his disciples faces a mid-life transition. He sends him on a journey to wholeness, a quest to the Western Wall, the last remaining wall of the Temple in Jerusalem, to plead mercy from the *Shekhinah*, who is identified in the Kabbalah as the Bride of God. There Rabbi Abraham has a vision of the *Shekhinah*, in which he first sees her as an old woman who emerges from the wall "dressed in black, deep in mourning." Soon after this he faints and has a vision of the *Shekhinah* as a celestial bride.

Central to understanding this mystical tale is the concept of the *Shekhinah*. The term is first found in the Talmud, codified in the fifth century, where it refers to the Divine Presence, that is, the presence of God in the world. It is linked, in particular, to the sacred quality of the Sabbath. But by the sixteenth century the meaning of the term *Shekhinah* had evolved considerably. It came to be identified with the feminine aspect of the Divinity and took on mythic independence. Myths can be found in the *Zohar* and other kabbalistic texts that portray the *Shekhinah* as the Bride of God and Sabbath Queen who once made her home in the Temple in Jerusalem and later, when the Temple was destroyed, went into exile with her children, Israel. At this point the mythic figure of the *Shekhinah* becomes entirely independent of the Divinity and takes on a separate identity. Nor will her exile end until the Temple has been rebuilt, which Jewish lore links with the coming of the Messiah, since the rebuilding of the Temple is said to be one of the miracles that will occur in the messianic era.

The two appearances of the *Shekhinah* that Rabbi Abraham envisions at the Wall, that of the old woman in mourning and of the bride in white, are the two primary aspects associated with her; she appears as a bride or queen or lost princess in some texts and tales and as an old woman mourning over the destruction of the Temple in others. In "A Vision at the Wailing Wall" she appears in both forms, signifying that his encounter with her is complete.

From our perspective, the *Shekhinah* can be recognized both as a mythic and archetypal feminine figure, very close to the purest vision of Jung's concept of the anima, the symbolic feminine aspect of every man. In "The Vision at the Wailing Wall" the Ari recognizes that if Rabbi Abraham continues on his present path, he is going to shortly meet his death. That is to say, his life has reached a dangerous transition, and in order to survive it, he must undertake an extraordinary task. Therefore the Ari sends him on a quest to find the *Shekhinah* in the logical place where she could be found—the Wailing Wall, the remnant of her former home. Rabbi Abraham encounters her there both as a grieving old woman and as a radiant bride, and afterward he is a new man, who through this visionary experience has rediscovered his lost anima and reintegrated his feminine side. That is why he is able to live for another twenty-two years, one year for each letter of the Hebrew alphabet, representing a whole new cycle of his life.

There is much to learn from this tale about how to read rabbinic tales to discover the psychic truths at the core of them. First, however, it is necessary to learn how to interpret their symbolic language. Identifying the *Shekhinah* with the anima is the first step toward translating this language into an archetypal framework.

The next step is to recognize that the quest of Rabbi Abraham is primarily an inner one. After all, as the Ari makes very clear to him, he must save himself. All the actions he undertakes, from wearing sackcloth and mourning to walking to Jerusalem, are mystical techniques intended to put him in a proper state of mind to receive the vision at the Wailing Wall. In this sense Rabbi Abraham might be seen as not only preparing himself for the vision, but inducing it as well. Or the Ari can be seen as having planted the seed of the vision when he sent him on the quest. This quest and its corresponding vision, although expressed in terms of religious symbolism, is essentially an exploration of the world within.

Indeed, the folk structure that best expresses the essence of transition is that of the quest, which represents the inner journey that must be taken before the transition can be completed. It is no accident that as many as half of all fairy tales are quest tales, where the quest represents just such a psychic transition. This is true, in particular, of Jewish fairy tales, since the motif of exile is one of the dominant themes of Judaism, echoed in the biblical accounts of the expulsion from the Garden of Eden and the Exodus from Egypt, as well as in the Babylonian exile that followed the destruction of the Temple, and the expulsion from Spain in 1492.

Of all the Jewish quest tales, the most significant is almost

certainly Rabbi Nachman of Bratslav's "The Lost Princess,"[2] which
concerns a quest to find a princess whom the disciples of Rabbi
Nachman readily identify as the *Shekhinah*. More than any other
tale, "The Lost Princess" presents the myth of the *Shekhinah* in
fairy-tale terms that make it universally recognizable.

Rabbi Nachman of Bratslav holds a unique place in Jewish lore.
The great-grandson of the Baal Shem Tov, he is widely acclaimed
as the greatest Jewish storyteller of all time. "The Lost Princess"
was the first story he told to his hasidim when he began to tell
stories. There are thirteen primary tales in all and a few dozen
other scattered tales.

On the surface the tale of "The Lost Princess" appears to be a
conventional fairy tale, and as such it is a compelling one. But it
was actually intended to serve as an allegory of a primary Jewish
myth, that of the exile of the *Shekhinah*. It was Rabbi Nachman's
method to disguise his mythic, kabbalistic tales in the form of
intricate fairy tales, with many tales within tales, about kings and
queens, princes and princesses. He hinted that he did this in order
to conceal the mysteries revealed in these tales. His hasidim knew
how to explore these mysteries by examining their symbolism
and translating it to the appropriate mystical doctrine.

This, in brief, is the tale of the "The Lost Princess":

> There once was a king who had six sons and one daughter. His
> daughter was especially dear to him, but one day he became angry
> with her and said, "Go to the Devil!" and the next day she was
> gone.
>
> The heartbroken king then sent his most loyal minister on a
> quest to find her, giving him all that he might need to accomplish
> the quest, including a servant. The minister searched everywhere
> in the world but failed to find the princess. At last he came to a
> remote palace where he discovered her, and he managed to talk to
> her. She told him that she was being held captive in the palace of
> the Evil One, who took her when the king sent her to him, and that
> in order to set her free, the minister must long for her release for a

---

2. *Sippure Ma'asiyot*, by Rabbi Nachman of Bratslav, edited by Rabbi Nathan
Sternhartz of Nemirov (Warsaw: 1881).

year, and at the end of that year, fast for one day, neither eating nor drinking, and then she would be able to return to her father, the king.

The minister remained there for a year, longing for her freedom, but on the last day, when he was supposed to be fasting, he saw an apple on a tree that was so appealing that he picked and ate it. After this he fell asleep and slept for seventy years. At the end of this time he awoke and was told by his servant of his long sleep. Then, heartbroken, he returned to the lost princess, who told him to repeat the year of longing, but this time he was permitted to eat—but not to drink—on the last day. He repeated the year-long vigil, but on the last day he saw that the waters of a familiar spring had turned red, and he could not resist tasting them. They turned out to be a delicious wine, and he drank his fill and once again fell asleep.

This time, while he was sleeping, the princess left the palace of the Evil One and rode past him in a carriage. She got out of the carriage and tried to wake him, but when she could not, she wept into her scarf and left it with him. When he finally awoke seventy years later, his loyal servant told him all that had taken place and showed him the scarf. He held it up to the sun and discovered that the tears of the lost princess had written a message on the scarf, in which she told him that henceforth she could be found in a palace of pearls on a golden mountain.

So it was that the heartbroken minister set out on a second quest, which turned out to be far more arduous than the first, because no one he met had ever heard of a palace of pearls on a golden mountain. He searched for many years, and his quest brought him at last to a great desert where he encountered three giants—one in charge of the animals, one in charge of the birds, and one in charge of the winds—all of whom were brothers. Each of the giants carried a giant tree as a staff. These giants called together the animals, the birds, and the winds, but none had heard of the palace of pearls. At last a late wind arrived, and when rebuked by the giant for being late, it explained that it had been carrying a princess to that very palace of pearls.

The giant then gave the minister an enchanted bag with an endless supply of gold and ordered the wind to bring him to the foot of the golden mountain. There the story ends, with Rabbi Nachman's assurance that eventually the minister did free the princess, although he does not reveal how this took place.

This appears in all respects to be a characteristic fairy tale, with a king, a lost princess, a quest, three giants, and an enchanted palace. As such, it can be interpreted from a Jungian perspective as a universal fairy tale, where the quest for the lost princess can readily be recognized as an inner journey. This is also the essential Jewish meaning of the tale, when the symbols in it are translated into their Jewish equivalents.

Such an interpretation can be found in the Bratslaver commentaries on "The Lost Princess," for this tale, and the others that Rabbi Nachman told, were examined by his hasidim with the kind of intense scrutiny reserved for the sacred texts. It was an article of faith with them that his stories could best be understood allegorically, and indeed "The Lost Princess" lends itself to such an interpretation. The key is the king who has six sons and one daughter. The king is easily recognizable as God, who is traditionally represented as a king in a multitude of rabbinic parables. The six sons and one daughter can be readily identified as the six days of the week and the Sabbath. And the identification of the Sabbath with a princess naturally evokes the Sabbath Queen, which, along with that of the Bride, is one of the primary identities of the *Shekhinah*.

The apple that the minister picks recalls the forbidden fruit of the Garden of Eden, and in eating it on the final fast day, he repeats the sin of the Fall and must wait for another generation, symbolized by the seventy years he sleeps. Indeed, the stages of the story can be seen to represent the biblical chronology. The princess is linked to the seven days of Creation. The episode of the Garden of Eden is echoed by the eating of the apple. The episode of the water turning into wine can be linked with the story of the Flood and the sin of Noah in becoming drunk. Also, the three giants that the minister encounters in the desert can be identified as the three towering patriarchs, Abraham, Isaac, and Jacob, while the trees they use as staffs can be identified with the Torah, as in the passage *It [the Torah] is a Tree of Life to those who cling to it* (Prov. 3:18). So too does the minister's search for the palace of pearls repeat the Israelites' search of the Holy Land. As for the scarf with the words written by the tears of the lost princess, it represents the sacred writings of the Torah. These symbolic parallels to the biblical chronology demonstrate that

"The Lost Princess" can also be understood as reflecting the collective Jewish experience, reliving the archetypal experiences represented in these key biblical episodes. That such a collective interpretation of the text was intended is found in the Haggadah for Passover, where it is stated that "In every generation each person must regard himself as if he himself went forth out of Egypt."

So too can this seminal story be understood on the level of personal inner experience. Once the link has been perceived between the lost princess and the *Shekhinah*, the allegorical meaning of Rabbi Nachman's tale reveals itself as a fairy-tale retelling of the myth of the exile of the *Shekhinah*. The king's angry words, which result in the disappearance of the princess, are equivalent to the destruction of the Temple in Jerusalem and the subsequent exile of both the *Shekhinah* and the Children of Israel. At the same time, they are equivalent to the expulsion from the Garden of Eden, the wandering in the wilderness, and other variations on the myth of exile, which is another of the primary Jewish myths.

Thus the figure of the lost princess in Rabbi Nachman's tale can be recognized as an anima figure. As such, she represents, in personal terms, a crucial missing element in the psychic equation, which the minister seeks to restore in his quest. In collective terms the exile of the *Shekhinah* can be seen as a psychic dislocation of the Jewish nation brought about by their exile from the Promised Land.

Rabbi Nathan of Nemirov, Rabbi Nachman's scribe, confirms the identification of the lost princess with the *Shekhinah* in the introduction to *Sippure Ma'asiyot*, Rabbi Nachman's primary volume of his tales.[3]

> Behold, the story of the princess who is lost is the mystery of the *Shekhinah* in exile. . . . And this story is about every man in every time, for this entire story occurs to every man individually, for everyone of Israel must occupy himself with this *tikkun* (act of redemption or restoration), namely to raise up the *Shekhinah* from her exile, to raise her up from the dust, and to liberate the Holy

---

3. Ibid.

Kingdom from among the idolaters and the Other Side among whom she has been caught. . . . Thus one finds that everyone in Israel is occupied with the search for the lost princess, to take her back to her father, for Israel as a whole has the character of the minister who searches for her.

The significance of Rabbi Nathan's comment that "everyone in Israel is occupied with the search for the lost princess" should not be missed. Here is the clearest statement indicating that the process of searching for the lost princess, who is identified with the *Shekhinah* and thus with the anima, is an inner one. We must marvel at the psychological insight of Rabbi Nachman and Rabbi Nathan. It is clear from Rabbi Nathan's statement that Rabbi Nachman's tale is presumed to be allegorical. Thus the recognition of a complex symbol system is not only linked to a mystical theology but to an inner quest that "everyone of Israel is occupied with."

There are three strong possibilities as for the identity of the loyal minister: The minister can be identified with the *tzaddik*, the righteous one, who must search and find the lost princess and bring her back to the king, or, symbolically, to God. Or the minister can be identified with the nation of Israel whose task it is to search for the lost princess, or the *Shekhinah*, in her exile. Or the minister can be identified with the Messiah, and here the linkage seems quite natural, for kabbalistic myth holds that the exile of the *Shekhinah* will not end until the Temple is rebuilt, which is not destined to take place until the advent of the Messiah. And the reason "The Lost Princess" is left unfinished is because the Messiah has not yet come.

All three of these interpretations of the role of the minister seem quite accurate, and each permits the tale to be seen from another important perspective. When the minister is seen as the nation of Israel, the responsibility for finding the lost princess rests on every Jew, and the importance of this doctrine to each individual is emphasized. When the minister is viewed as a *tzaddik*, the key role of the *tzaddik* in bringing about the reunion of *Shekhinah* and Messiah is underscored. And by identifying the minister with the Messiah we can recognize that Rabbi Nachman has combined two primary Jewish myths, that of the *Shekhinah* and that of the

Messiah, into one mythic fairy tale, thus demonstrating their interdependence. Nor is it necessary to narrow these interpretations down to one. One of the beautiful things about the process of commentary in Jewish texts is that multiple readings are not only permitted, but encouraged. Therefore we can easily accept the legitimacy of all three interpretations.

As for the Jungian symbolism of the coming of the Messiah, it can be identified with the individual's process of psychic growth—the individuation process. Just as individuation is an ongoing process, so too is the waiting for the Messiah, as is indicated in the twelfth of the Thirteen Principles of Maimonides, from his *Commentary on the Mishnah:* "I firmly believe in the coming of the Messiah, and although he may tarry, I daily wait for his coming." Thus the messianic era is the culmination of the series of transitions that constitute the history of the Jewish people, and represents a time when all the people will have returned to a state of wholeness and when the journeys of the individual and the collective will each equal the journey to wholeness. We note also that both the *Shekhinah* and the Messiah are in exile, and therefore they have to be found and brought into consciousness. Also, it is apparent that the arrival of the messianic era will be the equivalent of a return to the Garden of Eden since it involves a return to a prelapsarian condition. Therefore, arriving at the messianic era represents a full return to the beginning, the meaning of the Hebrew term *teshuvah*, which means both "return" and "repentance." Such a return can also be viewed as a return to the primordial state we experienced at the beginning of our lives, which is represented by the Garden of Eden.

For the most part, the myths concerning the *Shekhinah* and the Messiah are separate, but they converge at the same conclusion, which is the End of Days. For one of the consequences of the coming of the Messiah will be a miraculous re-creation of the Temple, exactly as it was. Therefore the coming of the Messiah is essential to ending the exile of the *Shekhinah*, and the two myths are eternally bound together.

There is another Hasidic tale that draws on the themes of the *Shekhinah* and the Messiah. This is a tale of Rabbi Eizik of Kallo, a famous Hungarian Hasidic master, called "The Sabbath Guests":

Two traveling Hasidim arrived in the city of Kallo on the eve of the Sabbath and sought out the hospitality of the Rabbi of Kallo, about whom they had heard so much. Already tales were being told of his miracles throughout Hungary, and the visiting Hasidim greatly anticipated spending the Sabbath in his company.

Soon everyone had gathered together to celebrate the Sabbath, and all looked toward the Tzaddik of Kallo for the signal to welcome the Sabbath Queen. But the Tzaddik did not stir. Not a single muscle moved. Every eye remained upon him, yet he seemed detached, in deep concentration.

The visiting Hasidim were startled at such behavior, for no one ever delayed the beginning of the Sabbath for even an instant. Could it be that the rabbi had lost track of time?

All at once there was a knocking at the door, and when it was opened a couple came in. The young man was dressed in a white robe, as was worn in the city of Safed. The young woman, who was also wearing white, was hauntingly beautiful, with very dark eyes, her head covered with a white scarf. The Tzaddik rose, at the same time signaling for the Sabbath to begin. The Hasidim began singing *Lecha Dodi*, the song that welcomes the Sabbath Queen, as the Rabbi of Kallo went to meet his guests. He treated them with every kindness, paying as much attention to the woman as to the man. This was too much for the visiting Hasidim, but they were guests, and there was nothing they could do.

After the meal the Rabbi of Kallo rose and said, "This couple has come here to be wed this day. And I have agreed to marry them." Now these words were a deep shock to the visiting Hasidim, for weddings are forbidden on the Sabbath. And they began reciting psalms to themselves, to protect themselves from the desecration of the Sabbath. At that moment the Rabbi of Kallo turned to the two Hasidim and addressed them. He said, "Of course, the consent of everyone present is necessary, if the wedding is to be performed. Please tell us if we may have your consent?" And there was almost a pleading tone in his voice.

Now it is one thing to witness such a desecration, and quite another to perform one. But the two Hasidim did not dare turn the Tzaddik down. Instead they each dropped their eyes and continued reciting psalms, and a great fear was in their hearts.

At last, when they raised their eyes, they saw that the couple was gone. The Rabbi of Kallo was slumped in his chair. For a long time there was silence. At last the rabbi said, "Do you know who they were?" Each of the visiting Hasidim shook his head to say no.

And the rabbi said, "He was the Messiah. She was the Sabbath Queen. For so many years of exile they have sought each other, and now they were together at last, and they wanted to be wed. And, as everyone knows, on the day of their wedding our exile will come to an end. But that is possible only if everyone gives his full assent. Unfortunately, you did not, and the wedding could not take place.[4]

In this tale of Rabbi Eizik of Kallo, the Messiah and the *Shekhinah* arrived unexpectedly at his house on the Sabbath as a couple who wish to wed. The Rabbi of Kallo recognizes who they are, but the visiting Hasidim do not, and because of their blindness, the opportunity to bring the messianic era is lost. Just as Rabbi Nachman's tale of "The Lost Princess" links the myths of the *Shekhinah* and the Messiah, so does this tale identify the pair as a bride and groom, suggesting that their union would herald the End of Days, the rabbinic vision of the messianic era. In a sense, this tale of Rabbi Eizik makes the convergence of the two myths of the *Shekhinah* and the Messiah complete, as symbolized by their desire for union. Such mythic fusion is common, and often results in the creation of a new myth. From a Jungian perspective, this tale seems to advocate the fusion of the male and female "inner beings," as represented by the *Shekhinah* and the Messiah. Such a union can be viewed as the full integration of the male and female archetypal figures, and a symbol of psychic wholeness. Unfortunately, the tale tells us, the marriage has not taken place because you, the visitor to the realm of the unconscious, haven't given your approval for it. Thus the conclusion of the story can be interpreted as if it were a dream, reporting the present state of psychic balance. From this perspective the story reports a lost opportunity for psychic unity, while from the traditional perspective it is a tale of why the Messiah has not yet come. Such stories explain how there are opportunities in every generation for the Messiah to come, if something does not go wrong. And there are many such tales, for the longing for the Messiah has been very great.

---

4. *Tortenetek a "Kalloi Cadik"—rol* (Hungarian) by Albert Neumann (Nyiregy-haza, Hungary: 1935).

That the quest of uniting the *Shekhinah* and Messiah is primarily an inner one is well illustrated by the concept of *tikkun*,
meaning "redemption" or "restoration." This is the very term that
Rabbi Nathan, Rabbi Nachman's scribe, links to the exile of the
Shekhinah when he says that "everyone of Israel must occupy
himself with this *tikkun*." Here *tikkun* is directly understood as an
internal process of healing and repair, and it is understood that it
takes place on a personal and a collective level at the same time.
That is why it is known as *tikkun olam*, repair of the world.

The concept of *tikkun* is itself the subject of a vivid 16th-century
myth, which was the last major myth to be added to Jewish
tradition. This myth, created by the same Rabbi Isaac Luria who
sent Rabbi Abraham on his fateful quest, represents the core of
the Ari's teachings and his greatest gift to Jewish tradition. It
illustrates the Jewish vision of the very process of restoration and
transformation. According to this cosmological myth, God sent
forth vessels bearing a primordial light at the beginning of time.
Had these vessels arrived intact, the world would have remained
in its prelapsarian condition. But somehow—no one knows
why—the vessels shattered and scattered their sparks throughout
the world, especially on the Holy Land. This is the first stage of
the Ari's cosmology, known as "The Shattering of the Vessels." It
is the symbolic equivalent of other cosmic catastrophes such as
the expulsion from Eden, the destruction of the Temple in
Jerusalem, and the expulsion of the Jews in Spain in 1492, which
took place just forty-two years before the Ari was born.

The second phase—and it is the existence of this second phase
that makes the myth so remarkable—is called "Gathering the
Sparks." Here the object is to collect the fallen sparks and raise them
up. This is the very definition of the process of *tikkun*, of healing
a world that has become unraveled. The process of raising up the
scattered sparks involves the first explanation and justification of
the ritual requirements specified in the Torah, known as the
mitzvot. Each time one of the *mitzvot* is fulfilled, according to the
Ari, scattered sparks are raised up and redeemed. Ultimately,
when enough sparks have been gathered, the broken vessels will
be restored, and this is the symbolic equivalent of the messianic
era. Thus the myth of the Ari states unambiguously that a
person's deeds serve directly to transform and restore the world.

And at the same time, of course, this process of transformation occurs within the individual as well. Thus the Ari's myth is a healing one, focused on the processes of breaking apart and restoring to wholeness.

Perhaps the most remarkable aspect of the Ari's myth is how it, too, combines two primary Jewish myths, that of Creation and that of the messianic era, into one. Rather than present a view of original sin, as is found in Catholicism, the imperfections in the world are made the direct responsibility of God, removing much or all of the blame from the human realm. So too is the role of the Jews defined: to gather the scattered holy sparks and raise them up. This memorable myth spread rapidly throughout the Jewish world and brought kabbalistic principles to the Jewish masses for the first time. Today it remains one of the most haunting and relevant of Jewish myths.

From a Jungian perspective, the shattering of the vessels might be identified in individual terms as the equivalent of a breakdown. It represents a breaking through of the unconscious at a time of psychic transition. On the collective level, the shattering of the vessels represents a time of upheaval, such as that resulting in the destruction of the Temple in Jerusalem, or the expulsion from Spain in 1492—or any of the dozens of crises in Jewish history. The gathering of the sparks represents the process of restoration both on the individual and collective levels that ultimately achieves the kind of psychic balance known as Individuation. And we note that the developmental sequence of the Ari's myth requires the shattering to take place before the restoration can be achieved, indicating that the shattering is an essential, as well as inevitable, phase of this process.

In both teachings and tales, the primary role of the master or *tzaddik* is to guide his disciples on the path of the Torah. The myth of the Ari does this, explaining that following this path will result in personal and cosmic restoration. And in the tale of Rabbi Abraham, the matter is framed in terms of Yom Kippur and the long-established tradition that a person's future is decided on that day, while the quest on which the Ari sends him grows out of the myth of the exile of the *Shekhinah*. As a result, Rabbi Abraham survives a difficult and crucial transition in his life and emerges not only renewed, but, in a very real sense, reborn.

Thus it can be seen that the roles of the *tzaddik* and the therapist are parallel. Just as the *tzaddik* brings his disciples to recognize their personal connection to Jewish myth, as in the story of Rabbi Abraham's vision at the Wailing Wall, the therapist helps an individual recognize that others go through a similar process and that the stages of personal experience that lead to individuation take place in a personal, as well as universal, sphere.

In the tale of Rabbi Abraham, the transition he confronts is identified as a matter of life and death, and this is often the case. By putting the transition in these terms, we can easily recognize its importance. In most of these tales the key events take place during times of transition, involve major life events such as birth, marriage, and death, and are often linked to one of the holy days. That is when Jews are most subject to Divine judgment.

Judaism, of course, offers a multitude of rituals and ceremonies to ease and define life transitions. The ceremony of the *brit* (circumcision) adds an eight-day-old boy to the community of Israel; *bar* and *bat* mitzvah serve as initiations into adult life; an elaborate wedding service, followed by seven days of celebrating the *Sheva Berakhot* (seven blessings), leaves a couple feeling very married; and the extensive rituals linked to death, beginning with those of *shivah* (seven days of mourning) and continuing with the reciting of the Kaddish for an eleven-month period, have the effect of providing consolation to the one who is grieving, and a meaningful structure at a time of chaos in their lives.

At the same time, Jewish tales portray a transition provoked by a time of danger, of either inner or outer origin, in which the conventional ritual structure is not enough and the presence of some kind of guide is required in order to survive. The figure who then miraculously appears is usually identified with one of the patriarchs or prophets, especially Elijah, who often appears in a time of dire need. Furthermore, the kind of survival indicated in these tales often requires radical transformation of the self in order to achieve the psychic balance found in Individuation.

A good example of such a tale is "A Kiss from the Master," collected in Israel by the Israel Folktale Archives.[5]

---

5. IFA 612, collected by S. Arnest.

During the days when the shrine of Rabbi Shimon bar Yohai was still open, the wise men of Safed would enter it on Lag ba-Omer. Once a rich man who was visiting in Safed on the eve of Lag ba-Omer was invited by his host to visit Rabbi Shimon's grave in Meron. When they arrived, he saw that the sages were sitting inside the shrine of Rabbi Shimon bar Yohai, rejoicing. They invited the rich man to join them, and they gave the rich man an honorable place among them.

Then, one at a time, they read passages from the *Zohar*, as was their custom. But when the guest received the book, he had to put it down, for he could not read the Aramaic in which it was written, and he was deeply ashamed.

After they finished reading, everyone but the rich man returned to their tents. But he remained in the shrine, weeping bitterly for his lack of knowledge of the Torah, until at last he fell asleep. And no sooner did he sleep than he dreamed that Rabbi Shimon bar Yohai appeared to him in a dream and comforted him, and before he departed he kissed him on the mouth. And that is when the rich man woke up.

From the moment he opened his eyes, the rich man felt as if a new spirit were within him. He picked up the book of the *Zohar* and opened it to the first page. There he found, much to his amazement, that he could now read the Hebrew letters. Not only that, but the true meaning of every letter rose up in his vision, for the spirit of Rabbi Shimon had fused with his soul. In this way his eyes were opened to the hidden meanings of the Torah and its mysteries were revealed to him.

Later the others returned to the shrine, and they began to discuss a difficult passage in the *Zohar* that none of them could comprehend. Then the rich man spoke and explained that passage to them as if it were elementary, and their eyes were opened to its true meaning. Even more, they were amazed at his wisdom, for they knew he could not even read the language and yet what he said could only come from a master of the Torah.

Then the sages demanded that the rich man explain how this transformation had taken place. And the rich man revealed his dream about Shimon bar Yohai. And when the sages heard this dream, they understood that a miracle had occurred and that the rich man had been possessed by an *ibur*, the spirit of a great sage who fuses his soul to the soul of another and in this way gives it guidance. So too did they know that this sage could be none other than Shimon bar Yohai, since that was the very place where he was buried.

After that the rich man found that all he had to do to call forth the soul of Rabbi Shimon was to open the book of the Zohar. And then he would be able to understand the mysteries of the Zohar as if they were the *aleph bet*. And in the days that followed, the sages invited him to remain in Safed and to bring his family to join him. This he did, and before long they made him the head of the kabbalists of Safed, for they knew that he spoke with the wisdom of Shimon bar Yohai.

What this tale suggests is that the spirit of Rabbi Shimon bar Yohai returned in the form of an *ibur*, literally an impregnation, a positive kind of possession in which the soul of a great sage who has died binds his spirit to one of the living in order to increase that person's wisdom and faith. This is in contrast to possession by a dybbuk, where the evil spirit of one who has died takes possession of one of the living. Here the spirit of Shimon bar Yohai comes in a dream to a man uneducated in the Torah. The spirit kisses him, and afterward the man discovers that he has become a master of the Torah, possessed with the spirit of Shimon bar Yohai.

It is characteristic of these tales that the possession by the *ibur* is not permanent but is triggered by something, such as the study of a particular text or the wearing of *teffilin*, the phylacteries worn by men during the morning prayers. There is a story, for example, about the *tefillin* of Rabbi Hayim ben Attar, who was known as the Or Hayim. These were purchased after his death by a wealthy man, who discovered that the spirit of the Or Hayim would emerge whenever he wore them, giving him a spiritual awareness far beyond anything he had previously experienced. In both of these tales, that of Shimon bar Yohai and that of the Or Hayim, the *ibur* represents the inner being that emerges to guide a person through a difficult time of transition. The fact that the presence of the *ibur* must be triggered in some way indicates that the presence of this inner being only emerges when it is required by internal or external circumstances.

One of the most tantalizing indications of the presence of an *ibur* concerns Rabbi Abraham Isaac Kook. It was well known among the followers of Rav Kook that a great change had come over him when he came to the Holy Land. So great was the transformation that even his handwriting changed, as if he had become a different person. And, indeed, Rav Kook was once heard to say: "I am the soul of Reb Nachman." Rav Kook's statement is a mysterious one, which suggests a direct connection between the souls of the two great rabbis. Above all, it demonstrates how greatly Rav Kook admired Reb Nachman and how strongly he identified with him. Among the followers of Rav Kook, this statement was understood to mean that the soul of Reb Nachman had come to Rav Kook as an *ibur*. and the two souls had fused. This, then, explains the changes that came over Rav Kook when he arrived in the Holy Land and links him to Rabbi Nachman, whose love for the Holy Land was legendary. Furthermore, Rabbi Nachman regarded his journey to the Holy Land as the completion of a quest started by his great-grandfather, the Baal Shem Tov, the founder of hasidism. So here we have a quest started in one generation by the Baal Shem Tov, continued in another by Rabbi Nachman, and extended into yet another generation by Rav Kook.

The concept of the *ibur* has broad psychological implications. A person possessed by an *ibur* has become transformed—the new soul has fused with the old. The result is a soul guided by the spirit of a sage, which brings forth wisdom and strength to a wavering soul facing a virtual abyss that has to be crossed. From a Jungian perspective, the man has activated the archetype of the Wise Old Man in himself. As a result of this transformation, he can now read in a language that was foreign to him. This means that he can now communicate with that part of himself whose previous messages were not received. Furthermore, his ability to comprehend the true meaning of these messages is greatly enhanced.

The Zohar itself, the book that opened to this man because of the possession of the *ibur*, is the key text of Kabbalah. It contains many tales about Rabbi Shimon bar Yohai, a great talmudic sage of the 3rd century, who was the reputed author of the Zohar until Gershom Scholem and other scholars demonstrated that the primary author was Moses de Leon, who lived in Spain in the 13th century. Anyone who has spent any time with the Zohar will confirm the great difficulty of its text. Furthermore, the text is above all a symbolic one, drawing on a rich kabbalistic mythology, and in the process transforming the meaning of many concepts from the way in which they were understood in earlier sacred texts.

Following the earlier discussion about the need to learn to read the symbolic language of these tales, this one embodies a solution, addressing the very issue of learning to read a foreign language by finding the solution in a dream, a message from the unconscious to the conscious. The dream is the key vehicle in Jewish tales for messages to be delivered from the Divine realm to our own. So too does the dream of the man in the shrine bring with it the power of the Wise Old Man who lies dormant until activated. Because the new soul is so closely identified with Rabbi Shimon bar Yohai, the man who receives this soul has no difficulty acknowledging its inherent wisdom. Thus he is open to the wisdom ultimately emanating from his unconscious self. In a nutshell, the message of the tale and the dream can be summed up as follows: The knowledge and wisdom you seek can be found within.

Here is another tale, this a hasidic one, in which a dream guides a man to a patriarchal figure, who provides salvation. This tale is "The Cave of Mattathias," and was also collected orally in Israel, demonstrating the continued vitality of the oral tradition. It is a tale about a hasid of the Rabbi of Riminov, as follows:[6]

In a village near the city of Riminov there was a hasid whose custom it was to bring newly made oil to Rabbi Menachem Mendel of Riminov, and the rabbi would light the first candle of Hanukkah in his presence.

One year the winter was hard, the land covered with snow, and everyone was locked in their homes. But when the eve of Hanukkah arrived, the hasid was still planning to deliver the oil. His family pleaded with him not to go, but he was determined, and in the end he set out across the deep snow.

That morning he entered the forest that separated his village from Riminov, and the moment he did it began to snow. The snow fell so fast it soon covered every landmark, and when at last it

---

6. *Sefer Sgulat Moshe*. Also found in *Toldot Rabbenu Hayim ben Attar*, edited by Reuven Margarliot (Lemberg: 1904) and many other sources.

stopped, the hasid found that he was lost. The whole world was covered with snow.

Now the hasid began to regret not listening to his family. Surely the rabbi would have forgiven his absence. Meanwhile, it had become so cold that he began to fear he might freeze. He realized that if he were to die there in the forest, he might not even be taken to a Jewish grave. That is when he remembered the oil he was carrying. In order to save his life, he would have to use it. There was no other choice.

As fast as his numb fingers could move, he tore some of the lining out of his coat and fashioned it into a wick, and he put that wick in the snow. Then he poured oil on it and prayed with great intensity. Finally, he lit the first candle of Hanukkah, and the flame seemed to light up the whole forest. And all the wolves moving through the forest saw that light and ran back to their hiding places.

After this the exhausted hasid lay down on the snow and fell asleep. He dreamed he was walking in a warm land, and before him he saw a great mountain, and next to that mountain stood a date tree. At the foot of the mountain was the opening of a cave. In the dream the hasid entered the cave and found a candle burning there. He picked up that candle, and it lit the way for him until he came to a large cavern, where an old man was seated, with a very long beard. There was a sword on his thigh, and his hands were busy making wicks. All of that cavern was piled high with bales of wicks. The old man looked up when the hasid entered and said: "Blessed be you in the Name of God."

The hasid returned the old man's blessing and asked him who he was. He answered: "I am Mattathias, father of the Maccabees. During my lifetime I lit a big torch. I hoped that all of Israel would join me, but only a few obeyed my call. Now heaven has sent me to watch for the little candles in the houses of Israel to come together to form a very big flame. And that flame will announce the Redemption and the End of Days.

"Meanwhile, I prepare the wicks for the day when everyone will contribute his candle to this great flame. And now, there is something that you must do for me—when you reach the Rabbi of Riminov, tell him that the wicks are ready, and he should do whatever he can to light the flame that we have awaited so long."

Amazed at all he had heard, the hasid promised to give the message to the rabbi. As he turned to leave the cave, he awoke and found himself standing in front of the rabbi's house. Just then the rabbi himself opened the door, and his face was glowing. He said: "The power of lighting the Hanukkah candles is very great. Whoever dedicates his soul to this deed brings the time of Redemption that much closer."[7]

Like the tale of the master's kiss, this one uses a dream as a vehicle to encounter the Wise Old Man, who is identified here as Mattathias. This is clearly the case because his messianic expectations were so great, as were those of the Riminov hasidim. Indeed, the message from Mattathias is that the messianic era is almost upon us, hinting that the Rabbi of Riminov can have an important role to play in this event. But the real importance of this dream is the way it provides salvation to the hasid trapped in the snow. By creating the conditions to save himself, using the oil for the Hanukkah candles, he saves himself from freezing and is able to sleep, and thus to dream. The dream first transports him from a cold place to a warm one, and then brings him face-to-face with Mattathias. This dream meeting is a fateful one for the hasid, for when he awakes he finds himself at the rabbi's door. A miracle has once more taken place, as it did to Rabbi Abraham when he had a vision of the *Shekhinah*, and as it did to the rich man who was kissed by Shimon bar Yohai. This miracle indicates that the abyss has been crossed and the transition completed.

From these last two tales, and from a multitude of others, we can recognize that there is a pattern to the role of the Wise Old Man. This figure is inevitably identified with one of the great Jewish patriarchs or sages, whose arrival at a time of danger heralds a miraculous event. In every case we can recognize in this pattern the presence of the archetype of the Old Man who, like the *ibur*, brings wisdom and the strength to survive a difficult transition.

Yet, for those who fail to recognize its importance, this encounter with the Wise Old Man can be disastrous. "The Cottage of Candles,"[8] a remarkable Jewish folktale from Afghanistan, presents a vivid demonstration of such an encounter:

---

7. *Hag La'am*, edited by Eliezer Marcus (Jerusalem: 1990). Told by Shimon Toder. The original legend about Hanukkah is found in B. Shab. 21b.

8. IFA 7830, collected by Zevulon Qort from Ben Zion Asherov.

There once was a Jew who went out into the world to seek justice. Somewhere, he was certain, true justice must exist, but he had never found it. He looked in the streets and the markets of cities but could not find it. He traveled to villages and he explored distant fields and farms, but still justice eluded him. At last he came to an immense forest, and he entered it, for he was certain that justice must exist somewhere.

He wandered there for many years and he saw many things— the hovels of the poorest peasants, the hideaways of thieves, and the huts of witches in the darkest part of the forest. And he stopped in each of these, despite the danger, and sought clues. But no one was able to help him in his quest.

One day, just as dusk was falling, he arrived at a small clay hut that looked as if it were about to collapse. Now there was something strange about this hut, for many flickering flames could be seen through the window. The man who sought justice wondered greatly about this and knocked on the door. There was no answer. He pushed the door open and entered.

As soon as he stepped inside, the man saw that the cottage was much larger on the inside than it had appeared to be from the outside. In it he saw hundreds—or was it thousands—of shelves, and on each of the shelves were a multitude of oil candles, burning brightly.

Stepping closer, he saw that some of the flames burned with a very pure fire, while others were dull, and still others were sputtering, about to go out. So too did he now notice that some of the wicks were in golden vessels, while others were in silver or marble ones, and many burned in simple vessels of clay or tin. These plain vessels had thin wicks, which burned quickly, while those made of gold or silver had wicks that lasted much longer.

While he stood there, marveling at that forest of candles, an old man in a white robe came out of one of the corners and said: "*Shalom aleichem*, my son, what are you looking for?"

"*Aleichem shalom*," the man answered. "I have traveled every-where, searching for justice, but never have I seen anything like all these candles. Why are they burning?"

The old man spoke softly. "Know that these are soul-candles, as it is written, *The soul of man is the candle of God* (Prov. 20:27). Each candle is the soul of one of the living. As long as it burns, the person remains alive. But when the flame burns out, he departs from this life."

Then the man who sought justice turned to the old man and asked, "Can I see the candle of my soul?"

The old man nodded and led him into the depths of that cottage, which the man now saw was much larger on the inside than it appeared to be on the outside. At last they came to a low shelf, and the old man showed him a line of tins on it. He pointed out a small, rusty one that had very little oil left. The wick was smoking and had tilted to one side. "This is your soul," said the old man.

Then a great fear fell upon the man and he started to shiver. Could it be that the end of his life was so near and he did not know it?

Then the man noticed that next to his tin there was another, filled with oil. Its wick was straight, burning with a clear, pure light.

"And this one, to whom does it belong?" asked the man, trembling. "That is a secret," answered the old man. "I can only reveal each person's candle to himself alone."

Soon after that the old man vanished from sight, and the room seemed empty except for the candles burning on every shelf.

While the man stood there, he saw a candle on another shelf sputter and go out. For a moment there was a wisp of smoke rising in the air and then it was gone. One soul had just left the world.

The man's eyes returned to his own tin. He saw that only a few drops of oil remained, and he knew that the flame would soon burn out. At that instant he saw the candle of his neighbor, burning brightly, the tin full of oil.

Suddenly an evil thought entered his mind. He looked around and saw that the old man had disappeared. He looked closely in the corner from which he had come, and then in the other corners, but there was no sign of him there. At that moment he reached out and took hold of the full tin and raised it above his own. But suddenly a strong hand gripped his arm, and the old man stood beside him. "Is this the kind of justice you are seeking?" he asked. His grip was like iron, and the pain caused the man to close his eyes.

And when the old man released his grip, the man opened his eyes and saw that everything had disappeared: the old man, the cottage, the shelves, and all the candles. And he stood alone in the forest and heard the trees whispering his fate.

This tale is an example of a Divine test, such as that of the Garden of Eden, or that of the binding of Isaac, or that of Job. The

man seeking justice attempts to fulfill the biblical injunction
Justice, justice, shalt thou pursue (Deut. 16:20) by setting out on a
quest to find justice. At last he arrives at the cottage of candles,
where the old man permits him to view the candle of his soul. The
identity of the old man remains a mystery, although his supernatural aspect is quite clear. As the Keeper of the Soul-Candles he
functions as an Elijah-type figure who is hidden in the forest in the
model of the *Lamed-Vav tzaddikim*, the Thirty-Six Hidden Saints
who are said to be the pillars of the world. Above all, he is the
incarnation of the archetype of the Wise Old Man.

The test that takes place in the cottage surely does so at the
behest of God, so it remains a Divine one. One way of reading
the tale is to see that in arriving at this cottage, the man is on the
verge of completing his quest to find justice, but he is first tested
to see if he himself is just. Instead of proving worthy, he attempts
to destroy another's life to save his own. But he is caught and
made to face the consequences of his action. In this sense he does
find justice at last, for justice is meted out.[9]

It is apparent from the story that the man who is seeking justice
is at the very end of a long quest, as indicated by the fact that his
soul-candle is about to burn out. If he were able to pass the test in
the cottage of candles, he would have received his just reward. But
he fails the test at the very end, demonstrating that he is not a true
seeker of justice after all, since he does not abide by that justice for
himself. Thus he falls prey to the powers of the *Yetzer Hara*, the
Evil Inclination, which must be overcome in order to achieve
justice, which is represented in this story as a kind of inner
harmony and acceptance of one's fate.

Thus we have seen how archetypal figures, such as the anima
or the Wise Old Man, appear in Jewish lore and are transformed
into mythic figures such as the *Shekhinah* or a patriarch. Indeed, all
of the tales discussed here draw on the collective Jewish myth.
Just as individuals go through a series of transitions in their lives,

---

9. It is interesting to note that the man's quest in "The Cottage of Candles" is
in many ways parallel to that of the man from the country in Kafka's famous
parable "Before the Law," found in his novel *The Trial*, who comes seeking justice
at the gates of the Law. And in both tales the man fails to find the justice he is
seeking.

so have the Jewish people gone through a series of collective experiences, not only those recounted in the Scriptures, but the collective experience of the people in every generation. Therefore these tales can be understood in terms of both the collective Jewish meaning and the individual's psychic experience. So too is there a deeper collective level where these tales can be recognized in purely archetypal terms. These three levels of meaning exist simultaneously in all of these tales and provide them with a profound depth of meaning.

What is found, then, in these rabbinic tales, is the projection of unbridled imaginations set in a mythical world reflecting the conditions of their inner lives, drawing on a complex system of symbols that have a remarkable parallel to the Jungian constellation. That the symbols used by the rabbis have an archetypal character is confirmed by the tales of Rabbi Nachman of Bratslav. The traditional Bratslaver commentary on these tales clearly demonstrates they were understood to have a direct correlation to key mystical figures such as the *Shekhinah* and the Messiah and to many other mystical concepts. A study of how this mystical system was understood and what purposes it was intended to serve reveals that it was a method of spiritual purification, drawing on many mystical techniques, including prayer, fasting, ritual immersion, and, as discussed, allegorical readings of sacred texts. Dreams were recognized as Divine messages as well, and attempts were made to interpret them, since it is written that "a dream that is not interpreted is like a letter that is not read."[10]

Certain key Jewish myths, such as that of the *Shekhinah* and that of the Messiah, have a direct correlation to recognizable archetypal patterns and figures, and when considered from this perspective they readily open themselves to interpretation. The Jewish tales that draw on these myths can be seen to mirror a complex psychic process involving the interaction of a constellation of archetypes. Such an analysis reveals the central role of psychological processes, especially those concerned with patterns of change, in Jewish mystical teachings and tales.

In conclusion, there is a recurrent pattern in Jewish tales of a

---

10. B. Ber. 55b.

person in mid-life reaching a crisis that is resolved by the inter-vention of some celestial or saintly being. In Jungian terms, these beings (anima/*Shekhinah*, Wise Old Man/Elijah) are inner beings, introjections of the person's own soul/self who emerge to help the person through the crisis and assist in a transition to a higher state of personal psychic development, that of Individuation.

Nehemia Polen

Turning Darkness into Light: Teachings of the Piaseczno Rebbe

The following is a translation of a derashah (homily) from *Esh Kodesh*, a collection of hasidic teachings by Rabbi Kalonymos Kalmish Shapiro of Piaseczno (1889–1943). *Esh Kodesh* is the last work of Hasidism written in Poland. Rabbi Shapiro was a master of hasidic educational philosophy, who was especially famed for his abilities in working with the estranged and alienated Jewish youth of twentieth century Poland. Refusing opportunities to escape at the beginning of World War II, Rabbi Shapiro was caught in the devastating events of the Holocaust. He lost almost his entire family in the first weeks of the war but continued his work of spiritual leadership and teaching throughout the period of the Warsaw Ghetto. He recorded his discourses in his own hand, and when it became clear that he was not likely to survive the war, he buried them. After the war they were dug up and eventually published in Israel as *Esh Kodesh*. (My own interest in *Esh Kodesh* was sparked by Reb Zalman Schachter-Shalomi, who pointed out the significance and spiritual profundity of the work to me and encouraged me to take this work as the topic for my doctoral dissertation.)[1]

The homily was delivered on November 25, 1939 (*Parashat Vayishlah*, 5700). The biblical text is the story of Jacob's struggle with an enigmatic individual at the river Jabok. According to tradition, the figure with whom Jacob struggled was actually the guardian angel of Esau, identified with Samael, the personification of evil[2] Rabbi Shapiro's exegesis is rooted in the hasidic emphasis

---

1. This translation and commentary has since been printed in Polen, Nehemia, *The Holy Fire: The Teachings of Rabbi Kalonymus K. Shapiro* (Northvale, NJ: Jason Aronson, Inc. 1994).
2. See *Bereishit Rabbah* 77:2–3; *Tanhuma Va-Yishlah* 8; *Zohar* 1:146a. Cf. the

on God's imminent presence in all things. In the hasidic view, no sector of reality can be excluded from the presence of God. From this perspective, evil is not viewed as an independent realm of substantive power, nor as a mere privation as the philosophers would have it, but as a misaligned or unbalanced version of divine goodness, which can be raised up or "sweetened" by the consciousness of the individual who knows how to trace its source in the divine realm.

But this hasidic notion, which was usually associated with the practice of sublimating extraneous thoughts in prayer, now confronted a far more virulent problem: physical actions of human cruelty, perpetrated by sadistic, implacable enemy, designed to inflict maximum pain, suffering, and degradation. How could these be raised up or sweetened? In *Esh Kodesh*, Rabbi Shapiro maintains the hasidic viewpoint on evil, not from a posture of detached theorizing, but while staring into the very face of darkness.

[Esh Kodesh, p. 13]

And he said, I will not let you leave, unless you bless me (Gen. 32:26).

Let us understand: Why did our father Jacob deem it necessary for Esau's guardian angel to bless him? Did not God already bless him? Furthermore, why did the angel ask Jacob "what is your name?" (v. 27) Did he not know his name?

We may suggest the following answer. It is a well-known principle that the deeds of the Patriarchs are a sign for their descendents.[3] Jacob encountered the angel and struggled with him, and the angel touched the hip socket of Jacob's thigh. When the angel desired to go, Jacob said to himself, "Will this same pattern occur to my children? Will it happen that, after enduring troubles and mishaps, their salvation will be limited to the fact

---

discussion in Gershom Scholem, *Major Trends in Jewish Mysticism* (New York, 1946), p. 239, and nn. 115–116; also idem, *Kabbalah* (New York, 1978), p. 128.

3. Cf. Nahmanides on Gen. 12:6.

that their enemies will not overcome them, that they will not fall into their enemies' hands, but will return to the situation which prevailed before the crisis? This can't be!" So he cried, "I will not let you leave, unless you bless me. After the sufferings are over, God must liberate my descendents decisively, not just remove them from their immediate crisis."

Now we now that Esau's guardian angel is Samael. In the messianic future, the letter *mem* of his name—which symbolizes death—will be removed, because "death will be swallowed up forever." (Isaiah 25:8) What will remain are the letters of *Sa–el*, the *Gematria* of which is equivalent to that of the Tetragrammaton added to that of *Ado-nai*. This means that he will then be a holy angel, one of the celestial princes. After Jacob struggled with him, he repaired the aspect of himself which was in the angel, thus preparing him for the future redemption. At that point in the narrative, then, the angel was already sanctified, was already seeking good for Israel. So the angel asked him, "What is your name?" And He Said, "Jacob." The angel then replied that the name Jacob is related to the time when *His hand was grasping Esau's heel* (Gen. 25:26); all the acts of deliverance which Jacob had known up to that time had come after Esau had treaded on him with his heel; [the deliverance had consisted of] slipping away from the oppressor's heels. [So, the angel went on,] "Your prayer is that this cycle continue—that after the trouble arrives, the deliverance might follow. But enough of that whole cycle! From now on your name is Israel: deliverance will be yours *ab initio*. You have indeed triumphed!"

Furthermore, we note that the word *sarita* (You have struggled) is related to *sar* (prince, great one). Thus, by saying, "You have struggled with a divine being and with man, and have prevailed," the angel suggested to Jacob that he first became great, though he only later prevailed. The angel stated in effect: Even before you prevailed, even when your troubles were very great indeed, *you became great*. Your inner spirit did not fall; even then, inwardly, you were a prince.

Rabbi Shapiro's message of hope and encouragement is clear. To the hounded Jews of Warsaw he gave a reminder that they were, and would always remain, princes. But what is most extraordinary about this teaching is his vision: of Samael redeemed, mended, transformed into a force for good, a sacred angel whose desire was now to bless Israel.[4] To have had that vision, to have had the courage and audacity to publicly expound it at *that* time and in *that* place, was itself the ultimate triumph over, and transformation of, evil. By his example and by his teaching, Rabbi Shapiro did indeed prevail.

---

4. Rabbi Shapiro's statement that Jacob "repaired the aspect of himself which was in the angel" is also striking in context, for it suggests that there was some deep, intimate connection between the Jews and their persecutors, who were perpetrating a colossal evil, but might yet be rectified into a source of blessing. Compare *Esh Kodesh*, pp. 61–62, and see my "Hasidic Theology in the Face of Evil," *Proceedings of the International Conference on Religious Jewry and Religion During and After the Holocaust* (forthcoming).

PART III

Created Them: On Gender and Relationship

Leah Novick

Rebbetzin Malka, Queen of Belz

Introduction: In Search of Malka of Belz

This story about Malka of Belz represents an important part of my search for my female ancestors. Like other Jewish women looking for a usable past, I was directed to the biblical heroines: women prophets and queens, wise women and warriors. Re-immersion in biblical *Midrash* indicated that there is indeed material on the legendary women of our ancient past. I found, however, that recovering the biblical heroines was insufficient to fill the gap in my longing to know more of historical Jewish women's lives. I was haunted by a feeling of emptiness exemplified by my experiences in *Beit Hatefusot*, the wonderful Diaspora Museum outside of Tel Aviv. For years their only exhibit with a female figure was an unidentified woman lighting Shabbat candles! Despite the museum's remarkable chronicling of the lives of diaspora Jewish communities, the focus was on the masculine Jewish experience. Women in photographs were either nameless or identified as mother of, wife of, or daughter of, whoever the man in the picture might be.

We all know, from personal and sociological sources, that our diaspora foremothers provided direction in the family and the community. They certainly provided spiritual guidance to their children and to other women. Until recent years, with scholarship spurred by a growing Jewish feminist awareness, there was little documentation of their roles in ritual, because they were excluded from official leadership positions. As more data emerged, it became apparent that during all stages of our history, and in all the countries where we lived, there have been women who wrote and led prayers and knew liturgical music. While most of them seemed to lead only women in prayer, they were part of the

Ashkenazi and *Mizrachi* experience. Others, like Malka of Betz, had both male and female followers. In her case, she made her contribution through her clairvoyance and giving personal advice as "wise-woman" and *tsaddeket.*

Ironically, much of my search for Rebbetzin Malka's story came from immersion in biographies of her husband and other chasidic masters. Fortunately, folklore on the early chasidic teachers has retained references to the women in their family circles. In the early years of the movement there were more opportunities for women's participation and more acceptance of their healing and prophetic work (as in the case of Eidel—the Baal Shem's daughter, Feige—her daughter and the Mother of Rebbe Nachman of Bratslav, the Maggid of Mezrich's daughter-in-law, Freda the daughter of Schneir Zalman of Liadi etc. also Malka "die Trisk-erin" who became Rebbe in her father's place and other women of that genre). Except for the Maid of Ludomir, who comes on the scene later in the nineteenth century, most of the recognized women were members of accomplished families. Girls in rabbinic families were more likely to have received—or absorbed—substantial Jewish education, and those who married rabbis often did their spiritual teaching as *Rebbetzin.*

During the 1980s, when I started looking for material on these women, whom I sometimes refer to as "Jewish Boddhisatvas," I was leading a regular *Rosh Chodesh* group. During our monthly gatherings I taught about these *Tsadikot* and sometimes asked the participants to collectively meditate on them. As part of this process, we discovered our grief over not having full names for the female ancestors. It was in one of these gatherings that someone "received" the first name of "Shoshana" for "Bat Ha Levi of Baghad," the twelfth-century Yeshiva teacher, usually referred to as the learned daughter of the *Gaon*, Rabbi Shmuel Ben Eli. The name felt right for the young woman, venerated by Iraqi Jews, who made pilgrimages to her grave after her mysterious and early death. (There is a first name given for her fiancee, who died after their betrothal, but none for her.) She was described in the diaries of Rabbi Petachiah of Regensburg as having taught behind a window so the male students would not be preoccupied with her great beauty. Centuries later, the "Maid of Ludomir," Chana Rachel Werbemacher, would teach from behind a door.

I continued to explore the group meditation technique in my workshop in different locations in North America. As I would prepare the stories for presentation, a specific ancestor would seem to come through stronger than others, as though she were connected to individuals in those cities or to the atmosphere of the place. At Byrn Mawr College—a setting replete with statues of august women founders—my workshop group connected with the spirit of Doña Garcia Nasi, the famous sixteenth-century Jewish philanthropist and visionary who rescued hundreds of thousands of Jews from the Inquisition and pioneered the resettlement of Tiberias. In a workshop in Toronto, we felt the influence of the Maid of Ludomir, the late nineteenth-century chasidic rebbe known for her kabbalistic knowledge and unique skills as a healer and preacher. In Eugene, Oregon, where my collaborator Shonna Husbands-Hankins lives with her husband Rabbi Yitzchak, we felt the presence of Rebbetzin Malka Rokeach and her husband, Reb Shalom, the great Belzer Rebbe.

Although I was gaining the confidence to use these insights, I never gave up on the music of the mind and the need for data to establish the roles of women spiritual teachers in Jewish history. Early in the summer of 1990, I was chosen to be a Coolidge Fellow at Harvard University. I was blessed with a month at the Episcopal Divinity School, access to the superb Harvard Libraries, and the company of two dozen supportive Christian and Jewish colleagues. During that brief halcyon period, I continued my search for material on Rebbetzin Malka of Belz and Dulcie of Worms, the twelfth-century *tsadeket* who was martyred along with her children. Daily, I plowed my way through dozens of books about the periods in which they lived as well as books by and about their husbands.

During my first night in Boston, I had a delightful dream in which a former colleague of mine from UC Berkeley, where I taught for some years, appeared dressed like Sherlock Holmes. He assured me, "Don't worry . . . the sleuth is with you!" I must admit that the research did feel more like detective work than study, complete with some great "a-ha" experiences. For example, when I found the edition of *Chochmat Halev* (The Wisdom of the Heart), Rabbi Eleazar of Worms' thirteenth-century book, which contained his poem celebrating his wife's life, I sat in the sultry hot Widener Library among the aging books and wept for hours. The same library provided "pay-dirt" in my search for Rebbetzin Malka and opened up some special gateway to the spirits of the holy couple from Belz. It seemed that I started to connect with the Rebbe in the library among the *sforim*, whereas I had been "receiving" the Rebbetzin out of doors in the California woods, especially on her *Yahrzeit*.

In my reveries, I had imagined Malkele first as a young, energetic girl with secret outdoor places where she went to meditate and pray, and look for herbs and flowers. I pictured her as having guides who introduced her to the plants that would later become her main method of healing. To me, she was sparkling and curious, a clever and attractive girl with reddish glints in her chestnut hair. Then I saw her as a young married woman with a kerchief on her head, covering the luxurious tresses. She was moving among the pots and pans in her kitchen, feeding her seven children, caring for the Rebbe's students, dealing with the visitors and *schnorrers*. And while her tall strong body rested on the earth, her spirit soared with the *Shekhinah*.

Blessed with growing trust in the intuitive process, I was guided to take my search for Rebbetzin Malka into another domain, the one we sometimes refer to as "channelling" or the ability to receive from other dimensions of reality. It is this process I relied on for the section of the story I have entitled "Malka and Reb Sholem in the World to Come." For myself as a former left-brain "junkie," this process of acknowledging the validity of intuition (and sharing it with others) has come late in my life, and not without struggle. However, as the experiences with the souls of the heroines became powerful sources of insight and inspiration, I realized that connecting with the female ancestors who were clairvoyants is my way of honoring the work I do as a rabbi whose lineage is through them.

For what has also become available to me is a kind of shower of energy from the great rabbi consorts and increasing imaginal material about the process Reb Zalman refers to as "co-Rebbe-ing"—using and reuniting the male and female energies to do the sacred work. The integration of mind, body, and intuition as an expression of spirit has been an important part of Reb Zalman's teaching. With the encouragement I received from him, I started

on a process that feels like constructing a patchwork quilt; Malka's
story is one square.

The Story of Rebbetzin Malka

Malka Rokeach, who would later be known as Malka of Belz,
grew up in Sokai in the Ukraine where her father, Issakhar Dov
Ber Rokeach, was the community's rabbi. Since he was an
opponent of the teachings of the early Chasidim (ecstatics and
mystics who revolutionized Judaism of that time with their focus
on participatory spirituality and closeness to nature), it is not clear
how the young "Malkele" managed to develop her pro-Chasidic
ideas. It appears that she had an independent spirit as a girl and a
teen that was later reflected in her independence as *Rebbetzin*. She
seems to have had a strong religious education and opportunities
to experience the spiritual teachers of the area, which included
Rabbi Shlomo of Lutsk. The early Chasidim are said to have
included women in their teaching circles; perhaps her mother,
who is not mentioned in any of the stories, was sympathetic to
their work. If so, she would have been an important influence in
Malka's life as the Rebbetzin would be later on in the lives of her
own children.

Shalom Rokeach, who was Malka's cousin, came from the
Galician city of Brody to live with her family after the death of his
father, Rabbi Eliezer Rokeach. Reb Eliezer, who died at the age of
thirty-two, had been a follower of Rabbi Hayyim Halberstam of
Zanz. When Shalom's mother remarried, she sent her son to
receive guidance from Malka's father so that he would receive a
proper religious education. A descendant of illustrious rabbis,
various sources cite Shalom's lineage on his father's side to Eliezer
Rokeach of Amsterdam (1735), and his mother's family to the
Maharal of Prague. The young Shalom lived up to his learned
ancestors and became a great Talmudist and miracle worker.

While there is little information about their childhood together
or their courtship, the folklore is consistent in presenting Malka as
the one who introduced her cousin Sholem to *Chasiduth* and
foresaw his future as *tsaddik*—even in the early days of their

marriage when he still wanted to be a businessman. The Rebbe also had talent as an architect and is said to have designed and built the famous Belz synagogue with his own hands.

She was the driving force behind Shalom Rokeach's early studies, particularly in the area of Kabbalah. According to one legend, she held the candle over his books for a thousand consecutive nights (which would have given her access to the material as well) until Elijah the prophet himself came and initiated Shalom Rokeach into the mysteries of the Creation. Other folktales portray her as secretly letting him out of the house each night, down a ladder, so that his immersion in kabbalistic study would not be publicly known. And, it was Malka who had directed him to Shlomo of Lutzk, Reb Shalom's first Chasidic teacher. He would then go on to study under various celebrated teachers including the Seer of Lublin, Uri of Strelisk, Abraham Yehoshuah Heschel of Apta, and the Maggid of Kozienice. Reb Sholom became very devoted to the Seer of Lublin who was responsible for arranging his appointment as Rabbi in Belz.

From the beginning of their marriage, and later when her husband became *rebbe*, Malka never stayed in the background. She chose to participate in her husband's activities and even ate at the same table with him, which was considered quite radical. A woman of vision (*eyshet chazon*), her husband consulted with her regularly on spiritual matters. In addition, she had devotees of her own in the court, which included prominent men who came to her for advice and healing. They also funded her charitable activities, which probably focused on feeding the poor. Her intuitive powers coupled with her supreme faith have been celebrated in a number of tales of her clairvoyance.

The extent of her "private practice" is not clear as she was also responsible for the care and sustenance of the inner circle of the Chasidic Court, and of her seven children—five girls and two boys. It is probably not a coincidence that her daughter Eidele assumed the functions of rebbe during her marriage to Rabbi Yitzchak Isaac Rubin of Sokolov, son of Rabbi Asher of Ropcyzce. Eidele's husband, Reb Yitzchak, who died in 1876, was reputedly shy and retiring, so she delivered the learned discourses on Shabbat and distributed the *Shrayim* (blessed food from the Rebbe's table).

Eidele also received contributions which she used to feed the poor, generally conducting herself like a rebbe. Her father is said to have remarked affectionately that all Eidele was missing in that role was a rabbi's hat (*Is feilt ir nor a shpudik*).

One of Malka's other daughters, whose first name is unfortunately not cited, married Rabbi Henich of Olesko who was a leader in the Court of Belz. Malka's youngest son, Joshua (1825–1894) became his father's successor after Reb Shalom died in 1855 on 27 Elul 5615. Although convention would have favored the older son who did indeed want his father's post, the conflict seems to have been resolved in a miraculous manner by the appearance of Reb Shalom's spirit before his awed followers.

There is a consistent pattern in all of the stories of Malka of Belz, citing her extraordinary powers of inner vision, her ability to know the divine plans, and even on occasion to be able to intercede in the heavenly court to reverse or alter celestial decrees. One story, which tells of how she averted a plague against the domestic fowl of the area, suggests that her powers were known and recognized by Rabbi Meir of Premishlan, a neighboring *tsaddik*.

Another theme throughout all the stories of Malka and Shalom is their mutual devotion. At all stages of their lives, the Rebbetzin provided the devoted support which enabled the Rebbe to achieve his greatness. Malka's efforts expanded when the Rebbe lost his vision later in his life, at which time she became his "seeing eyes," providing him with renewed insight and inspiration. The Rebbe celebrated Malka's wisdom and saintliness. While their division of labor reflects their nineteenth-century background, Reb Shalom's description of her attributes indicate a deep respect for her abilities and admiration for her intelligence. She appears to have been truly regarded as a *tsaddeket* (saint) and wise-woman who had opportunities to express both wisdom and insight.

Expecting to outlive his wife, Reb Shalom was beyond consolation when she died. Many famous rabbis and scholars visited him in an effort to assuage his grief. According to the stories, his tears, which issued forth in great streams, did not stop until he was reunited with his beloved Malkele in the world to come.

Malka and Reb Sholem in the World to Come

When Reb Sholem left the planet on 27 Elul 5615 (1855) there was great rejoicing in the heavenly courts. Great choruses of angels sang in celebration of his arrival and subsequent reunion with his beloved Malkele. Their divine souls, which had always vibrated as one light-being, were now betrothed to each other once again at the celestial level. While the Rebbetzin already had a temporary assignment—to greet the souls of saintly women healers in the Garden of Eden—Reb Sholem's arrival signalled a new era. It was decided that they could appear together before the heavenly court after Reb Sholem's initial intake was completed.

All the divine beings in attendance agreed that the Rokeachs as a *zivuga kidusha* (holy dyad) had reached a very high level through prayer, meditation, healing, and good works. The question was whether their mutual love and devoted "co-rebbe-ing" would qualify them for exemption from the obligation to reincarnate. Reb Sholem was at first surprised to learn how many of his rabbinical colleagues were sent back to earth in women's bodies to learn the lessons they had missed. It seemed that few of the sages had been blessed with the kind of marriage that the Rokeachs had. In fact, when Reb Sholem looked into the future, he was even more surprised to see how little of his example rubbed off on his followers. Later, toward the end of the twentieth century, he could see a descendant of Belz—Rabbi Zalman Schachter—beginning to practice "co-rebbe-ing" publicly.

Because the *Kadosh Baruch Hu* was deeply concerned about the future of the Belzers, and the recurring anti-Jewish sentiments in much of Eastern Europe, it was decided that he and Malkele would now be given the opportunity to spread their *nitzatzot* (sparks) among many individuals on the planet. Reb Sholem had past experience with this process of *Ibbur* and had once told his brother (who wondered how Sholem had gone from an ordinary youth to a *tsadik*) that he had received a visitation and an infusion of sparks from the soul of his holy grandfather when he reached his Bar Mitzvah. Additionally, once a year on Rebbetzin Malka's

Yahrzeit (honoring her especially, since so few famous women's dates were known and observed) the holy couple could appear anywhere to individuals who called upon them or seemed to need their assistance. Using that special *Yahrzeit* power, Malka and Sholem engineered the liberation of the Belzer death camp by the allied forces following an agreement signed by Himmler to surrender the concentration camps (27 Adar or 16 March 1942). And they brought about many other miraculous events including the famous Camp David peace treaty signed by Begin and Sadat 27 Adar 57 or 26 March, 1979.

Since the end of the second world war, their souls had been drawn to Eretz Yisrael and usualy hovered over the cities in Israel where many of the remaining Belz descendants now live. However, in the 1990s, Rebbetzin Malka noticed that the Chasidic community was becoming less open to spontaneous appearances of ascended souls. Unlike their original followers (who had seen Reb Sholem's neshamah appear before his oldest son and bar the disruption of the younger son's appointment as Rebbe) these contemporary Chasidim, like other Israelis, were becoming a little more difficult to reach. The Rebbetzin, always curious and a bit adventurous, as she had been when on this planet, began to roam around the minds of the freer "Neo-Chasidic" souls that were clustered around the leadership of Reb Zalman Schachter-Shalomi in Philadelphia, who did, after all, have some kinship with them. The Rebbetzin loved those creative spirits and adored Zalman's sense of humor. The Rebbe, who had healed schizophrenics and hysterics in his time, was fascinated by the counseling techniques that Reb Zalman and his students used.

Rebbetzin Malka, who had grown up in the Ukrainian forests, was still most attracted to beings who resonated with nature and the outdoors. (In fact, there was a rumor that she had learned her herbal therapies from non-Jewish shamans in the Ukrainian mountains.) So it was natural that she would be drawn to the *Shekhinah*-worshipping women that abounded in the Pnai Or Aleph circle. Like herself they were devoted to meditation and prayer; some also used channeling, herbs, incantations, and laying on of hands. She loved the way they gave birth to their babies and absolutely reveled in their leadership in music and dance. She had hardly imagined such a possibility in Belz as these women rabbis and cantors. Midwives and visionaries she had seen in her time, as well as great healers, and her own daughter Eidele functioned as a rebbe, but it was considered most unusual. These women who were officially leading prayers for the whole congregations—that was a real *chiddush*.

Given Malka's connection to the female teachers, it was perhaps inevitable that she would gravitate towards Reb Leah, one of the West Coast's roving rabbis. Despite her ambient nature, Leah always stayed home for Rebbetzin Malka's *Yahrzeit* which she celebrated with a plethora of candles and a special meditation circle with *Eishet Chazon* (women of vision) members around the United States (an amazing group of healers and visionaries who celebrated their connection at the biennial Pnai Or Aleph gathering, where they acknowledged each other's accomplishments in moving rituals). A number of these women had been introduced to Malka of Belz through Leah's devotion to the Rebbetzin and her efforts to make Malka's life better known.

On Malka's *Yahrzeit*, 27 Adar, they would sit in silent meditation at the same time, despite the varying time zones, and focus for about an hour on "receiving" the Rebbetzin's spirit. During these annual gatherings, Malka (and sometimes Reb Sholem, too) would playfully recall the details of their Chasidic life and send them over the thought waves to the participants in the circle. Some of the recipients kept notes so they could convey their experiences to you, the readers of this tale.

What did they experience? Many of them envisioned Malka as a young woman, full of loving energy for her children and all who came to her for help. One of the rabbis in the circle saw Malka as a full-figured older woman, reading from the *Tehillim* and *davenning* in Yiddish—addressing God as "Tata Zisa." (Yiddish for Sweet Father). She thought that the Rebbetzin did *Tehilim* (Psalms) every day in Yiddish, in addition to her regular davenning. She saw that Malka used a seven-day plan, covering the book weekly and praying specifically for those who needed help at the physical and spiritual levels. Her insight is consistent with the story about Malka healing a disabled man by her interpretation of the Psalms (*Ner L'Ragli*).

The same respondent envisioned Malka healing the poor and the sick, kabbalistically, through the preparation of food and herbs, doing each step of the process with special *Kavanah* (spiritual intention). She would go to the market, davenning along the way and then put her healing intentions into the buying, preparing, cooking, feeding, and serving of the food. Because these were typical female activities, her actions had the appearance of simple kindness and generosity, rather than the expression of great healing powers. (There is a story of Malka seeing the future of a certain man's soul while she was serving kasha to the poor.) Likewise, because of the times in which they lived, Malka may have channeled in a lot of the information for Reb Sholem who was able to apply it in healings as part of his recognized role as *Tsadik* and healer.

This same respondent saw Malka taking long solitary walks in nature as part of her *hitboddut* (meditation/contemplation). Malka seemed to be independent and strong—a very powerful, yet very soft woman with a smiling, glowing face. Another participant, who studies Tibetan Buddhism, saw Malka in the woods, communicating with and through the evergreen trees of the Ukrainian forest. She imagined Malkele receiving teachings from non-Jewish healers in that area. Other participants also felt the Rebbetzin's powerful connection to nature and her openness to all life and to all beings. Honoring that deep reverence for all that grows, Leah always goes outdoors for part of Malka's *Yahrzeit* and speaks to her, from the heart, in wooded areas.

One woman artist in the circle saw Malka as a young girl holding a ball of light. Perhaps Malkele, even as a child, already understood the golden light with which she healed others. Later, this friend experienced her as a young woman in a large bed, making love with Reb Sholom, rolling over and over. Others who experienced them making love felt them to be one soul, one living, breathing organism united at the highest levels. They experienced the harmony in the relationship between the Rebbetzin and her husband. It was as if they were always one being united in a sacred marriage, over many lifetimes. For all, there was a great longing to share that unity, and to have it in their own lives. That bliss is the reason why the author continues the search for Malka, the Queen of Belz, and lights candles in her memory, every year on 27 Adar.

References

Selected Sources in English

Aron, Milton. *The Worlds of Six Hassidic Masters.* New York: Citadel Press, 1969.

Buber, Martin. *Tales of the Hasidim: Later Masters.* New York: Schocken Books, 1947.

Horodetzsky, S. A. *Leaders of Hassidism.* London: Hasafer Agency for Literature, 1928.

Langer, Jiri. *Nine Gates to the Chasidic Mysteries.* New York: David McKay Company, 1961. Reissued New Jersey: Jason Aronson, 1993.

Mintz, Jerome R. *Legends of the Hasidim.* Chicago: University of Chicago Press, 1968.

Newman, Louis I. *The Hasidic Anthology.* New York: Charles Scribners Sons, 1934.

Rabinowycz, H. M. *The Word of Hasidism.* London: Valentine Mitchell, 1970.

Taitz, Sondra, and Henry, Emily. *Written Out of History.* New York: Biblio Press, 1983.

also: Encyclopedia Judaica, Jerusalem: Keter 1971, pp. 451–455.

Carol Rose

Walking the Motherpath: An Update

Approximately ten years ago I designed a set of cards, with artist Lu-Ann Lynde, called "Walking the Motherpath." The cards were our attempt at "midrash making" about the lives of biblical women. On each oval card there's a sketch of one of the matriarchs accompanied by a poetic interpretation. There are also one word "qualities" or characteristics assigned to each of the women in the deck. My hope was that these cards would serve as "mirrors of identity," or doorways into a greater personal aware-ness, that women (and men) would use the cards to unravel the stories of the ancient mothers to gain greater insight into their own life processes.

> Since midrash contains many possible interpretations (all presented non-dogmatically and often side by side on the same page) the person using the cards, could sort through this raw material and, as tradition allows, could begin to make educated choices about which interpretations to accept and which to discard.[1]

Our research included text study, some exploration into existing midrashim, and our own dreams and imaginings. In some cases, we used the interpretations gathered from women in our respec-tive women's groups.

What we were trying to do (like Marion Zimmer Bradley's *The Mists of Avalon*) was to shift the emphasis of an entire body of

---

1. Carol Rose, "Walking the Motherpath," in *LIVING THE CHANGES,* ed. Joan Turner (Winnipeg: The University of Manitoba Press, 1990), pp. 106–113.

history to include the experiences of women. Our task was complicated because we were trying to do this with so-called sacred text, with text respected for its continuity. And we were trying to do this as "insiders," as those who felt directed and commanded by the wisdom of the past.[2]

Over the years, the cards have been used by women in many different faith communities. They have become a vehicle for making the lives of our foremothers accessible. Individuals have used them in study groups (as educational material), or they have been used alone, as meditative tools. We have heard from people throughout the United States, Canada, and Israel who have found the cards helpful in sorting out just what it is that they can believe about their biblical foremothers, and discerning what these women's lives have to say to them, in the midst of their own spiritual wanderings. Recently Ulla Ryum, a visiting Danish playwright, discovered the cards. She is currently trying to bring me to Denmark to do a "Walking the Motherpath" workshop there. It is her belief that the cards represent a way of imagining text that is missing in European interfaith study circles.

The cards are my response to the challenge of remaining faithful to my tradition while at the same time, making changes from within . . . All of the women represented are portrayed in their fullness; they are neither overly weak or unrealistically powerful. They are individuals; each has her own integrity and uniqueness. In the workshops, I use the cards and a variety of (imagery) exercises, beginning with an examination of what we have been taught (about the matriarchs) in the past. We discuss the images of women that we have been carrying, and we create a ritual to restore our vision. Then, free of fear, we look at the lives of our biblical mothers and, indeed, at the lives of all those women who have influenced us, and we put forward our own intuitions. The hope is that we will create a new oral tradition, one that is inclusive of the contributions of women and, therefore, healing . . . We tell new stories about the lives of capable, strong and inspired individuals. We create stories that present women and men honestly, and that illustrate their relationships, their frailties and their

2. Ibid.

importance in the divine scheme. Traditional images of the feminine facet of the divine are reintroduced. Images of the One who is called Goddess, or Shekinah, or Sacred Mother become part of our telling.[3]

The cards are still changing. Because our original intent was to "remain true to the inside," we produced them as they came to us—sketch-like and technically imperfect. They were meant to evoke responses from those who interacted with them. We have been told that they have power, though certainly, they are not the last word. My teacher in imagination, Madame Colette Aboulker-Muscat, has described them as "a delightful game, an exercise." Currently I am working on a booklet to accompany the cards. I am also trying to refine some of the poetry. R'Zalman has playfully called them "the Jewish Tarot." He has suggested that they become "the pathways between the Sephirot, a women's *Kabbalah*." Whether they will work out to match the exact number of pathways is hard to tell. Just this year we added another image—*Abigail*—for a new workshop that I call "Listening to Our Inner Prophetesses." This workshop uses seven identified prophetesses: *Abigail, Deborah, Esther, Hannah, Huldah, Miriam,* and *Sarah* as models for personal growth. The hope is that these seven prophetesses will serve as our guides as we journey inward to the source of our own wisdom.

Like "Walking the Motherpath," this workshop uses imagery exercises, movement, writing, and mandala making, to help bring the stories of biblical women to life. As these stories unfold and take on subjective reality, workshop participants observe the ways in which the matriarchs have dealt with life's most challenging issues, and they see how these responses can still be effective in bringing about change in their own lives. Participants are given seven cards, each with an image of one of the prophetesses. They shuffle the cards, turn them face down and then, after a directed exercise, they choose one of the prophetesses as their guide. The exercises are designed to take them through the seven energy systems in the body. Each "guide" brings information from

3. Ibid.

the energy center that she has been chosen to address. Consequently, every person in the workshop receives a unique message.

I am grateful to R'Zalman for recommending the book, *The Personal Totem Pole* by Eligio Stephen Gallegos, Ph.D.[4] Indeed, it was R'Zalman who first recognized the similarities between Gallegos' system and the work that I was doing with the prophetesses. I have since adapted many of Gallegos' ideas for use in my workshops. In both cases, the body is the sacred source of wisdom. The energy centers are believed to house the many parts of the self that crave communication. Gallegos has his clients create a "personal totem pole" using mythical animals to set up the possibility for communication between these parts. "Listening to Our Inner Prophetesses" uses biblical women as guides. These "guides" permit workshop participants to make contact with the energy centers, to gather the information stored there, and to reflect upon the importance of this information to the whole "body/mind/spirit" system.

Both "Walking the Motherpath and Listening to Our Inner Prophetesses" are laboratories in which the stories of biblical women can be explored experientially. They are opportunities for increasing our "image pool," for expanding our tradition by allowing women to reinterpret and re-vision the wisdom of our matriarchs, from a woman-centered perspective. They are part of *Tikkun Olam*, healing the unbalanced presentation of our shared past. Carol Christ calls opportunities to tell women's stories from a woman's point of view revolutionary.

> Women live in a world where women's stories rarely have been told from their own perspectives. The stories celebrated in culture are told by men . . . As women become more aware of how much they must suppress in order to fit themselves into the stories of men, their yearning for a literature of their own, in which women's stories are told from women's perspective, grows. That is why the new literature—fiction and poetry—written by women who are aware of the gap between women's experience and men's stories is so important . . . The simple act of telling a woman's

---

4. Eligio Stephen Gallegos, Ph.D., *THE PERSONAL TOTEM POLE* (Santa Fe, New Mexico: Moon Bear Press, 1987).

story from a woman's point of view is a revolutionary act: it has never been done before.[5]

At the conclusion of her presentation as scholar-in-residence at the University of Manitoba, noted feminist Bible scholar Elisabeth Schussler-Fiorenza read a poem from the "Walking the Mother-path" deck. She talked about the wonderful scholarship that she has found among her students at Harvard, and she lamented the fact that students still seem to lack the ability to be imaginative with the text. In a very real sense then, Walking the Motherpath cards (and the workshops constructed around their images) are an attempt to awaken the imaginative process. As such, they are another facet of our continuing efforts toward a lively and vital Jewish Renewal.

---

5. Carol P. Christ, *DIVING DEEP AND SURFACING; WOMAN WRITERS ON SPIRITUAL QUEST*, (Boston: Beacon Press, 1986), pp. 4–7.

Yosef Wosk

A Proposal for the Annual Observance of Bat-Yiftach

This proposal is based upon the disconcerting story in Judges 11:34–40 that discusses Yiftach's sacrifice of his daughter—or, as it is sometimes interpreted, her forced lifetime confinement.[1] The biblical text concludes, "It was a statute in Israel. From year to year the daughters of Israel went to lament the daughter of Yiftach the Gileadite, four days in the year."

Which four days? Neither the text itself nor any of the classical commentators identify the dates of the four days. The only mention of time is the two months that Bat-Yiftach asked of her father prior to fulfilling his vow (Judg. 11:37). A closer reading of the text, however, does hint towards a more definite dating.

Verse 29 describes Yiftach's vow as one of thanksgiving for having achieved a military victory and saving his people. It states that "whatever comes out of the doors of my house to meet me . . . I will offer it up for a burnt offering." Spring, soon after the winter rains, is a time propitious for battle; it also witnesses the birth of many lambs and goats, whose nature is to be frisky and curious about anyone approaching. Animals are well aware of the presence of others—whether another animal, a human, or even a spirit—many moments before humans notice the approach of another being.

Yiftach, therefore, must have reasoned that it would be a lamb or kid goat that would skip out *mi'daltai baiti* (from the doors of my house) to meet him. By specifically mentioning "doors" in the

---

1. Originally published in *Neshama* (Winter 1991) as a response to Judith Antonelli's article "Bat Yiftach: Reclaiming a Lost Jewish Women's Ritual" published in *Neshama* (Fall 1990).

plural, he is further implying animals—including sheep and goats—that often lived in the homes. He may also have been alluding to the barns and stables, all part of his homestead—his extended "house." He planned to offer a thanksgiving sacrifice of a kosher animal; not his dog and certainly not his daughter (Judg. 11:35). The only thing he did not reason, so he thought, was choosing which animal to offer.

He left this last detail for God to choose through a type of divine lottery. Using divine chance was not uncommon in ancient Israel. Two examples of such a lottery from the biblical text are the Yom Kippur goats, "one for Y-H-V-H and one for Azazel" (Lev. 16:8), and the distribution of the land among the twelve tribes (Num. 26:55). In the Scroll of Esther we see Haman using "lots," *purim*, to determine the most auspicious date for his scheme. Yiftach's neglect in choosing an animal may have been careless and irresponsible since there were so many unknown factors involved, but he nevertheless did it with faith and trust in the Guiding Principle of the Universe.

When his beloved daughter, instead of the projected animal, appeared first to greet him he felt obligated to sacrifice her (Judg. 11:35).[2] His decision has been consistently condemned by every-one ever since. Although Yiftach was the only one strong enough to save Israel in those days (c. 1135 BCE), he gained a reputation, even in his lifetime, as the worst of Israel's judges. His wanting to sacrifice his daughter makes him not only the worst of the leaders but the worst of anyone in Israel. It is to the credit of the editors and canonizers of the Tanakh that they did not edit such an extreme event from our history. The entire Bible is written with such great, sometimes unflattering, realism.

---

2. Compare to the story of the Akeda, Abraham's binding of his son Isaac (Gen. 22:1–19) and to the Greek mythological story of Iphigenia, the eldest child of Agamemnon who sacrificed her in order to gain favorable winds of the Greek fleet on its way to Troy. *Iphigenia in Aulis*, by Euripides (c. 405 BCE), is perhaps its most famous version.

A Title or Name for the Observance

I suggest calling this unique time simply by the words used to describe them in the text; that is, the Four Days, *arba'at yamim* (Judg. 11:40). This is a plausible title for these days of remembrance for three reasons.

1. It is taken from the original text.
2. It is akin to other observances that are known by the period of time they encompass. For example, there are the "Three Weeks" (between 17 Tammuz and 9 Av) and the "Ten Days" (of Repentance—*Aseret Yemai HaTeshuva*—between Rosh Hashana and Yom Kippur).
3. Yiftach's vow—to sacrifice the first living thing that came out of his house to greet him upon his successful return from battle— was made to that name and aspect of God known as Y-H-V-H, the Tetragrammaton (Judg. 11:30).

The attributes associated with this name generally imply mercy. For Yiftach to offer such a cruel sacrifice to such a benevolent spirit is even more insensitive and abhorrent than if he had related to the more judgmental aspect of God, identified with the name Elokim.

By invoking the Tetragrammaton, it is as if these four letters of the divine name of mercy associate themselves with the four days of mourning for Bat-Yiftach.

A fuller version of the name would be "The Four Days of Bat-Yiftach," *arba'at yamim Bat-Yiftach*. Perhaps over time the name of the observance will even evolve to simply invoking her name, Bat-Yiftach, so that we will ask each other, "What are you doing for Bat-Yiftach this year?"

The Four Days

Let us return to the dating of the Four Days. We first speculated that Yiftach returned home from battle around Pesach, a time when the newborn lambs and kids would be playing. A second hint based upon a *gezera shava* (rule of Talmudic interpretation) strengthens the spring dating.

Bat-Yiftach *rushes out* to greet her father with drums and cymbals (*b'tupim u-vimholot*) or "timbrels and dances" an instrument used to accompany dances (Judg. 11:34). The same language is echoed in Exodus 15:20, referring to Miriam and the women of Israel *going out* to sing and dance with drums and cymbals (*b'tupin u'vimholot*). The root word *tsai* (to go out) is used in both stories, and the description of their instruments is identical.

According to the hermeneutical rules of interpretation based upon similar wording in two disparate statements, we can assume the following: Just as Miriam and the women's celebration was on the seventh day of Pesach, so Bat-Yiftach went out to celebrate her father's victory with drums and cymbals on the seventh day of Pesach.

Pesach begins on 15 Nisan; the seventh day falls on 21 Nisan. If we add the two-month grace period Bat-Yiftach secured from her father before the sacrifice, we arrive at 21 Sivan as the projected day of sacrifice or confinement. The Four Days might be observed, then, from 21–24 Sivan.

The Torah reading for most years during the week of 21 Sivan is Shlach (Num. 13–15) and the Haftorah features the story of Rachav in Joshua 2:1–24. A powerful triangle of female personalities is therefore suggested by the reading: Bat-Yiftach, Miriam, and Rachav.

Suggestions for Observance of The Four Days

1. Since Miriam and Rachav are also implicated in the Bat-Yiftach story, they should also be included in the observance to some extent, either through study or ritual (such as Kos Miriam).
2. The main focus, however, would be on Bat-Yiftach. This could be observed through text study and appropriate rituals. Since she was either killed or forced into isolation, these four days — filled with actions serving as an antidote — might be ones of increased *gemilut chasadim*, acts of kindness, for women who

have suffered verbal and physical abuse in their lives, women who are victims of incest, degradation, and violence.

It would be a time to visit women in our society who feel lonely and isolated, who are shut-ins due to age, jail, health, or mental/emotional handicaps. It could also be a time of increased efforts to help single women and men desiring a relationship find each other. The loneliness and fear that many of them experience—at least some of the time—is similar to what Bat-Yiftach may have felt at times, in isolation for so many years.

Perhaps the good works achieved during the Four Days might even develop into an ongoing Bat-Yiftach Society of women helping other women.

3. Another aspect of the observance might be a form of *hitbod-dadut*, a deep, self-reflective meditation leading to transcendence towards a universal consciousness of being.

May Bat-Yiftach's life, her love, and enthusiasm—as well as the tragic circumstances that eventually surrounded her—never be forgotten. Through observing these "four days in a year" we might just bring some solace and hope to the many Bat-Yiftachs in our society. Perhaps the story has been preserved all these centuries so that our generation, at last, can act in some small measure in partnership with the Creator *letakein haolam* to repair a wounded world.

Dawn Rose

The Step into Nothing Need Not Be: The Search for a Jewish Women's Spirituality

Many long years ago (*ve-yesh omreem,* and some would say, in another lifetime altogether), in a faraway, mystical, magical land called Northern California, I was asked to participate in a women's ritual that was to be filmed for a Women's Studies seminar on spirituality at a California State University. The theme of the ritual was "healing," the setting to be in nature. Otherwise, the ritual, both in form and content, was wide open to our imaginations.

The location we selected was a 100-year-old mineral springs set deep in the heart of the coastal mountain range. Although we did plan the ritual in one of their ancient hot tubs, we did not film it in one. Rather, we hiked a little ways up the quiet creek that flowed on the edge of the spa, and found at last a perfect place, a cozy clearing surrounded by thicket at the base of a cliff. On the top of that cliff was a picturesque plateau where sheep grazed year round.

The ritual we conceived was quite simple. I was the image of a woman in mourning. Dressed in black robes and a white mask, I was the image of Mother Earth in pain, or the *Shehkinah* in exile. The film began with me, kneeling in the clearing. Head bowed, masked face in my hands, my entire body rocked back and forth in unarticulated grief. Another masked woman in a many-colored robe appeared, and upon seeing me and witnessing my grief, took my hand and bid me silently to rise. She then led me to an altar, built hastily from found wood, and there presented me with a feather, a crystal, and earthen bowl of water from which I drank, or pretended to do so, through the mask.

The ritual ended there, with two robed women standing at the base of a cliff, one holding a feather, a crystal, a now empty bowl. From there the cameraman panned away to the thicket, then took a long, long look at the muddy creek waters disappearing around the bend.

It was all quite lovely, this made-up ritual, a grabbag of sorts collected from Native American (we presumed), Christian, Jewish, and what I like to call "California" spirituality. As a key participant, however, I was embarrassed afterwards, and glad that my identity and my discomfort would go unrecognized behind the mask.

Looking back, I find I have even grown angry. Were I truly a woman in sorrow, unable to feed my children, husband lying terminally ill, were I really a woman in mourning, my daughter or son dead, my father encancered, were I really a woman in grief, my life destroyed, career ended before it began, were I any of those women, really, I would have despised us in our flowing robes with cameraman in tow. What would that feather be to me? Would it make my sorrow float softly down and be gone? What was that crystal more than a rock, sharp in my hand? What was that earthen bowl? Of what meaning was any part of that offering? The only meaning I found was that of a woman, divorced from any tradition, reaching for the female universal and attaining the generic.

Is it true that to find women's spirituality, particularly Jewish women's theology, we must wander far from our homes and the homes of our ancestors, to someone else's mother's garden, to everyone else's symbolism and meaning? Must we indeed dream the dream of a common women's language, a language ignorant of the words *bubba* and *zadie*, *aba* and *ema* as if we had no mothers of our own, no stories to recount, no history to retell? Did tragedy truly find our grandmothers so naked of resource? Have all our counterparts historically and geographically been so shallow, or have we jaded moderns so internalized the tradition's patriarchal focus on our own feminist critique that it is we who presume vacuity?

I wonder.

I wonder, first, if were we to search for this Jewish women's tradition, this wellspring of strength and wisdom and (dare I say) ritual, that I suggest—half on logic, half on faith—does indeed exist, where would we look? How would we find it, and so finding, recognize it? How would we relate to it? How would we accept, appropriate, integrate, honor it?

It is a large and multifaceted question, this issue of resources, and deserves far more straightforward discussion than it has hitherto enjoyed. For example, as Jewish women, most of us do not *know* our own history very well. We do, however, already *feel* everything from ambivalence to rage about that story. While all of those feelings are real and important, some inspire action, others impede. All accrue to a panorama of vision with an attending range of distortions (as does all vision—historical, religious, even academic). This we need to discuss also, for these emotions and distortions are a filter, an aspect of our interpretation, a factor in our appropriation: even, perhaps, a barometer of our acceptance of our mothers/grandmothers/foremothers/ourselves.

Here I have perhaps put the cart before the horse, for we have not yet begun to identify those resources to which we might respond. What are they and where are they to be found? In broad strokes, we might say they are the evidence—archaeological, anthropological, literary, oral, and personal—of Jewish women's lives, historically and contemporaneously. By using the term "contemporaneously" I intend a dual meaning: international and local/personal. This last designation is by far the most available, inevitably the most problematic, and inescapably the most important. It is ourselves as resource, commentator, the here-and-now focal point in the continuing dialectic, interpreters of the past and translators for the future. What we discover and develop now must be passed on in ways, God willing (given our material/ economic/political resources), much more concrete than the ephemera we have inherited from the past.

Moreover, the resources for a Jewish women's spirituality need not, by any measure, be limited to that part of the tradition which might be traced squarely back to foremothers. However we will come to conceive of the spirituality of our foremothers, parallel, interactive, springing from and adding to, all these paradigms bespeak of an integrative part of a whole. The entire tradition, then, is our resource as it was theirs, but under two conditions: accessibility (perhaps less limited now than before, given the rise in Jewish women's scholarship), and acceptability (perhaps, in the light of the feminist critique, more limited than previously).

But what of those resources which have, on the other hand, sprung more directly from the hand and the heart of Jewish women? With the ever-expanding research and scholarship being carried out by academics, authors, and artists, the question of how-to-find resources by and for Jewish women is much less a problem than the question of the next steps of interpretation and integration. The extraordinary volume entitled *Four Centuries of Jewish Women's Spirituality*, edited by Ellen Umansky and Dianne Ashton, is a perfect case in point.[1] This book of poetry, letters, prayers, autobiography, speeches, and essays, testifies to the range of "spirituality" or theological thinking selectively indicative of the Jewish woman's life—interior and exterior—for a significant range of years. Important to our discussion, however, are the kinds of material resources. It is a rare piece in this anthology which deals directly, systematically, with the topic of spirituality or theology. For Jewish women, there is no canon of literature (yet) that parallels the philosophical or mystical traditions of the patriarchal "side" of Judaism. Rather, our pool of resources might better be understood to belong to the long, very Jewish tradition of commentary, in which theology and spirituality is encouched in a far less systematic form responding to a specific point. Unlike rabbinic commentary, however, this commentary is catalyzed less by Toraitic text and more by lived experience. In other words, it is the existential situation of the Jewish woman which here demanded and received response. Embedded within that response in its myriad forms, awaiting careful exegesis, is the evidence of the emotional, spiritual, and intellectual interior lives, which constitutes the spiritual/theological world view, even religious survival strategies of those women we might call our foremothers. Another way to explain the above might be to propose that the rabbis in their Torah commentary likewise spoke from the nexus of their world view and situation. Their response, however, was

---

1. Ellen M. Umansky and Dianne Ashton, ed., *Four Centuries of Jewish Women's Spirituality: A Sourcebook* (Boston: Beacon Press, 1992).

played out in relation to text. The response of Jewish women (and non-rabbinic Jewish men, for that matter) comes in genres less esoteric, more interpersonal rather than intertextual.

And so we have this anthology of works. Umansky and Ashton have already performed two critical tasks in the apprehension of resources, that is they have identified and arranged. While these processes appear simple enough, I propose they are far from simple, carrying significance beyond the academic and religious and into what feminists would call the political. First, in a tradition which canonizes particular genres by specific groups as religiously significant, the identification of genres and authors outside of these groups is revolutionary. It constitutes a radical act of reclamation and is accomplished by a reading which is sensitive to alternative modes of expression indicative of marginality. This literary and religious sensitivity is culminated in an act of naming which bestows new value, constituting a challenge to and a redefinition of traditional value structures.

Having identified and amassed these writings, the editors in the preface tell of their struggle to appropriately arrange or present those works:

> We initially intended to organize the book around the themes of God, Torah, and Israel: the three central categories of Jewish religious thought. Yet, as this volume took shape, it became clear to us that these materials we had collected could not easily be subdivided into three thematic sections. Indeed, almost all the writings seemed to reflect on all three themes. On the other hand, there also seemed to be important differences among the writings, differences based on historical periods in which the pieces were written. (p. xiv)

Instead of attempting to force these works into the discrete categories of traditional Jewish male theology, Umansky and Ashton were able to respond to the literature as itself, unfolding its own story over time. This suggests an important methodological point: Any systematization or systematic presentation of Jewish women's resources needs to occur *b'deavad* (after the fact) rather than *b'hathilah* (prior to accumulation). Traditional categories, gleaned from the traditional cannon will not explain, but rather pervert the actual content of these pieces. Fortunately or unfortunately, this denies us all the easy parallelism sought by reductionists and teachers of introductions to Jewish theology. We will not find ready parallels to (over)simplified patriarchal thought, but are instead forced to acknowledge a far more complex and nuanced universe of meaning and symbol. Full engagement will require an entering in rather than a sampling of.

Having come to this body of literature, then, we discover a multi-genred collection divided by the editors according to historical period. This division is consistent with the notion of women's writings as primarily in response to lived experience as opposed to ahistorical text. They are overtly situated in their place and time. Moreover, Umansky, in the title of her rich introductory essay on the history of Jewish women's spirituality, "Piety, Persuasion, and Friendship," offers what may be the closest parallelism possible between the traditional categories of God, Torah, and Israel, with some important, and I think startling, differences. "Piety, persuasion, friendship" are not proper nouns. Though they might relate, sequentially, to the concepts of God, Torah, and Israel, they do not present themselves as categories of thought, but instead as highly personal and interactive states of being. They are nouns which point to active relationships, including and going beyond traditionally specified arenas of religious thought. Therefore, we might characterize these writings more fully as situated in place, in time, and in relation.

Here, I suggest, we find also the beginnings of a method (and perhaps attitude) of approach to and interpretation of these texts. First, they are written within a historical and geographic framework and ought to be read with the clearest understanding possible of the authors' actual life situations. At the crudest level, such information may not only provide the most honest portrait, but also lend necessary (I have found) apologetic buffer against the understandable, albeit unfortunate, knee-jerk response of modern Jewish women at the perceived, and often real, obsequious tone in the earlier writings. This response, important and well-earned, too often means the relationship ends there in rejection and eschews the possibility of deeper appreciation and understanding.

It is at this very point that we might explore the practice and the meaning of a methodological stance as unacademic and unsystematic as compassion. Invoking the same license so often afforded the rabbis (to be loved and revered in spite of statements and attitudes for which, were they moderns, they would be roundly rejected), we would approach these texts, these foremothers, with similar honor, presupposing significance and meaning in their lives and writings. Our task, then, would not be to judge, nor defend against judgment, but rather to uncover that meaning, through methods historical, exegetical, or as yet undiscovered. Most important, however, is the very presupposition of meaning, which begins with compassion and moves towards honor, neither of which has yet been afforded women's lives and writings in our tradition. It is upon us to unlearn the stumbling blocks occassioned by our own anger over their disenfranchisement, and ours.

Situated thus in place and time, is it truly possible these texts may be of value to us in our place and time? Here we may invoke the very essence of religious tradition, a concept which assumes some measure or kind of relevancy which transcends existential specificities. I propose that these texts, and countless others yet unanthologized, contain such relevancy. For these women's texts this relevancy may best be found in their third situative aspect; that is, in relation. More specifically, we would want to explore the apparent fact of "relationship" as a primary avenue of spiritual/theological expression, and further, then, the nature of those relationships exegetically for the actual religious values as they are played out within the interpersonal matrix. Engaging the texts from the latter perspective would require a further act of naming; that is, to envaluate (or invest with value) these authors as moral and/or religious agents operating within the scope of their perhaps limited universe of relations.

Such a reading of fictive or biographical women's text is not without precedence in the contemporary women's movement. Katie Cannon, in her book, *Black Womanist Ethics*, offers just such a reading of both the life and works of the African-American anthropologist/novelist Zora Neale Hurston.[2] Positing that traditional white or "dominant" ethical values presuppose a range of

---

2. Katie G. Cannon, *Black Womanist Ethics* (Atlanta: Scholars Press, 1987).

options and an autonomy of free will unavailable to depressed minority communities, Cannon turns to the literature of her community; in this case Hurston's works, to plumb the depicted relations and response for those ethical or moral virtues that provide both for the communal survival and the personal integrity of the minority members. In this study, likewise a radical act of reclamation and naming, she uncovers three primary virtues which may be discerned from Hurston's life and works: "invisible dignity," "quiet grace," and "unshouted courage." These virtues, I would suggest, are identified and named as the product of a first-level exegesis. A second-level investigation might flesh out more clearly the religious or spiritual core (call it theology) from which the characters, overtly religious or not, have obtained these ethical stances.

While the content of the literature by Jewish women bares little relation to that of African-American women, we may still consider the existential situation to be analogous in the same way that many minorities experience marginality and disempowerment. One of the most fertile resources, then, is this ecumenical and racial comparison for finding what women of other religions have done methodologically with their own resources. Here, Cannon, for example, initiates an unusual method for her "unusual" subject, Black women's ethics. She "starts with *experience* instead of with theories or values or norms." (p. 5, emphasis mine) Experience per say being an unwieldly object of investigation, she turned to black women's literature because:

> . . . this literary tradition is the nexus between the real-lived texture of black life and the oral-aural cultural values implicitly passed on and received from one generation to the next (p. 5).

Can we not posit, at least for investigation, that Jewish women's literature carries a similar complex of meanings? Moreover, I find Cannon's articulation of her specific goals in this study to be especially pertinent:

> My goal is not to arrive at my own prescriptive or normative ethic. Rather, what I am pursuing is an investigation (a) that will help black women, and others who care, to understand and to appreci-

ate the richness of their own moral struggle through the life of the common people and the oral tradition; (b) to further understandings of the differences between ethics of life under oppression . . . (p. 5–6).

A suggested approach then, to historic Jewish women's literature in its various forms, might be to discern patterns of moral/ethical agency (or actualization) both in the context of interpersonal relations and the broader relations of the socio-religious community. The goal beyond and behind that agency is to reconstruct the motivating and sustaining religious/spiritual world-view, or *Weltanshaung*. As Cannon explains, this investigation would not be for the purpose of proposing prescriptive ethics or theology (probably inapplicable to our place and time), but rather providing descriptive information which might inspire and inform our struggle today. Moreover, the very act of identification and naming might further the revolutionary envaluation of women's lives and literature as *canonical*, worthy of canonization, and subsequently, of study by women and men. Just as special reading techniques are required to read rabbinical commentary for its spiritual/theological content, so too a hermeneutic for approaching women's texts must be discovered. The work of Umansky and Ashton, along with Katie Cannon, and with other feminist scholars in their own traditions, points the way.

In our search, however, for resources for a Jewish women's theology/spirituality, we are in no way confined to literary texts from the past and the hurdles, hermeneutically and personally, which they pose. The possible contributions of Jewish women's lived experience spans the globe as well as the centuries. Just as modern "traditional" or "androcentric" Judaism comprises an intercontinental amalgam of law, debate, thought, and customs, so too does our women's tradition. One of the most outstanding (and accessible) examples of this kind of research to date can be found in the work *Women as Ritual Experts: The Religious Lives of Elderly Women in Jerusalem* by Susan Sered.[3] This book, from her dissertation for Bar-Ilan University, is a study of the spiritual life

---

3. Susan Starr Sered, *Women as Ritual Experts: The Religious Lives of Elderly Women in Jerusalem* (New York: Oxford University Press, 1992).

and attending ritual practices of a small group of elderly Kurdish
women. Her introduction begins with this remarkable description:

> A bent old woman, wearing two colorful kerchiefs, indiscrimi-
> nately kisses books in the back of the House of Study, and then
> kisses the shelf on which the books rest. Her friend, making an
> eloquent gesture with her arm, blesses all of the young men who
> are engaged in studying sacred texts. These same women will
> return home, spend hours preparing traditional Jewish foods, and
> then in the evening go to synagogue to attend a prayer service of
> which they understand no more than a few words. At several times
> during the service, they will hold their hands palms upward, kiss
> their fingers, and beseech God to grant their children, grandchil-
> dren, and all of the Israeli Defense Forces, health and happiness.
> Following the service, they will distribute perfume to the other
> women in the ladies' gallery of the synagogue, and all will anoint
> themselves with the perfume, proudly declaring the Hebrew
> blessing said for sweet smells. Despite their own poverty, on their
> way home from synagogue they will be careful to give small sums
> of money to every beggar that they pass (p. 3).

The very choice of these old women as research subjects, with
their kisses and kerchiefs, reminiscent of many of the quirky old
ladies found in many old schules here and abroad, is in itself a
radical departure from the almost universal attitude and understanding regarding what constitutes acceptable Jewish practice
and spirituality. Sered has made a most profound and iconoclastic
challenge: in these kisses and gestures, this cooking and choreog-
raphy, these women have developed a ritual language that
sacralizes women's experience in the otherwise male-dominated,
Jewish religious world.

Interestingly, following the daily lives of several closely connected widows in a Kurdish neighborhood in Jerusalem, Sered
found that it is the fact of their widowhood which provides these
women with the autonomy and time to assume the greatly
anticipated level of ritual and religious involvement previously
denied them by family duties. Widowhood, for these women,
means attending the synagogue when before they would have
been engaged with care of child, husband, or housework, and it
means giving *Tzedukkah* now because it is their money to give.

Having attained, through personal tragedy, personal autonomy, they transform their twilight years into a time of heightened spiritual endeavor.

Moreover, the system of daily and weekly rites that this small community of women perform and pass on to newly widowed women, not only addresses their lives and concerns, but dares to claim cosmic efficacy far beyond women's sphere. These women see their kisses and prayers and blessings and petitions as important, indeed necessary, to the well-being of men studying sacred text, performing (men's) ritual, even protecting the nation. Indeed, even the significant amounts of Kosher cooking done before each holiday is understood by them to be not so much in preparation for, but rather in creation of, that holy day. Their experience of cooking is a sacred experience:

> For these women food preparation is sacred because it embodies, concretizes, dramatizes, and ritualizes the central elements of Judaism, as understood by the women themselves. The basic ritual building blocks of their religious world include sorting, cooking, serving, and cleaning—tasks that are simultaneously and insepa- rably essential to both physical and spiritual fulfillment. *The women both domesticate religion and sacralize the profane* (p. 102, emphasis mine).

While traditional Judaism itself, as many religions, might in fact be understood as the "humanizing of the sacred and the sacraliz- ing of the profane," there are a number of elements here which make this study revolutionary. One, the sacramental experience of the women in the synagogue and in the home is a shared experience accompanied by shared understanding of the sacred- ness of that experience. Due to this interpersonal as well as intergenerational aspect, it qualifies as an independent or alterna- tive tradition. Two, this arena of sacralized lived experience is specific to women, a fact which both points to the lacunae of sacralizing rituals within normative Judaism for women, and to the reality of alternative ritual frameworks both currently existent and realistically possible. Like Umansky and Ashton above, through the simple acts of identifying these women's synagogue and kitchen activities as ritual, Sered has performed the most primary act of reclamation in spiritual/theological construction: she has named the hitherto unnamed or misnamed. And in those simple acts of naming, examining, and illuminating as ritual, she has completely restructured the context in which we may perceive and interpret Jewish women's spiritual lives. And, I would suggest, our own.

Just as in our search for resources, ideas, traditions, raw material into which we might dig our hands and fashion ritual and meaning and wisdom for today, just as in that search we must give name to the anonymous historically, identify the unknown contemporaneously, so too must we now name and identify our greatest resources: each other, ourselves. It would constitute a singular hypocrisy were we to adorn ourselves with any thinner mantle of authority than that with which we strive now to honor our foremothers, our counterparts. We are in fact Jews, are we not, living, learning, navigating our modern society, seeking answers, feeding children, loving partners, even offering prayers in and out of synagogue? We must therefore learn to read, hermeneutically, our own lives, discerning our own patterns of moral agency and the core of faith or knowledge that agency enacts. And we must learn to build on that which we discover within, finding the moments of our women's lives which already are sacralized with covert/overt ritual, name them, and move on to those other moments crying like an infant for that same gentle touch of the divine.

It is easy to say, though, for many it's almost impossible to do. We Jewish women and most modern Jewish men do not experience our own religious knowledge as pertinent to the ongoing debate. We have not been taught to recognize and understand our own personal spiritual authority. That honor is reserved for rabbis and scholars of ages past. The problem is that they were not women and they did not live now. And we are too many and have lived too much to really know so little.

So now that we understand a broader question of resources—after historical research and cross-cultural analysis, after the identification and the naming of others—how can we identify and name ourselves? It may be said that our spiritual disability as Jewish women is indicative of a broader malaise of changing identities and roles, yet a firmer spiritual base may well provide a foundation from which to approach all others. All these factors are connected, in place, in time, and in relation.

And we must seek these connections, as did Esther Broner, in *The Telling*.[4] This book, or chronicle, telling the story of the "Feminist Seder" over the course of some fifteen years, beautifully illustrates both in content and in form the process and the profit of the identification of each other and each self as religious authorities and ritual experts. The reality of the ongoing existence of this seder alone is of significance both religiously and politically. Yet the fact of this chronicling of the seder—the lists of the participants, what they said, wore, cooked, how they grew and occasionally argued—is in many ways even more revolutionary. The fact of the book, with its trivia and its sublime, points to and creates another reality; that is, it is important when Jewish women gather to do Jewish ritual. It is worth writing down and preserving. It is worthy of telling and retelling.

---

4. E. M. Broner, *The Telling* (San Francisco: Harper, 1993).

Ya'acov Gabriel and Cindy Gabriel[1]

Rei'im Ha'ahuvim: A Couple-istic Renewal of the Tenaim for Marriage

In studying the laws and customs of Jewish marriage, one is struck by their diversity and elaborateness. Practices vary from country to country, and each period in history adds its own layer of *minhag* and creativity to this community building *Simchah*.

In exploring its origins, one sees how rooted Jewish marriage is in *kinyan* (acquisition) and in contract law. The man "takes" the wife before witnesses, and the woman acquiesces to it. According to the Talmud (*Kiddushin* 2A), a wife can be acquired in three ways: by accepting something worth money, by accepting a written document in which the man promises to take care of her, or by the couple sleeping together. Of these three methods, the third, *Beeyah*, seems to have the greatest potential for egalitarianism. In love-making, the giving and the taking can be mutual.

One can extrapolate from the concept of *Beeyah* that a couple has the right to mutually consecrate their commitment to each other. How a wedding is formatted, what is said in the *Ketubah* (marriage document) and in the pre-nuptial *Tenaim* (agreements), are the ways this can be done. We looked for sacred rituals and symbolism to support our creation of an equal partnership. We then evolved the following processes to precede our *Erusin* (engagement), *Kiddushin* (sanctification), and *Nissuin* (our marriage's consummation).

1. Ya'acov (Jack) and Cindy met as a result of their independent connections with Reb Zalman: Jack was studying with Zalman to become a rabbi. Cindy was living an active, Jewish life in Mount Airy, in Philadelphia, with P'nai Or at its center. They were married in Elul 5750 (August 26, 1990).

Preparation for Marriage

Tenaim

There is a custom that the bride and groom's family create *Tenaim* (agreements concerning the wedding) as an engagement ceremony. Traditionally, people wrote a document to clarify when and where the wedding would take place, and to specify what material things each family would contribute to the new union. We transformed this ritual to reflect what we brought to each other psychologically and spiritually. Our *Tenaim* consisted of our expectations and needs, what we wanted our partner to know in advance, to protect us both. We used a "four worlds" approach, analyzing issues from the point of view of doing, feeling, thinking, and being. Ultimately, we developed eighteen areas of sensitivity, issues that required consciousness if our marriage was to flourish.

We spent many hours over many months talking about these *Tenaim*. We were commuting twice a week between Shenorock, New York and Philadelphia (a three-and-a-half hour trip) and wrote most of the agreements during that time. Specifically, the process went this way:

We would begin by brainstorming, listing all possible areas we wanted to talk about. The ground rules for brainstorming are that no idea is to be initially judged, that everything is written down and analyzed later.

When we felt we had addressed every possible issue, we combined categories until we had eighteen (חי in Hebrew) representing *chai*, life. We came up with the following categories:

1. General Assumptions—Ideas and areas of commitment and communication that frame our agreements, including statements about financial, emotional, intellectual, sexual, and spiritual domains.
2. Personal/Relationship Growth—Specific ways we will support each other's healing from childhood and family traumas.
3. Conflict Resolution—Ground rules for stopping destructive behavior patterns in our future fighting.
4. Relationship to Extended Families—A game plan for visits,

and for responsibilities towards our parents, children, sisters, their partners and their children.

5. Relationship to "Exs" and "Wanabees"—What constitutes healthy and appropriate behavior toward ex-spouses and toward people who single one of us for private attention.

6. Use of Money (savings, earning, spending)—A budget outline of who will provide for what in our relationship, and how earnings will be allocated to expenses, leisure, and savings.

7. Ritual Observance—How we will deal with issues of our differing approaches to *Kashrut*, Holiday observance, and Jack's role as a rabbi in a community.

8. Scheduling Daily Life—How we will keep aware of each other's needs and activities through a daily calendar.

9. Household Nurturing—How we will delegate and divide responsibilities for paying bills, shopping, cooking, doing laundry, and house cleaning.

10. Physical Health (exercise & eating)—Ways of supporting each other in staying conscious around food and in taking care of our bodies.

11. *Tikkum Olam* (*tzedakah* & environment)—A plan to divide up time and resources for worthy causes we support.

12. Continuing Education/Creative Expression—Emotional and financial support for each other's learning and skill development in the future.

13. Vacation Planning—A long-term plan for scheduling times for travel and relaxation.

14. Changing Locations/Traveling—Rules for safe driving and for preparing for trips less stressfully.

15. Family Planning/Children—A plan for deciding whether or not to have children, and if not, how to keep a connection to children, through friends and family.

16. Sharing Thoughts/Working Together—How to not monopolize friends in conversations, and how to create work together.

17. Other Promises—A list of specific promises about issues that have created conflict in the past, such as clutter in the house, and taking initiative in planning projects.

18. Openings—Space for family and friends in the community to add their advice and insights.

We began to work on each area. We took turns talking about our expectations of ourselves and our expectations of each other.

We continually reminded ourselves that our responses should not be what we thought the other wanted to hear, but what we ourselves wanted and expected. The few times that our expectations were in conflict, we negotiated until we were both comfortable with the resulting statement.

The process was intense and very rewarding. We hoped to avoid future conflicts by honestly articulating fears and expectations at the outset. We strongly believed that the language we chose would be a major step in creating our shared vision of life together.

The Tenaim Ceremony

The day of the reading of the *Tenaim* was 28 Av. The word formed from the number twenty-eight in Hebrew is *Koach* (power) and Av in Hebrew is formed from the first two letters of the alphabet, the *aleph* and the *bet*. What we were symbolically saying was that we draw up these agreements to invoke *Koach b'Av*, the power in words. Language and declaration have power to shape future actions. The week before we were married, as Shabbat ended, we invited friends and family to witness our *Tenaim*.

We created a Havdalah service. Jack spoke about the separation and distinction between being single and being married.

Cindy then introduced the *Tenaim* and explained how we had used the concept to create our own process for making agreements. We asked that each person present be a witness, to challenge us if they thought that any of our agreements were not specific or not realistic. We handed out the eighteen sections, one to each person, and our friends and family read them out loud in order. There was discussion by the group after each reading. People shared their own experiences of resolving conflicts with their partners, of dealing with "wanabees," and all the other issues. At the end, we asked each witness to write his or her own piece of advice to us and to sign our agreements. Also, in light of our impending marriage, Cindy's mother broke a plate, symbolizing the breaking of one family unit and the creation of another.

This ceremony was a very intense ending to our "singlehood," and the people present said it was a powerful, community-strengthening experience for them.

Conclusion

We have described our *Tenaim* in order to show how explicit a premarital arrangement can be and have appended a few detailed sections. Hopefully, this will encourage people contemplating marriage to look at the range of elements they need to address *before* proceeding with the *Erusin* and *Kiddushin* (engagement and marriage ritual). These *Tenaim* continue to be an important tool in our lives. The incidental benefit of having needs and expectations catalogued so carefully is that we can review them often. They are a helpful reminder of where stress might intrude in our relationship. Thus, they continue to have a healing function as our marriage evolves.

We submitted this paper to this collection honoring our transcendent, beloved Reb Zalman, because he is a continuing inspiration to us in the area of creating *Kavannah* (intentionality) in living and in ritual. We would never have realized it was possible to tailor *Tenaim* so that they would become so personally meaningful, without Reb Zalman's earlier, brilliant use of psychohalachic process in transforming rituals for life cycle events and for *davenning*.

May his holy insights flow through us to many, many more people, and may we all continue to be blessed with the elevated quality of life generated by Reb Zalman's ideas.

1. General Assumptions

We will have our wedding on August 26, 1990
at 11 A.M. at Juliet and Phil's house in Bala Cynwyd.

We will both take on the name "Gabriel" as our family name
for its Jewish and mystical symbolism,
from the angel associated with music and learning.

We do this in the spirit of feminism, acknowledging that marriage
is an identity change for both men and women. We also do this to
strengthen and deepen our commitment to our Jewish Hebrew heritage.
We encourage people to use that name for us.

We define our relationship as a deepening partnership:

Financially, we will combine our resources and responsibilities.

Emotionally, we will be each other's primary support.
We will share confidences with each other.

Intellectually, we will enthusiastically support and are
willing to participate in each other's learning process.

Sexually, we are committed to an exciting monogamous relationship.

Spiritually, we honor each other's connection to
The One, The Source of all Being, and enjoy assisting each other on our paths.

We are committed to keep talking/communicating, even under stress.

We are committed to working on projects together and to playing together.

When we fight, we will stop and see the conflict from each other's perspective.

Laughter will be a significant part of every day.

We will take care of each other in times of sickness.

Our goal is to see the possibility in every day.

We acknowledge that these and the agreements that follow are
part of a process that is evolving in our relationship.
We will re-evaluate and modify these agreements
over time, to our mutual satisfaction.

8. Scheduling Daily Life

*We will maintain a calendar on our
refrigerator which lists meetings, activities,
and travel plans. We will both keep it up to date.*

*We will make a separation between work space
and non-work space in our home.*

*Jack will stay aware of his tendency to over commit his time.
When someone asks him to do something, he will practice a first response
of "I'd love to—let me check my schedule and I'll get back to you."*

Cindy will not work more than 8 hours a day at the computer.

*We will check in with each other as a way of
time-reality check before committing to a major project.*

We will check in each morning or the night before about the day's schedule.

We both will take responsibility for planning social time with friends.

We will strive to broaden friendships beyond the congregation.

*We will check in with each other regarding
what we watch on TV.*

16. Sharing Thoughts/Working Together

We recognize that we are both passionate,
articulate people. Nonetheless, in our excitement at
sharing stories and news with others, we will be conscious
of giving each other room to finish thoughts and sentences.

If either of us feel we have been interrupted, we will
kindly and politely remind the other that "I'm telling this story."

We are interested in developing ways of working together,
designing facilitating seminars and workshops on
Jewish and non-Jewish issues.

We are committed to Midrashic Torah style dialogue, which includes the
possibility of more than one right answer to any question.

Our goal is to naturally, and non-competitively
share our thoughts and learning.

Reuel Falcon Karpov

The Voice of My Beloved: The Torah

This is an exploration of the gender issues and the romantic issues that arise when a woman, as opposed to a man, reads Torah. It articulates what many women have sensed, but have not been able to talk about.

Once our beloved is under our skin, our whole world is changed. We walk around humming jazzy little tunes, sing poems and exaggerate for emphasis the most special words. This new language of love arrives to us on music's carrier-wave. So it is when your beloved is Torah. And it is this shared encounter with ecstasy, the sacred intimacy at Jewish communal worship's heart, that I want to explore and celebrate.

The archetype of the dynamic between ceremonial Torah-reader and Torah as essentially marital, with ecstatic love-making as a metaphor for Torah-reading, is traditional. How is a lover relationship possible with Torah, for both men and women Torah-readers? Torah as an icon is feminine, allowing us to relate to her as a bride, a queen, a woman. Torah as text, on the other hand, the collective memory of tribal narratives and legalities I encounter in learning and in Torah-reading's shared remembering, is a primarily masculine consciousness. The *hakafos*, our sacred circle-dances of *Simchas-Torah*, our autumnal Torah festival, parallel closely the sacred ceremonial circlings of the *kaleh* (the bride) about the chosen (the bridegroom). My experience with Torah is again an encounter with an opposite sex's consciousness, and the lover relationship's polarity remains.

Torah is alive; the behaviors customary for interacting with Torah acknowledge this. For a Torah scroll to be *kosher*, it must be handwritten on sheepskin parchment, skin of Jewish sancta's totem animal. A Torah scroll, to be *kosher*, must radiate animal presence.

A Torah scroll's ceremonial cover is intentionally a seduction garment, clothing whose design tacitly invites removal. Its features honor and acknowledge the contained beauty we longingly imagine—too intense for us to expose continually, too compelling for us not to want to undress. We ceremonially undress Torah with respect's grace and precision.

Words impeccably handwritten barely skim physical Torah's heavy parchment. The ancient Hebrew words are the skin of the breathing life whose surface they skim, whose pulsing consciousness binds us as mirror and friend. Our beloved's skin's lines and patterns road-map that consciousness's imagination, inviting us and opening to us that territory of spirit, releasing a powerful voice from within us and from beyond us.

Jewish tradition tells us that with every word of prayer, an angel is born. If we mispronounce the word, the angel is born deformed. If we go back and correct the word, the angel is healed. *Trop* itself—Torah's specified sacred tune—is similarly a prayer form, providing opportunities for the same sacred precision. Our certainty opens us into a beauty more apparent, into patterns more beloved, into a desire intensified, through repeated knowing. When we truly and accurately *lein* (ceremonially chant) Torah—according to the masoretic text's preordained signals—the angels thus created ascend whole, clothed in garments of dignity and proper symmetry.

The Masoretes' text confides to us what hearing and naming Torah's life force require to actively blossom under our touch into deeper self-revelation. Learning Torah text's and tune's ceremonial enactment involves a fascination with delicately precise inner workings, parts intimately scanned in text's and memory's mutual committing. Sacred discipline's strictness enables and sustains the flow of *kavonoh* (directed sacred intention) between ourselves and Torah.

Our intensely detailed imagining of this moment launches Torah's magnificent calling-forth. The ceremonial Torah-reader, anticipating this encounter, internalizes this intimate knowledge, so as to convey truly the letters' most hidden spirit. Our attentiveness helps nourish our beloved and ourselves into a being deepened through sharing, fully enlarged with love given and received.

Through *trop* (markings indicating prescribed tune) the masoretic Torah text specifically tells us: Here is the precise gesture I need; here is its precise timing. Here are how the gestures themselves best precede and follow one another. Now I need you to respond here with a faster gesture, here with a slower one. Here is where I want the same set of gestures to repeat, then break free from repetition. Here is how I can best be loved, for my breathing life to respond released into its towering height of voluptuous consciousness.

Inviting the specifics of our loving, the text has pre-informed us: here, and here, and here, is where I ask you to allow my love voice through gestures resembling, respectively, a small rising, a great rising, a quadragon, a scattering, a clustering as of grapes, a moon one-day-old, a heifer's horns, a chain. The text confides to us how, when, and in what sequence, more dramatic moments are welcomed.

The ceremony of *Krias*-Torah (public performance reading of Torah) includes a *gabbai* simultaneously silently reading identical masoretic text including vowels, punctuation marks, and *trop*, all of which the Torah scroll contains only implicitly. The function of the *gabbai* in *Krias*-Torah is like the spotter in gymnastics. Both human minds, the one experiencing, the second actively, identically imagining, do not join but coincide, simultaneously body-surfing the incoming wave of consciousness.

Coinciding also with both minds in *Krias*-Torah's ceremony are not only those physically present, but all those involved since the beginning. We can feel those collective *n'shomos* (spiritual minds) present, blessing with us. We can feel that deep life's vortex of energy with us, surrounding us, underlying and supporting us from the deep place in the Cosmos where Torah first caught life and its spirit ignited.

Here to bless with us are those who invented the folk narratives informing this text. So, too, are all who stood together at Sinai—

as are all who stand with us now—receiving Torah at our continuing Sinai revelation.

Here to bless with us are sacred Scripture's priestly editors. So, too, are those who argued about it in the sacred discourses appearing as commentary even before the canon's closing, before the text's final letter's writing.

Here to bless with us are those who, before us, intoned Torah. So, too, are those who taught it and were murdered for doing so, including Rabbi Akiva and the others whose deaths, burned alive wrapped in Torah's parchment scrolls, our *Yom Kippur* martyrology recalls.

Here to bless with us are those desiring Torah but prevented from Torah study. Some never reached an age of maturity to make Torah study possible in this lifetime, other than their nine pre-natal months of Torah study memories with Elijah the Prophet, memories tapped out of them at birth by his accurate forefinger beneath their noses. Some, in this life, were deprived through ongoing anti-Jewish persecutions. Or Jewish religious civilization itself may have denied them, as all of the Jewesses not permitted to read Torah.

With us at this moment in spirit, encouraging the community of hearers, are those who taught us to appreciate Torah. All present, whether or not physically incarnate, are so proud that you have come in sacred attentiveness, respecting the sacred consciousness that Torah contains and has accumulated through history.

Tradition tells us that Torah's written text, black letters against light background, is "black fire on white fire." In this moment where eternity's constancy intersects with history's restlessness, our combined silence is active, knowing. We may find ourselves forever receptive and forever new. And that moment can reward us, bearing our renewed discovery along mutual pleasure's carrier-wave, turning us finally into the revelation of the white fire surrounding written Torah's openly visible black fire.

Leining, Torah's sacred cantillation, is not intended to be—as Italian opera's shared sung oratory, belted out to an audience—a public declamation. The ceremony is open, but more in a shared privacy than in a stage event's public place. Like the voices of India's ceremonial singers, or those of the Native American church or other Native American ceremonialists, the voice is intoned, not sung. *Leining*, rooted in our primal life before Torah, bounces off the soft palate, lighting up all of the *chakras*.

It is for the Lover of Torah to sense what the beloved intends, however subtly. It is for the Lover of Torah to sense what the text demands, assuming nothing too quickly, knowing when to push what part of the text a bit further, grasp and strain it almost to breaking, bend it under our voice into our best hearing of its truest need. It is for the Lover of Torah to hear when to back off, the moment before it would grow hard against us, slipping away, eluding us in an instant. By now, we must know that if we hold back it would betray us too. Torah as collective consciousness, the shared memory, intones us as much as we intone Torah.

Torah opens to us, and we open to Torah's voice, and we arrive to one another differently each time. Our senses, our voice, have given themselves over to our shared remembering, to this anticipated and repetitively imagined event. At such moments Torah's life, contrapuntal to our own, draws out our voice as other; receives our life and is received by it. Each coming moment breathes itself into what it has imagined, into a place from which new dreams emerge.

In each tryst with each return to a passage, wanting's blue steel edge is made molten again, wanting grown clearer and harder with the trust elicited by still grown cumulative through time. Learning the passage, and then publicly enacting it, is a collective love-making with that great voice. At the moment of *K'riah*, which means the reading or the calling out or the crying out of Torah, the focus of desire and its amplitude are the only thing in life that is for us, and that we are; we have consented for Torah to bend us into our joining's exact evolving shape. Committing the passage to oneness with our own consciousness, we know Torah intimately.

Torah is more expansive than any one or all of us. I can feel that great voice moving under my own like a great horse flying across a pasture, its life moving under me. Feeling the pleasure in moving with that voice's life in the best possible way, I am suffused with the parchment's feel, with the ancient words' scent. The tune's patterns change, changing my thought patterns as would the sudden changing of a living fire's sounds.

My voice, proceeding along sound's rim, suspended by precise design and an abandonment to desire, is privileged to explore, fulfill, and cherish line after remembered line of text wide with astonishment. Along our voices' paths, at moments we finally seem to hang motionless, only the air about us writhing, dark earth beneath us cantering us into fields of darkness and light. And in a moment of apparent pause, this moment of fierce quiet tension, our joined intensity gathering strength for renewed encounter, we begin again.

Sensation and experience become indistinguishable, with no momentary pause inquiring whether a turn in the tune is indeed a turn in the tune. Love of Torah arises beyond deliberate and punctual carefulness, and becomes its own voice again. The mind need no longer interfere to confirm that a mouth kissed is indeed a mouth kissed. Moses our rabbi's soul was thus taken through a kiss.

How is a lover relationship possible with Torah, for both men and women Torah readers? Torah as icon is feminine, traditionally allowing us to relate to her as a bride, a queen, a woman. But Torah as text, the collective memory encountered in learning and in Torah—reading's shared remembering, is primarily masculine. It is a collective tribal consciousness of predominantly masculine narratives and legalities. My experience with Torah is again an encounter with an opposite sex's consciousness, and the lover relationship's polarity remains.

Krias—Torah's ceremony deepens us into Cosmic Event. By reconstituting the written text into publicly shared, collective remembering, we caress our beloved's voice into casting a longer shadow in eternity. Like generations past, we too can be Lovers of Torah; that great Love continues.

With gratitude for all of my poetic teachers, including those who gave me Torah-Reading honors since 1969. Thank you all for letting me learn from you.

Harold M. Schulweis

Morality, Legality, and Homosexuality*

Here Rabbi Harold Schulweis offers us a compassionate and clear-headed look at homosexuality, based on both his grounding in traditional texts and his encounters in rabbinic counseling with the real concerns and anguish of individuals.

We are in this world and of this world and not of another. We are to be concerned with the creatures of this world, the creatures of the sea, the fowl of the air, the beasts and the cattle, everything that creeps upon the ground, and the human being.

The Bible focuses attention on the promise and failures, the sins and lusts, the dreams and desires, the creation out of dust of the human being endowed with the image of God. Judaism is married to reality, the whole of reality. It does not flinch from the encounter with sickness or death or guilt or despair. It does not avert its eyes from the condition of sexuality. In the middle of the holiest day of Yom Kippur at the Minchah service, the tradition chose from public reading not an episode about angels or saints but a section from the Torah that deals with the nakedness of the body, of incest, adultery, and homosexuality. Indeed in the Maftir of Leviticus 18:22, the explicit verse is found: "Do not lie with a male as one lies with a woman. It is an abomination." Leviticus 20:13 states: "And if a man lies with a man both of these have committed an abomination. They shall surely be put to death. Their blood shall be upon them."

---

* Reprinted from *Svara*, Vol. 3:1 (1993): 8–13.

If our tradition dares to speak of such matters on the holiest of days with candor, should I not speak to you about such concerns or should I smother my thoughts and mute my words? If Judaism is a way of life, a way of responding to reality, then the phenomenon of gay and lesbian relationships must be addressed. Every major church, every social critic, every newspaper, every journal is focusing on this phenomenon. The subject is now fixed on the American political agenda as evidenced by its obvious presence in last November's election.

Surveys report that ten percent of the general population is homosexual. Demographers suggest that the same percentage applies to other people including our own.[1] If then there are six million Jews in America it may be conservatively estimated that 600,000 gays and lesbians are in our midst. Six hundred thousand is a large figure, as many as all of the Jews in all of Los Angeles. Even if the lower estimates of four percent of the population are used, it would mean that 240,000 Jews are homosexual. The issue is being debated in the Rabbinical Assembly, the Jewish Law Committee of the Conservative Movement, and among biblical scholars and masters of the law.

But my choice of the topic at hand is not academic; it is more personal. She was a member of our congregation in her late fifties who sat in the congregation and exhibited a familiarity with both the Prayer Book and the Bible. She came every Sabbath and then at the end of one service she asked to see me privately. She sat across my desk. "You may remember my son; he attended Hebrew High School and was a student at the University of Judaism. He kept the secret of his orientation to himself. Whenever the issue of gays and lesbians came up, my son felt ridiculed, humiliated, hurt. I knew his sexual orientation and he knew how unhappy I was with the state of affairs. One day he announced that he was going to San Francisco for "the cure." A friend had suggested a therapist who would change him, who would teach him to be straight and normal. I kept receiving a number of letters from him. He was ebullient. Things were fine now. He had

---

1. Sol Gordon, "Homosexuality: A Counseling Perspective," *Judaism,* Fall, 1983, pp. 405, 429 citing C.A. Tripp, *Homosexual Matrix* (New York: McGraw Hill, 1975).

changed. He was a "new man." Then I discovered much too late that he was lying to me and to himself. My son took his life." She stopped speaking and looked at me. "I am here to ask you, Rabbi, was my son an abomination? Was he punished? Is that why he died?" She was visibly shaken, her eyes full of tears and pain, despair and anger. "I want to know," she continued, "what does Judaism say about my son? Was he guilty or was I? Was I too strong, too domineering a mother, and my husband too weak, too detached?"

I do not remember what it was that I said to her but her question never left me. It is one thing to read a scientific paper or to examine a rabbinic text. It is another to look into the pained eyes of a human being. Soon after her visit, the stigmatized issue seemed to come out of the closet. An article appeared in the Jewish press by Dr. Morris Mandel, a clinical psychologist who cites from a letter he had received:

> Before I take my life let me write you for advice. I am Jewish, Orthodox and most unfortunately, homosexual. Talk of marriage is thrust in my face as I am of marriageable age. The only trouble is that I am running out of excuses. I have done much repentance and prayer to God but He does not hear my prayers. I am a sub-human creature. Life to me is hearing more jokes about homosexuals. My heart bleeds and I pray to the God of my fathers that He never again thrust this poison into the House of Jacob.[2]

Since then I learned of several scientific studies indicating an unusual prevalence of suicide attempts among homosexual persons. The recent *Report of the Secretary's Task Force on Youth Suicide* projected that gay adolescents were two or three times more likely than peers to attempt suicide and accounted for more than thirty percent of completed youth suicides last year.[3]

Increasingly over these past years I have had visits from people from within the congregation and from without. Jewish young

---

2. Morris Mandel, "Learning to Hide: The Socialization of the Gay Adolescent," in D.A. Martin, *Adolescent Psychiatry*, Vol. 10 (Chicago: University Press, 1982) 52–65.

3. U.S. Department of Health and Human Services, *Prevention and Interventions in Youth Suicide*, Vol. 3 (Rockville, MD: GPO, 1986).

men and Jewish young women whom I know, who know me, whose parents I know, most of whom are members of the synagogue. At first they speak to me with downcast eyes and stammering hesitation. But finally there pours out of their lips revelations of terrible hurt and confusion and the feelings of worthlessness. They tell of the nagging clues of their felt difference during their early adolescence, feelings that they managed to repress. Their predilections for certain games and certain apparel and friends who were of the same gender were ignored. Then as they grew older a recognition of their erotic attraction to people of the same gender could not be denied. It was for them a deep, dark, shameful secret. They did well enough in school and had warm relationships with their parents but they were bleeding every day from jibes and jokes about dikes and butches and faggots and fags and *feigele-boychik [lit.,* bird-child]. Everyone laughed at the easy mimicry, the minced gait, the sissy lisp, the limp hand. It brought peals of laughter to everyone except to themselves. Why could they not laugh?

Those who came to me came into the study holding their breath. They came not knowing exactly for what. They were uncertain of my reaction. They came out of a need for confession and most often out of a concern for their parents.

I love my parents. I love my family. I can't bear to hurt them. I don't know what to do. Can I keep on hiding it from them? Should I run away? Should I leave the community? Should I leave the congregation?

I don't know what to say to the friends of my parents who want so desperately to fix me up. "How come you're not dating?" What must they think of me, that I have no sexual feelings, no romantic desires, that I am a eunuch? I love my parents. The other day my mother said "All I want is to dance at your wedding," and I winced with guilt.

Honesty is important in our family. I was raised to tell the truth. What do I say to my family and my friends about my sexual orientation? I have an important career that brings me close to people. Do I lie to them? Do I deceive them? Am I condemned to live like a fugitive forever running, dissembling, fearful of being discovered? Am I doomed forever to be embarrassed? Must I remain so guarded with everyone lest I give my secret away? Am I so guilty, is my love so shameful that I must forever cover the mark of Cain on my forehead? What do I say to you when you see me with my partner? How do I introduce my loving friend? No, I am not in a closet. I'm in a casket."

They are our tortured sons and daughters. Some have revealed their buried secret:

My parents don't look at me the same way anymore now that they know. I have disappointed them, destroyed their dreams. But I am the same son with whom they played as a child, whom they fed and clothed and in whom they rejoiced. I am the same son who brought home good grades, participated in the plays in Sunday School, in Hebrew School, in regular school. I am the same son who rejoiced with them at my Bar Mitzvah. I look at the faces of my dejected father and mother and I feel like saying to them: "Papa have you no blessing for me? Mama, do you see nothing in me but my sexual orientation? Am I not the same loving, caring, sensitive son to you?" Nothing is so terrible than to feel so distant.

I ask them, "Did you choose to be gay? Is this a matter of free will, your gay lifestyle?" The answers are much the same:

Rabbi, do you think that I would willingly choose my fate: that I would voluntarily choose a life that ostracizes me from my friends and family, that makes of me a pariah, that affects my career, my job, my house, my employment? Did you choose to be a heterosexual? No more did I choose to be gay. If I am confronting a choice today it is not whether to be what I am, but whether to accept my fate, whether to come out with my orientation or to bury it and recite Kaddish.

I read as much as I can and talk to others about the issue. I come across a great deal of material which indicates the genetic character of some if not all homosexual orientation. Professor Simon LeVay, a neuroscientist at the Salk Institute in LaJolla, scanned the brains of 41 cadavers, including 19 homosexual males, and found that a cluster of neurons in the hypothalamus, recognized as the center of sexual activity in the brain, was less than half the size in gay men as in heterosexual men, similar in size in gay men as in women.[4]

A few months later, additional evidence suggesting genetic origins of sexual orientation was published by psychologist Michael Bailey of Northwestern University and psychiatrist Richard Pillard of Boston University School of Medicine. Their research reveals that, if one identical twin is gay, the other is almost three times more likely to be gay than when the twins were fraternal.[5] I am not a scientist and I do not claim to understand all of the implications of this research. There remains a great deal of ambiguity about the etiology of gay and lesbian sexual relations. If sexual orientation is in the brain, John Money, a psychologist at Johns Hopkins asks, when did it get there? Was it pre-natal, neonatal, during childhood, or during puberty?[6] It is clear, however, that homosexuality is not simply a willed choice or an ideological commitment.

Scientific evidence aside, when I speak to these men and women they reveal that their preferential erotic attraction was not chosen, but discovered, and discovered with pain and anxiety. Their orientation is given, whether naturally or supernaturally. How can I call such powerful involuntary feelings immoral, justifying punishment? Surely a rabbi should know the rulings in *Bava Kamma* 28b and *Nedarim* 27a which read: '*Anus rachmanah patreiah,* meaning, "The Holy One exempts those who act under duress." In cases of compulsion, the Merciful One exempts. Who am I to condemn? Can I command you how to feel? Surely the object of a person's sexual arousal cannot be mandated. Do you choose the gender of your arousal? "Ought" implies "can." But they cannot.

What do other rabbis say? Biblical and rabbinic laws condemn gay behavior. You may not be able to control whether or not you are born homosexual but you can control your behavior. They say we cannot tell you how to feel but we can tell you how to act. So the chairman of the Conservative Jewish Law Committee in his

---

4. David Gelman *et al.*, "Born or Bred?" *Newsweek*, Feb. 4, 1992, p. 50.
5. *id.*, p. 46*ff.*
6. *id.*, p. 48.

responsum writes, "I have issued an invitation or perhaps a demand to the halachically concerned homosexual to refrain entirely from homosexual practice by remaining celibate and by not engaging in the common homosexual lifestyle."[7]

Rabbis as knowledgeable and as moral as I am argue that the law is the law, that the biblical verse cannot, must not, dare not be changed. To my argument, they counter that it is irrelevant to the law whether homosexuality is genetically or neurologically determined, irrelevant whether or not the "constitutional gay and lesbian" cannot meet his or her physical and emotional needs in heterosexual relationships, irrelevant that they are 'anusim— forced, coerced, compelled by nature. None of these factors justifies overturning the law. Whatever the etiology of homosexuality may be, whether it is due to hormonal imbalances, whether psychological techniques are shown to be incapable of changing a homosexual to a heterosexual person, whether homosexuality rises in number—all scientific, cultural and moral explanations are inconsequential: the law is irreversible. I respect their position.

But put yourself in my position. What do you say? How am I, as one who knows the Law, to respond to our sons and daughters who come for guidance? I must confess to you that I cannot look into the eyes of this man or that woman and say to either. "Abstain forever. Get thee to a monastery, get thee to a nunnery. Go and control yourself. Remain celibate for life."

I must confess as a rabbi, as a Jew, as a moral person I cannot seriously deny a human being created in God's image the intimacy, the love, the pleasure, the sensuality which is God's gift.

Why not? It runs against my Jewish sensibility, against my Jewish conscience, to bring misery, pain, torture, and anguish to innocent people who are created the way they are in the name of God and Judaism. The words from the Book of Job ring in my ears: "Did He that made me in the womb not make him? Did not the one who formed him form me too and shape us in one womb?" (Job 31:15).

I cannot, I do not, judge these people as sinners or their love as

---

7. Rabbi Joel Roth, unpublished paper of the Rabbinical Assembly Committee on Jewish Law and Standards, pp. 123–124.

abomination because such a judgment today, given our under-standing of the character of sexual orientation, is un-Jewish.

I cannot condemn them to ostracism or celibacy because the God I have been raised with is *El Male' Rachamim*—God who art full of compassion—the same attribute that Jews are to pursue: *rachmanut* [from the womb], *cum passio* [(Latin) with suffering].

More than compassion is involved. Jewish wisdom and the moral character of Jewish law are at stake. The Torah is a law of truth and of peace. Torah is no slab of stone thrown down from heaven. Rabbis have the right and the obligation to interpret the text so that it sanctifies God's name. That has been the Jewish tradition. The rabbis of the Talmud would not allow "An eye for an eye and a tooth for a tooth" to stand in the law of Judaism. They used logic and moral sense to free it from slavish literalism.

The Bible is rooted in history and history changes.

In the time of the Bible, the law of leprosy was based on the opinion that the disease was contagious and that it was a punishment for sins. But they did not know of Hansen's disease, they did not know that some forms were not contagious. Who today, knowing what we do, would treat the leper according to the presupposition of knowledge in that period of time?

According to early rabbinic understanding, a deaf-mute was considered to be retarded, mentally incompetent, an imbecile not able to serve or witness or to be counted in the minyan or able to affect marriage or divorce. But that ruling was based on empiri-cally false data. On a visit to the Vienna Institute for the Deaf and Dumb, Rabbi Simchah Sofer saw that their impaired speech and hearing had nothing to do with their intelligence and accountabil-ity. The law changed.[8]

Analogously, I would argue along with other scholars that the rabbis did not know of "constitutional" gay and lesbians who had no control over their sexual orientation. For them, homosexuality was a choice, contrary to nature. They were scientifically in error. And therefore, their judgment must be accordingly revised.

Likewise, it is not simply a matter of what the Bible says. We do not know exactly what *to'evah* meant. I would argue along with

8. Rabbi Simchah Bunim Sofer, *Shevet Sofer.* "*Even Ha'ezer* Number 21.

many biblical scholars that the biblical word for abomination, *to'evah*, refers not to homosexuality but to cultic prostitution. What the Bible inveighed against was the pagan tradition that paid obeisance to pagan gods by all forms of illicit sexual behavior.

And what do I say to that Jewish mother who came to see me after the suicide of her son? What do I say to the young men and women who come to see me asking whether there is in the heart of Judaism any blessing for them? To the mother I say, knowing what we do today, neither he nor his behavior are abominations.

What is abominable for the homosexual is what is abominable for the heterosexual. Promiscuity, coercion, rape, sexual exploitation, infidelity, adultery. What is abominable for one gender is abominable for another, what is abominable for persons of all sexual orientations is the disrespect for the personhood of the other. The flaunting, exploitive abuse of sexuality is as ugly in heterosexuality as it is in homosexuality. It is behavior, conduct, and character—not sexual orientation—that counts.

This summer I attended the gay and lesbian synagogue, Chayim Chadashim, and a man I knew from this congregation approached me, extended his hand to wish me Shabbat Shalom. He wrote me a week later confiding how difficult it was for him to approach me. "My heart stood still."

With what will we bless you? We bless you with the traditional blessing in Judaism. "Blessed art thou O Lord our God King of the universe who has created all kinds of creations. Blessed art Thou O Lord our God King of the universe who has created the human being in thine image."

You who are invisible and inaudible know that this is your home and that these are your people, that I am your rabbi, that this is our God, that you are welcome, that this synagogue is open to you, that nothing should be deprived to you. You are part of our family, you are part of our minyan, you are part of our blessings.

We are a congregation of Jews who are called to understand. We understand your suffering. We understand the primitive, homophobic discrimination, beatings and the humiliation afflicted upon the gay individual.

Jews should know the dangers of scapegoating and stereotypical caricatures. We should fight against the ugly perversions of the truth. We should fight against the notions that homosexuals, gay or lesbian, are all of one character, all one-night stand recruiters, caricatures paraded on the Geraldo Rivera freak shows. There are psychologically maladjusted homosexuals as well as psychologically maladjusted heterosexuals. But all forms of sexual harassment are violations of the spirit of divinity whether it is done by heterosexuals to women in the Navy at Tailhook or by homosexuals who violate the dignity of persons of the same gender. I would urge you to join in opposition to the Vatican's recent rulings that support discrimination against gay people in such areas as public housing, family health benefits, and the hiring of teachers and coaches. Sexual orientation is no abomination and no crime. It deserves no punishment from society.

Once it was written in the Book of Deuteronomy, Chapter 23, that eunuchs are not allowed to enter the House of the Lord. Then the prophet Isaiah arose to declare in God's name:

> [N]either let the eunuch say, Behold, I am a dry tree. For thus says the Lord to the eunchs that keep my sabbaths and choose the things that please me, and take hold of my covenant; And to them I will give in my house and within my walls a memorial better than sons and daughters. I will give them an everlasting name, that shall not be cut off. Also the children of the stranger, that join themselves to the Lord . . . even them will I bring to my holy mountain, and make them joyful in my house of prayer (Isaiah 56:3–7).

Joe August and Lawrence Bush

Brotherkeeping: Jewish Scripture and the Reconstruction of Masculinity

The sages portrayed in the Talmud were powerful men. When Rabbi Jonathan ben Uzziel would sit down to study Torah, "every bird that flew overhead would be instantly incinerated" (*Sukkah* 28a). Rabbi Chanina ben Dosa was known to vanquish a lion with words and frame the beams of a house with prayer. Rabban Gamaliel had a tube through which he could see at a distance of two thousand cubits across land or sea. Rabbi Akiva, a self-described ignoramus at forty, had acquired unmatched Torah learning and 12,000 disciples thirteen years later. He died rapturously reciting the *Shema* as Roman torturers flayed his skin.

"Any sage who is not as hard as iron," holds the Talmud (*Ta'anit* 4a), "is not a sage, as the verse states: 'a hammer that shatters rock' [Jeremiah 23:29]. Nevertheless," the passage continues, "a person should train himself to be gentle, as the verse states, 'Remove anger from your heart . . .' [Ecclesiastes 11:10]." Indeed, "training men to be gentle" might be called one of the definitive projects of Jewish law, for men are the ones whom the tradition perceives as needing the humbling, the community-mindedness, and the discipline that are among Judaism's major offerings. By contrast, notwithstanding their second-class status in the tradition, women are, within the context of marriage and childrearing, assumed to be more naturally inclined towards being "civilized."

Throughout the Talmudic tradition, therefore, it is less the sages' herculean powers than their virtues of restraint, discernment, surrender or egotism, and *teshuvah*, repentance, marked by tears, that prove their greatness and guarantee their leadership and longevity. These men embody an almost post-feminist masculinity of constructive power, harnessed by self-knowledge, that is a far cry from the violent, emotionally repressed male mystique of American culture. It is ironic, therefore, that few Jewish men seeking alternatives to the Sylvester Stallone/Arnold Schwarzenneger masculine model (and to the "tough Jew" mystique of Israel) are even aware of the *aggadic* (storytelling) literature of the Talmud. Typically, in fact, the very word, "Talmud," calls to the minds of most Jews not models of character and wisdom, but images of compulsive old men arguing over musty old texts before being humiliated by anti-Semites on the street. Piled on top of these stereotypes have been feminist polemics about the patriarchal, misogynistic Jewish tradition, and a surfeit of circumcision jokes told by *nebbish* comics. Malignment and parody have combined to make the notion that Judaism might serve as a resource for the reconstruction of masculinity seem almost absurd.

Clearly, there is a need to "rehabilitate" Jewish texts as a treasure trove for Jewish men who are questing to be "brotherkeepers." By "brotherkeepers," we mean men who are seeking, in community, to celebrate their powers, affirm their key masculine experiences, heal (or at least acknowledge) their injuries, and muster their energies to break free of narrowly defined gender identities. Modern Jewish men in particular need this kind of "brotherkeeping" in order to heal historically inflicted wounds, renew their life forces, and play active, committed roles in the renewal of both Jewish and American life and culture.

Why Jewish men *in particular*? It is not that we are a breed apart from non-Jewish men; we have suffered no less than others from the emotional repression involved in the construction of adult masculine identity, or from the loss of constructive outlets for male energies that Robert Bly bemoans in *Iron John*. Nor do we cause less suffering than other men through the violence and aggression that too often erupts when the "deep masculine," as Bly puts it, is buried and out of our soul's reach. Statistics show that Jewish domestic violence is nearly on par with that of the general American population and involves well over ten percent of Israeli households. Sexual harassment is as common within the institutions of the organized Jewish community as within the corporate world. Alcoholism, drug abuse, and other symptoms of a thwarted, caged inner life afflict Jews as much as the general population.

Yet Jewish men *do* contend with three unique influences that mark our masculine identities as different:

First, many of us live, with, or are strongly influenced by, feminist women. Jewish women have been pioneers in the American feminist movement, which has had the greatest impact upon middle-class, educated white women—a "type" to which a solid majority of Jewish women conforms. Chastened (if not converted) by this feminist presence in our lives, Jewish men have tended to lay low; to display enough sensitivity and restraint to feel exculpated of sexism, and then sit on our laurels, opting for a relieved feeling of innocence. As a permanent stance, however, "staying out of the way" can only engender isolation and fatigue. Many Jewish men are thus seeking a path of re-emergence that begins with the question: What does it mean to be a powerful man among a generation of newly empowered women?

Second, Jewish men have to contend with the role of anti-Semitism as a psychic force in our lives. The emasculated Jew— he of the circumcised penis, the plucked beard, the raped daughter, the shriveled frame in oversized concentration camp garb—is the very ghost that modern Jewish men have been seeking to exorcise through overachievement, assimilation, economic macho, intermarriage and every other means available. Notwithstanding the mighty reputation of the Zionist pioneer and Israeli soldier, Jewish masculinity itself remains a contested if not oxymoronic concept in our day, thanks to anti-Semitic stereotyping and the cultural impact of anti-Semitic oppression. The alienation from Jewish identity (and from Jewish women) that is common among many American Jewish men is bound up with this sense of emasculation. For Jewish men, therefore, the reconstruction of masculine identity involves a journey through painful psychic territory.

On the other hand, we are Jews—people who are "covenant conscious," who have chosen to live with a moral vision, to restrain destructive impulses, to contextualize our individuality within the community, to cultivate *mentshlikhkeit*. For many

Jewish men, this third unique influence in their masculine identity very much helps to open doors to self-exploration and consciousness.

In fact, Jewish-linked experiences are often great storehouses of manhood-linked memories. Whether it is the memory of a bar mitzvah, or of a father's relationship to a synagogue community, or of an inherited ritual object, there usually are, within the Jewish realm, crucial connections to a male parent or relative that emerge in few other realms. Such memories, whether painful or pleasurable, play a vital role in the healing aspects of brotherkeeping.

In short, for Jewish men, issues of masculinity and Jewish identity are interwoven in both troubling and empowering ways. At minimum, the use of Jewish scriptural texts as a resource enables Jewish men to investigate this linkage. Beyond this, however, the *Tanach* (the written Torah) and the Talmud, as well as the mystical texts of the kabbalistic tradition, are simply full of resources to inform and inspire the activities of "brotherkeeping" in our time. There are archetypal myths about heroic quests, about birth and death, about relations between father and son, mother and son, husband and wife, teacher and student, siblings, rivals, and friends. There are complex discussions about work, war, sexuality, youth and aging, temptations and spiritual fulfillment. There are stories that teach by inspiring us, and others that teach us by repelling us. There are stories that embrace most, if not all, human relationships, the full spectrum of emotions and all stages and transitions of life.

Already within the Jewish renewal community, the value of using Jewish text, especially in combination with Jewish ritual (mikveh, prayer, etc.) as "technology" for masculine healing and renewal, has been revealed through an embryonic, emerging Jewish men's movement.

This movement began at P'nai Or *shabbatons* and *kallot*, which provided an opportunity to create sacred space in which to gather, open hearts, tell stories, share anguish and conflict. Sometimes the work was focused on a theme, such as the father–son relationship at the First Annual Jewish Men's retreat, which was entitled "Our Fathers, Ourselves." Other times the work simply emerged spontaneously.

More recently, Joe August began to utilize biblical text in "droshodrama" form, using Torah stories as a basis for psychodramatic improvisation. (This technique has been used widely in Jewish renewal circles and also by master psychodramatist Peter Pitzele in a form he calls "bibliodrama.") One inspiration for Joe's work was Rabbi Rami Shapiro's book, *Embracing Esau: Reclamation of the Deep Masculine in Judaism*, which, in presenting a reinterpretation of Jacob's story as a heroic journey, suggested the potential of scriptural text as a resource for renewal. Another valuable source was Harry Brod's groundbreaking collection of essays about Jews and masculinity, *A Mentsh Among Men*.

At the 1993 *Kallah* in Berkeley, Joe led men in wrestling with the Jacob and Esau story and giving each other blessings that they would have wanted their fathers to give to them. A gathering of men went deeper into the same story at the Second Annual Jewish Men's Retreat in 1993, entitled "Jacob and Esau: The Mild One Meets the Wild One." The actual Torah portion for the date of that *shabbaton* retreat was *Vayetze*, which tells the story of the birth and early rivalry of Jacob and Esau. The retreat's design organically wove the textual material into the davening. For example, one Torah reading included a birthing experience in which each attendee wrestled with his "twin" and was reborn as either a "Jacob" or an "Esau," a character role they maintained for the remainder of the retreat. The dramatic high point of that retreat was the enactment of the reconciliation of the brothers (and the parts of oneself), which took place outdoors at sunrise as they met atop a great, expansive hillside. Overall, the retreat especially demonstrated the extraordinary potential of using the double-barreled Jewish technology of text and ritual.

In the summer of 1994 Joe August and Arthur Waskow led a course at Elat Chayyim, the Woodstock Center for Healing and Renewal, entitled "Becoming Brothers, Becoming Brotherkeepers." This week-long workshop focused on the stories of Cain and Abel (conflict and murder), Jacob and Esau (conflict and reconciliation or "live and let live"), Jonathan and David (the spectrum of love and friendship possibilities between men), and Moses and Aaron (men collaborating and inspiring each other for a higher purpose).

The Third Annual Retreat in the fall of 1994, entitled "Isaac

Unbound," focused on making sense of the legacy and the tradition we have received from our fathers and on redefining this legacy for ourselves and our children.

As this process of "brotherkeeping" emerges, its integrity and its broad scope as a transformational activity becomes all the more clear. There is great need for *tikkun*-making between Jewish men (gay and straight, fathers and sons, friends and competitors); between Jewish men and Moslem, Christian, and African-American men; between Jewish men and women (wives, lovers, mothers, daughters, sisters, friends). Conflicts throughout our world have components that can be distinctively addressed through "men's work." Brotherkeeping is therefore not a reactive process of turning inwards; it is a new tool of progressive community building.

Rabbi Zalman Schachter-Shalomi's approach to Torah, to leadership, and to the building of Jewish community has inspired many creative uses of Judaism as a resource for healing and consciousness-raising. One biblical figure who has won his enduring affection and admiration is Aaron, brother of Moses:

> I like the sense that the priesthood is . . . [about] caring for the people. Aaron is a loving person; he reconciles people to each other. If you come to Moses and say you've sinned, Moses says, 'Oh, there's a terrible, terrible punishment . . . ' If you go to Aaron, he says, 'All right, we'll make a little sacrifice and reconcile you to God—I'm sure you're sorry for what you've done . . .'

Yet the figure from Scripture that has been "most consistent for the last forty years of my life," says Reb Zalman, "is Rabbi Yochanan ben Zakkai, who took Jews through the paradigm shift of the destruction of the second Temple." By being smuggled out of the besieged city of Jerusalem in a coffin and winning from the Roman oppressor the privilege of establishing a Jewish academy in the village of Jabneh, Yochanan ben Zakkai, the youngest of Hillel's eighty disciples, saved the Jewish religion from the fate of the Jewish nation. Reb Zalman comments:

> At the end of his life he was asking if he had done right; if he was bound for *gehenna* or *gan eden* (hell or heaven). Here he has had to reform Judaism from a temple-based religion to something home-

based; I'm sure there were some people saying, 'You should have asked for the Temple, for Jerusalem itself, you shouldn't have gone for an academy, you should not deal with the Roman enemy, General Vespasian, you should have done this, you should have done that . . .'

There are moments today when I'm told, 'Zalman, you did it wrong. You've gone too far. You're going to go to *gehenna*.' Well, I'm not sure I'm not going to go to *gehenna*, hm? Cutting this corner, cutting that corner, saying this bit of Judaism is important, this bit is not important—how do you know?

I judge from my intuition. But how do you know your intuition is not the *yetzer hara* (evil impulse)? This is the dilemma faced by Yochanan ben Zakkai when he was called upon to perform this feat of Jewish renewal.

Yet the compliers of the Talmud decided very much to affirm Rabbi Yochanan ben Zakkai's difficult choice by reporting a blessing bestowed upon him by Hillel, years before the tragic destruction of Jerusalem, in which the great leader of the Sanhedrin hails his youngest disciple, in the presence of all the others, as the "father of wisdom, father of generations."

As we have already begun to learn in our brotherkeeping work, a little affirmation never hurt anyone.

PART IV

All of Them Righteous: Dialogue Between the Traditions

Mordechai Beck

Tales of Reb Zalman

Reb Zalman snorts violently through his nose a number of times in rapid succession. The sounds, picked up and expanded by the microphone, fill the lecture room.

"Can you imagine?" he asks his bewildered audience, "if someone were to do this simple meditational exercise in a synagogue?"

The young people in the room laugh. The older people, and they constitute the majority, remain cooly quiet.

Reb Zalman was invited to deliver this talk at the Conservative Synagogue Center in downtown Jerusalem. It's not certain whether he was invited primarily in his role as a professor at a respectable American university or as a rabbi. He seems to enjoy the leverage this multiple identity offers him. His audience wants a lecture, advice. He prefers a confrontation.

"Once," he tells them, "I was asked to talk to some Jewish parents worried by their children's involvement in Christianity and Buddhism. They agreed to a question-and-answer format. But I insisted that only those who went beforehand to hear a Mass or to meditate in an Ashram could ask me questions. A few of them did so, and we limited the questions to them."

The audience moves restlessly in their chairs. The hot Jerusalem night has suddenly gotten hotter. Reb Zalman, grinning reassuringly, adds, "I asked the same of a group of nuns who came to inquire about yiddishkeit."

Smiles of relief all around.

All this seems far away from the experience of middle-aged, middle-class Israeli-Americans. Had they really, as one well-heeled member of the previous night's audience said, "understood more or less what the Rabbi was saying?" Wasn't the whole meeting incongruous, inappropriate? Reb Zalman confesses: "When I was walking away from that lecture I didn't feel quite clean. I felt that I had manipulated the audience, in a kind of spiritual vaudeville. That's what I undertook when I accepted their invitation. But I didn't want to let the event pass without introducing some level of real dialogue. If they felt they understood, I'm glad."

Some would argue that speaking so frankly about certain areas of experience could cause damage, madness even. Is it right that a healthy Jewish adult, let alone a youngster, should be exposed to such frankness?

Reb Zalman sighs. "People go and see crazy movies. They see 'Earthquake,' which is like Dante's first circle of hell, or 'Emanuelle,' which is a skin flick that takes you through the whole encyclopedia of sex—and that's O.K. That can be seen before the age of forty."

He sounds ironic, but he is probably just exasperated at people's lack of awareness of the barriers that they erect around themselves. So, when he speaks of mysticism, the unknown, or the unknowable to a group of middle-aged Americans his rationale is typical: "'Shlach lachmecha al penei hamayim,' Cast your bread upon the waters. I don't care what they do with the material. That's their own affair. Let's say that after they die, and go through the 'laundry,' they will be given a shabbos in Gan Eden (Paradise) and someone is going to say a word of Torah that will turn them on. One of them will say, 'Ah, yes, there was one evening in Jerusalem when I heard crazy talk like that.'" Reb Zalman smiles, as one who observes where the "bread" of his mouth had landed.

This is a far cry from the Polish-born Reb Zalman Schachter who, in 1947, reached the U.S.A. where he was ordained as rabbi by the Lubavitch Hassidic Movement. In the 1950s Reb Zalman wrote in "Commentary" that, at that point in time, the Divine Presence was most fully expressed in the personality of the Lubavitcher Rebbe. What happened to make Reb Zalman shift his allegiance, from being an ardent supporter to becoming an outsider, almost an outcast?

Reb Zalman's face pulls with strain and his large, luminous eyes close. He takes a deep breath as though to gather strength against an inevitable sadness: "There was first a matter of personal let-down," he explains. "If, as the Hassidim claim, the Rebbe cares for his followers, why did he not respond when my needs were acute and I was screaming for help? Even if he would have said 'Zalman, you have to work out this one yourself,' it would have been something. I needed a sign, but nothing came."

The rift between Reb Zalman and Lubavitch was deep and bitter. Some of his ex-comrades in the movement saw in his experimentation with meditation and alien religions the taint of heresy, even Sabbatianism. The criticism was not all one-way, however: "The message and educational aim of the Rebbe's broadcasted talks is not relevant to current life situations," observes Reb Zalman. "The approach is cold and abstract, mined with great skill and persistence, without which the speeches would have no real nourishment. It is an abandonment of the old way of *habad fabrengen*, which dealt with the inner life of the person, and with the aspects of the human-divine interaction. The burning questions—concerning peace, ecology, the use of materialism, the way in which a person may ascertain the divine will for this time, the rights and spiritual paths for Jewish women— these are mostly not dealt with, and if they are then only in ways that do not work for most Jews."

Lubavitch was not the only factor in this situation: "If the Orthodox establishment did their work, Lubavitch would be able to leave the mitza tanks and do its real and essential work— spreading the way of *hochma, binah* and *da'at* (different levels of understanding). This was the most important teaching I received at Lubavitch . . ."

"I think Lubavitch have a good school and I think I benefitted from the teaching. But when the Hassidim say, 'You dropped out,' I reply 'A good school graduates its students. If it didn't it would be a lousy institution.'"

Some say that Reb Zalman has gone too far, that he has blurred the distinct boundaries that separate not only himself from *habad* but also one faith from another, one "way" from the next. Again, it depends on how the reality is perceived:

"In Halil-Hebron—the city of God's friend (Halil-Haber)—I visited some Sufi friends, and asked them if I could do *zikr* with them. Zikr is the mention of the divine name and is done with the right breathing and body movement, in such a way as to let one's being be flooded with the awareness that *ein od milvado, la illaha illahu* (there is no one but God). The *eyn keloheynu* ('There is no one like our God . . .' from the morning prayer service) is a form of *zikr* . . ."

"They wanted to know if I was Moslem. I said I am a believer in the oneness of God, Blessed be He—*subhan Allah*. That I share with them of the holy levels of *tariqat, ma'arifat,* and *haqiqat* (which are the equivalent of the paths of the *yud*, the *hay*, and *vav* of the Hebrew name of God), but that I do not share with them on the level of *sha'ria* since, as a descendant of Isaac, I have a different *sha'ria* from that of a descendant of Ishmael. When they ask me about the *razuliyat* of Muhammad I said 'yes, I believe in it,' though it is not intended for Jews but for the *jahaliyan*—the unenlightened inhabitants of the Arabian cities. I told them that I didn't believe that *Muhammad* came to remove me from my path, but in saying so I was concerned to speak their language."

His approach had a predictable effect:

"Suddenly they hear their own expressions being used in this unusual way. One of them mutters, 'But the *razuliyat* is the key question!' They want to keep the surface tension high, whereas my whole purpose is to corrode the differences, or at least to reduce them."

Reb Zalman is just as quick to reduce the mileage in discussions within Judaism, especially if he knows of a shorter route else-where. "I was conducting a session with Shlomo (Carlebach)," he recalls. "He was tackling the question of personal responsibility and Divine guidance. It was a wonderful journey. Shlomo was quoting Rashi and hassidus, Talmud and Zohar. But if he had used the third chapter of Bhavaghad Gita he could have gotten there much quicker! Which is to say that a lot of things that we do in hassidus may be unnecessarily complicated and I'm not sure that I want to subject people to such an approach."

Reb Zalman's move into the academic world seems more than a little fortuitous. Students emerging into the radical 1960s were searching for exotic experience, meaning, and relevance. Part of this search meant turning away from the classical religions of the West and shifting attention to the East, with the help of meditation and drugs. In Reb Zalman they were to encounter someone who had been there and back, who was not answerable to any religious establishment, who—it was rumoured—had "turned on" with professors Alpert and Leary, and yet had remained strongly commited to being Jewish. To be Jewish was also to be 'turned on' spiritually as well as intellectually, through the emotions as well as through methodolgy.

If Zalman's spiritual wanderings confused the establishment they now provided a bridge for the counterculture. It was said that he brought back a Jew from Hinduism by showing him that *Krsn* (Krishna) appears in the scroll of Esther (1:14) as one of many secondary deities. In short, not only did he change from being Rabbi Schachter to becoming the "rebbe," Reb Zalman was also accredited with wonders; his students were no longer students, they were his Hassidim.

The "frum" world was not amused.

"I was with a group of NFTY (Reform) kids," he recalls. "We took a *sefer* Torah and passed it around. I asked whoever was holding the scroll to say a word of Torah—whatever they felt, whatever they wished to share. The 'frum' world heard this and was furious: Zalman is turning Reform kids into Hassidic rebbes!"

What particularly upsets Reb Zalman was not just the criticism—which was perhaps to be expected—but also the alternative as essayed by the same "frum" world:

"When I published *The First Step: A Devotional Guide,* I was accused by some Habadniks of wanting to give people the experience of taking delight in God, or experiencing Him with deep pleasure. "Well, it's true," I told them. "And if you can't do that, what's the point of this business? Their method, in contrast, is to make a promise: 'We have the way.' But when you ask: 'Did we reach the goal yet?' they say: 'It's not so easy. First you have to do this, then this, then that . . .' When I present a more direct method they resent it: 'You don't have such an exalted soul,' they say. If that's so, don't give me *Sefer shel beinoni,* (the book of an intermediate person—the standard text of Habad Hassidism); give me *Sefer shel Reshoim* (The Book of the Wicked)."

But just when you think that Reb Zalman has cut himself off from the mainstream, he flows back. His link with the "frum" world is still elemental, though as much psychological as theological.

"They're my anchor," he confesses. "Even though they give me a great deal of *tsores* and aggravation, I can't do without them."

Where, then, is the point of friction? Reb Zalman maintains that it is due to a misunderstanding of his special clientele: "If the 'frum' world knew to what ultimate end I work they would recognize it as their own." Ultimately, it's a question of strategy, since he wants to *mekarev*, to draw near the alienated.

One morning, Reb Zalman is on a bus in Jerusalem. He notices that there are special buses going to the grave of the Belzer Rebbe. He is very excited by this—where else can buses be commandeered for such a purpose? He asks a couple of the passengers if there is a provision at the grave for a cohen (since the priestly line, from which Reb Zalman is descended, is not allowed on the burial grounds). The black-hatted "frum" passengers are confused. Here is someone asking them a legitimate question, dressed in thigh-tight shorts and a thin shirt whose ritual fringes are discreetly hidden. Is this a puzzle! They look at him long and hard, but he escapes their neat categories.

Reb Zalman is not surprised, and perhaps the effect he had produced was deliberate. Nevertheless he wants the black hats to remain exactly as they are. "As long as we're speaking to each other, it's alright. What I can't deal with is the violent stuff . . . but of course they have to stem the tide on their side, although in the anxiety to maintain control over their young people, they lose their judgment and centeredness."

Reb Zalman uses the language of the Orthodox in order to confront them, sometimes playing devil's advocate, but more often than not believing himself to be on the side of the angels:

"Reb Zvi Elimelech of Dinov explains that there are new combinations of the Divine Name each month. If you know the combinations then your prayers will be answered. Thus, the High Priest, too, would go into the Holy of Holies each year to enquire after the combination of that year. I believe that Habad knew the combination for 1830—let's say—and that, ever since, they've been trying to make the world safe for that combination. They forget that new combinations are being made constantly."

"This is true not just of Habad but of Hassidim generally, whether they are in Williamsburg or Mea She'arim. They are pouring all their energies into reliving an anachronism, so much so that there is no energy left over to live in the present. This attempt at living out an anachronism prevents them, not only from interchanging with the world around them, but even from praying properly, or studying, let alone from perceiving the presence of their children or their wives."

"I'm not anti-tradition. On the contrary, I'll use anything that will help me get off. I've got a great deal invested in the materials of civilization, like language and vocabulary—*booba, zeida, cholent, tallis*—they're deeply embedded in the core of my brain, attached to my thalamus, not to the cortex. It would be foolish to deny that they're not part of my make-up. But, if someone says that I must believe in the God who was active at the time of Moses, or Yohannan ben Zakai or the Ba'al Shem Tov, my answer is no."

"The Besht says: 'What Luria knew was the Truth, but now it's me.' The Ba'al Tanya could say the same thing; so, too, could the Tsemach Tzedek. What is tradition but the wisdom that souls send down the path of history so that they might find the stores of wisdom when they are reincarnated? I am just making sure that the tradition I find when I return will be useful to further the realization of God."

Reb Zalman is engaged in a delicate balancing act that few of the rabbinate condone, let alone imitate. His insistence on the new, on fusing disparate elements of different cultures, of breaking from mechanical routines—demands continuous spiritual risks for which very few others appear capable or willing to undertake. But it is equally true that even some of his supporters in the Jewish counterculture have felt that he has gone too far, and that some of the risks he has taken have been unwarranted. How pliable is *halacha*, for example? How realistic is it to take from other peoples' sources without denuding the power that is in one's own? Will more than a tiny minority ever be able to benefit from his teachings and experiments?

Reb Zalman sees in this criticism a new conservatism, for which he had a ready answer:

"On a tree a new ring is formed each year, not in the center but on the edge—between the organism and the environment. That is where the danger lies, because it is there that the new stuff is happening. Those who are afraid of the new are usually the cancer types. They do not see that in order to grow, the metabolism must grow. In order to create there must be a process of destruction. In Hinduism these two principles are represented by Vishnu and Shiva. They are interdependent forces that are kept that way by Brahma, which is the pattern around which Shiva does not destroy what Vishnu rebuilds. These elements exist in a person, and remain constant. Similarly, in the laws of shabbat, to take away two bricks is the same 'work' as to add two bricks."

Reb Zalman's eyes narrow, concerned that I've understood. If not, he's prepared to go back and clarify. Often during our conversation, he has stopped and asked, "Can you hear what I'm saying?" This time I nod, and as I do so, he suggests a brief summation:

"I say, let that new stuff emerge—whatever is good, let it grow. Growing is what makes us live and die. It is what God does with us and to us." I am nodding more now and perhaps this gives him a sign to throw something else mysterious at me, as though to demonstrate that I haven't really started:

"We are just leaves on the tree, and it is the same tree."

Ma Jaya Sati Bhagavati

The Light of Every Candle

"Oh right," I thought, "another teacher in my life. My dead guru and my dead swami aren't enough. Now I finally got a live one, and a Jew at that. Why not go along with the good rabbi and his beautiful fiancée, and learn something on a Friday night? If nothing comes from it, at least I would have had a good Jewish meal and a night off from working with the dead and the dying."

Darshan had been called off and I was in my living room, which serves as a temple, altar room, living room, office and, this night, that Shabbos night in the winter of 1993, a dining room. It did cross my mind that the rabbi's schedule was as crowded as mine, and that he was giving up his precious teaching and writing time to be with me.

"Boy," I thought, "how I love this man, but I hope he doesn't start with the heritage crap." I'm a world-famous spiritual teacher and sure as hell know who I am.

The table was set beautifully by my students. Everything that could be put on one's plate representing a normal Shabbos night—in spite of us all being vegetarians—was in view. The matzo ball and mock chicken soup looked delicious waiting to be served.

"All right," I thought, "a night with the rabbi isn't so bad. We could always gossip about the latest in spirituality and about Ram Dass."

The good rabbi was doing Shabbos in my home on my ashram in Florida. He was doing it just for me. "Thank you very much," I wanted to say, "but I really don't care to do Shabbos—too much pain, too much sorrow, too many memories."

I had never sat at a proper Shabbos. I used to watch my grandmother light the candles in her private space in the cellar we called our home. But that space consisted of an orange crate, an old chair, and the two silver candelabras which belonged to only her and her memories of Minsk, Russia, and which Papa had his eyes on for years—to sell. I was the only one allowed to witness the strange rite. I yearned to touch the flame and feel my Jewishness, but I looked too much like my papa to have my Grandma let me that close to her or her candles. Still, I was the one she loved the best.

The four of us sat around the table, the rabbi staring into my eyes. I felt lost for a moment. "Hey," I thought, "I'm Ma. I touch; I'm not touched. Let's keep this on an impersonal level."

I kept still in the stillness.

"Ma, here is a present I had made for you in Israel."

I thought, "What can it be? I don't want anything that would commit me to this night. I'm only doing this for the rabbi"—as if the rabbi needed me to make Shabbos.

He handed me a beautiful shawl made special for me with my own colors on the borders.

"Don't cry, Ma," I said to myself. "This is all the Jewish drama that I expected. He is a good man and loves you. Just take the shawl the way you take any gift—with grace and dignity."

I touched the shawl, the gift having come from the rabbi's heart, and I started at once to shed a tear. "Stop," I said to myself.

The rabbi continued talking, ignoring my tears. He told the story of the Shabbos Queen. He placed the shawl around my shoulders and head and showed me how to light the candles, a gift to me from him. He placed the *Siddur* in my hands, and in that moment he gave me everything that I was and will be. Most of all he gave me the moment, the moment of every Jewish woman the world wide.

I was, this night, the Shabbos Queen.

I felt my whole ashram stirring with emotion; the temple doors felt swung open wide with completion. I felt the magnificent Jewish shrine, designed by Reb Zalman with the Ten Commandments etched in beautiful redwood, stir with a newness. I felt the pond, which we here at Kashi Ashram call the Ganga, which houses the ash of the many dead due to AIDS, flow into all hearts. I was lifted from the grief I carried like a large bag of sand in my heart and made whole in that moment of being the Shabbos Queen.

I guess something was missing in my life, and that something was my heritage. I was a Jew, I am a Jew, and I will always be a Jew—a Jew who bows to the feet of my Christ; a Jew with a big red ribbon tattooed for life on my left hand, the ribbon representing all the dead I have lost to AIDs; a Jew who is a Hindu and follows the monkey god of service, Hanuman; a Jew who loves the true tantra of man into God; a Jew who is a devotee of Mother Kali; a Jew who is the disciple of Neem Karoli Baba; a Jew who worships the Buddha and tries to follow his life of compassion, love, and kindness; a Jew who listens to the ancient teachings at the feet of one of the Sikh gurus, Guru Hargobind.

I could hear Parvati Sati singing in her profoundly sweet voice from the book that they'd placed in my hands, and my mind went spinning back in time and place.

I could see the child with long black hair down to her *tuchis* running on the beach and carrying a glass candle holder in each hand. The little girl was running as fast as she could. I looked closely at the small child, and I reached back into time as the sweet melody went on and around me.

"Are you OK, Ma?" I could hear Shodie ask from a distance.

"Leave her be." It was the Rabbi's voice. "My friend, let her be."

I was that little girl. I had walked the Boardwalk late at night, having sneaked out of the cellar window. I was seven and had been pretty much on my own since I could remember. It was about two in the morning, and I wanted to see my friends, the people closest to me in the whole world. They were the homeless who lived under the Boardwalk, and they shared their lives and their few possessions with me, making me feel wanted and loved. Most of all they shared their philosophy of life and gave me enough information in my young life to instill the feeling of safety and love.

I screamed at the top of my lungs so Henry could hear me and meet me down by the water's edge. I had been walking the boards for a long time after climbing out the cellar window. I went looking for my friends, but they were not there, and the place we called home under the boards was as empty as it ever was.

I continued walking the boards until I was almost under the big Parachute. I had come there often and felt quite safe in the crowd of mostly soldiers and sailors. It was 1947, and the armed forces were still mustering out. There was a big Air Force base in nearby Manhattan Beach, and we street kids grew up watching all the uniformed people take to Coney Island like fish to water.

Right in front of the Parachute was a bench where people sat and watched or waited to buy tickets. The line was always long.

"Hey, Joycey, whatcha doing out so late in the night?" asked Butchy, who had the night job running the Parachute. He was a handsome teenager who was also a cellar kid. All of us who lived in the cellars of the rich folks in Brighton Beach and Coney Island were called cellar kids. We made quite a rat pack.

"I felt like walking," I said, eyeing the two candles sitting by themselves on the bench. "What are those candles?" I asked, knowing they were the candles Jewish people lit for the dead. Grandma would light them every year for her husband and her papa, neither of whom I'd met.

"They're Jewish things," he said, forgetting I was a Jew. "Don't touch them. Those people killed Christ."

"Oh, Butchy, everyone says that, and I don't even know where Mr. Christ lived."

"Come on Joyce, don't be such a baby. No one means you. They mean your father and mother's great-great-grandparents." It had just hit him that I was a Jewish kid. Butchy was taking the tickets as he was talking to me. He turned for a second and asked, "Do you want them, Joyce?"

"Yeah," I answered indifferently.

"Well, go on and take them and get out of here. You're too young to go on the Parachute unescorted." He said this laughing; we had both grown up begging rides on the big chute and getting them when it wasn't too crowded.

I grabbed the glass candles with the Hebrew writing on them and felt sorry for the person who had forgotten them when he went on the Parachute. I ran the boards all the way to Brighton Beach, stopping for a moment to take a cool drink from the water fountain and to stare out at my ocean. The night was hot and sticky, the moon full and orange, and the sky clear and filled with falling stars. I stared at the ocean and was glad to be alive. I walked over to a couple holding hands on the bench and, like me, gazing out toward the ocean.

"Is this still Thursday, or is it Friday yet?" I asked. They looked startled.

"Well," said the young man, "it's after twelve, so I guess it's Friday."

"Thank you," I said to the young man, who had noticed that I was alone and much too young to be alone.

I began to run again with the slightest hint of a breeze in my hair. Reaching the corner of Brighton Beach Avenue and Coney Island Avenue, I flew down the steps to the beach and started screaming for my friends. I ran on the beach toward the ocean where, in the fullness of the moon, I could make out two figures sitting there in the heat with their heavy overcoats on. It must have been in the nineties, and I knew it could only be Big Henry and Old Hudson, wearing their entire wardrobes. They were sitting in the night sharing a bottle of Old Honor's homemade booze.

"Please, Mac," I said, "please, don't let them be too drunk." Mac was what I had called God ever since I could remember.

"Hey, Lady J," Big Henry called out, "whatcha screaming about?"

"Henry, Henry," I said throwing myself into his big arms, loving the scent of him and the scent of the beach, sea, and the night air. "Henry, we can *bentsch licht.*"

"Whatchat talking about little girl? What kinda language is that you're speaking?"

"It's English, Henry. My grandma *bentshes licht* every Friday, and the guy on the bench said that this is Friday and I want to be the Shabbos Queen. OK?"

Hudson shook himself out of his stupor and looked at me. "Little Joycey girl, come here." I went over to him and sat on his lap, avoiding the crutches lying beside him in the sand. Hudson had been in an accident, a hit and run, and he'd never received proper care.

"If you want to be that kinda queen, it's fine. I used to make a penny or two opening the lights on Friday nights for some mighty good Jewish folks, and I would see them getting ready for a feast.

They were kind to me and used to give me a lot of leftovers for my family after they were finished."

It was the first time Hudson had ever talked about his family, and I kept silent. He said, with his voice under control, "I would see those candles shining in the dark after I shut the lights for the night and wonder at it all. The old man once told me that it was the night of the Shabbos Queen, so little lady, if you wants to be that queen, you go right ahead."

I placed the candles on the sand, stood up, and gave my hands to my two friends. "Come on, let's go under the Boardwalk and light the candles." I pulled and pulled. They laughed and got up by themselves.

"Them there candles make good drinking glasses once they're burnt out and properly cleaned," said Big Henry.

"Yeah, but the wax has to be cleaned out real good," added Hudson.

I laughed. Both my friends and the rest of the under-the-Boardwalk crew could take a sentence and go on and on about nothing, and I loved it all.

We finally reached our home under the Boardwalk. Henry took off some layers of clothes and placed them in his house, a big fridge box. Hudson did the same. From his cardboard box Hudson brought out a piece of wood about a foot and a half square all around. He placed it in front of us like a small table. I put my candles on the board and asked for a match.

Just then Chews came along. My friend Chews and another woman, Chicky, made up the female part of my little under-the-Boardwalk family. Chews had a greasy paper bag in her hand.

"Whatcha doing?" she said as she stumbled over to us.

"Joycey is the Shabbos Queen," answered Hudson. "How's tricks?"

"Not too bad," answered Chews. "I got some leftover pretzels from Hazel." For a long time I had thought that Chews was a magician of some sort, because every time she came home someone would ask her, "How's tricks?" Only Big Henry wouldn't. In fact, he used to get real mad when anyone asked her that.

"What kinda queen, sweet thing?" she said as she gave me a big kiss on the cheek and handed me a pretzel.

"I'm going to *bentsh licht.*"

"OK, darling, whatever makes ya happy."

"Chews, do you have a match?"

She went into the little bag on a string around her neck and pulled out a butt and some matches. An old, small cross fell from the bag and just lay there next to the candles for the dead. Chews went to pick it up, but stopped and left it. "This was my baby boy's." That's all she said.

We all looked at her; we were so quiet. None of us ever heard Chews talk of family.

"Never you mind," she said smiling again. Her false teeth coming in and out of her full mouth as she talked reminded me of how she got her name.

"Chews," I said, "where's your baby boy now?"

"Why, darling, he's with Lord Jesus."

"Chews, I swear I didn't kill Jesus. I don't even know where he lives."

"I knows that darling, I knows that. Now light this butt for me while I take off some of these smelly clothes, and don't you dare inhale; you're much too young."

I lit the Camel but, inhaling deeply, and waited for Chews to come back. The men were getting sleepy now. Chews came to the little circle, her arms bare and showing track marks in the moonlight. I kept quiet as I gave her the lit butt, her black face looking beautiful in the night. I lit the *Yortzeit* candles, the candles for the dead, and thought it would be nice to light them for Chews' little boy. "What's his name?" I whispered into the night.

"Joseph," whispered Big Henry hoarsely.

I began the prayer with the only words I could remember from Grandma. *"Boruch Attaw Adonoy, Elohainu Melech Ho'olam.* And please, Mac, take care of little Joseph. And please, Mac, tell Jesus that my grandfather didn't kill him; and please, Mac, don't let me get caught being out; and if I do, let them care. Amen." Everyone joined in and said, "Amen."

Sitting there under the Boardwalk, cuddled up to my friends, looking out and up at the full moon and the falling stars, I was the Shabbos Queen. It was my first real Friday night.

I was swaying to the melody and the words around me. I could hear Reb Zalman singing in his booming, compassionate voice. I opened my eyes; Parvati Sati was holding me. Me—Ma, who holds the dying, the babies, the young men and women who very few would hold, let alone visit. Me, whose people are the junkies, the prostitutes, the crack addicts. Me, who always holds—I was now being held. I felt like that little girl again, only safe and free now on a Shabbos night.

I could see my ancestors from Russia before me, proud of the moment of the beginning of my renewal of Judaism. In my mind's eye I could see the little gold cross on the makeshift table. "For little Joseph," I whispered, "and all the lonely, sick, and homeless people." I was made the Shabbos Queen again that Friday night, and I was given back my heritage.

Every Friday night, wherever I am in this world, I light my little portable candles that the good, gentle, learned rabbi gave me, and I remember the little gold cross and little Joseph.

My God, what a gift my friend, Reb Zalman, gave me. He gave me Shabbos, and out of the candle-lit shadows of the past he gave me back Big Henry, Chews, and Old Hudson each and every Friday night of my life.

May the light of every candle ever lit light up your wisdom and your life, my dear friend, Reb Zalman Schachter. I love you.

Shalom.

Marcia Prager

Among Friends

Marcia Prager tells us about her work with Quakers, who are also called the Society of Friends, or Friends for short. The dialogue between the traditions is both about common values and roots, but also about sharing in areas where each tradition has placed more emphasis on development. Rabbi Prager also reaches Jews who have found a home in Quakerism with aspects of Judaism that they hadn't known existed.

The room is filled with light and silence. A complete quiet, yet the stillness is not one of absence, but of deep presence. Eyes are closed, hands gently held in a chain that encircles and unites all in the room.

This may seem like the opening meditation of a Jewish Renewal davvenen but it isn't. It is a Quaker gathering, and I am, for some, a now familiar guest. For others, this is their first gathering, known in Quaker circles as a "Meeting," led not by a Friend, but by a rabbi!

We have been in silence for some time now. I begin a soft niggun, while gently squeezing the hands I hold. The squeeze pulses in a chain about the room, each person calling the next back from their private meditation. The niggun continues. It moves through the room, building in intentionality and in intensity.

For Meeting, this is not the norm. Prepared for the challenge of introducing customs so different from Quaker practice, I'd spoken briefly, ahead of time, about my joy in being able to share wisdom from the Jewish spiritual path with a community which has come to feel like a second home to me, a community of fellow spiritual seekers whose paths I've grown to love and respect and whose welcome for me continues to be an unfolding gift.

I'd told them that I'd go with them into silence (wow, is sustained silence hard for Jews! But that's another story), and that we'd come out of the silence, not to talking, but into melody. A "niggun," a wordless melody, I said, which in my people's tradition serves a comparable role to that of silence for Quakers: a wordless vehicle crafted to carry us to deep centers of awareness, opening new possibilities for self-reflection and spiritual deepening. Within a niggun, we can open our hearts to feel life most deeply. We travel again to the places in our souls that hurt, and the places that sing with joy. Sometimes, if we are willing, those can merge and a great unifying light envelopes us. We feel an exaltation, and a nurturant love. We are lifted up, and along with us the melody floats higher and higher.

For a community that has foresworn ritual, liturgy, and (to a large measure) even song, this experience is new. And yet, being no strangers to the journey within, in only a few moments every voice has joined. The niggun flows like a river. I model "handdancing": beating the rhythm on knees, clapping, raising arms like branches towards heaven, bringing hands inward towards the heart. With eyes closed, a niggun can be traveled far and deep. I invite all who wish to do so to close their eyes, seated or standing, and intensify the niggun. With eyes closed we are alone while not alone, in private space yet aware of and supported by the presence of those around us. Later, after sharing more Jewish story and teaching, I will ask if anyone wishes to share their experience. I know the response will be wonderful! This is a community of seekers who welcome challenge and appreciate genuine spiritual work. While the Jewish idiom may be new, the style uncustomary, they are not new to the quest for God within and beyond, nor to the voice that calls to us as agents of God in the world.

Within the Community of Friends I have been invited to come share and teach. This has been a true journey of discovery for me. At the 1992 Friends General Conference, whose theme was "Live Love," I taught an eighteen-hour six-session workshop entitled "Ahavah Rabbah: With a Great Love You Have Loved Us." Jewish tradition, I said, is often characterized as a religion of law, not love. Is this so? I invited the community to come explore Jewish teaching about the abundant flow of Divine Love that calls us. In our sessions we blended storytelling, movement, meditation, and song to enter the Jewish experience of *Ahavah* (Divine Love), *Chesed* (Divine Grace) and *Rachamim* (Divine Compassion). We looked at Jewish liturgy, delved into Torah, sampled Jewish tradition's mystical teachings, and probed mitzvot as spiritual practices which address the complexity of human capabilities and needs. Each session began and ended in Quaker custom, with silent prayer. If any of you who are reading this are my Quaker colleagues, I want to say to you that your openness to me, and to this Jewish teaching that comes through me to you at this time, is an extraordinary gift. When you say to me: "This was the workshop my heart has been seeking for years," and other deeply moving words of praise, I feel gratitude that through your receptivity and desire to share I can be the vehicle for such an offering.

At Pendle Hill Quaker Center For Study and Contemplation I was privileged to join Rebecca Mays as a guest teacher in her course "Approaching the Gospels Together." In this participatory roundtable I shared a Jewish reading of Jesus' teachings, placing them in a Jewish spiritual and liturgical context. Together we worked on the Lord's Prayer, using Hebrew and Aramaic as doorways beyond the English translations into the depths of Jewish wisdom. How wonderful to find in the Lord's Prayer, so unknown to Jews and so poorly translated for Christians, a gem-like *t'fillah b'kitzur*, a moving and poetic condensation of major themes of traditional Jewish prayer!

I've spoken of my gratitude for the opportunity to learn and teach with Quakers, both those reared in Quaker tradition and those who've been drawn to Quakerism from other Christian and also secular backgrounds.

I now wish to speak of and to the Jews whom I meet in Quaker circles. I have been told that the Society of Friends estimates that twenty percent of Quakers are Jews. When I teach in Quaker meetings and other gatherings, I rarely need to ask who the Jews are. I usually see that you are crying as I speak. Afterwards you wait until the other well-wishers have spoken to me and are gone, and you come up to me on the path or in the hall to tell me about how much you appreciate my being there, and how much the Jewish You still hurts. I often hear you say that you have never, until now, heard a Jewish teacher speak of love or the heart, of the

feminine as part of God, or mitzvot having spiritual substance, of
Judaism as a deep spiritual path. You tell stories of bad teaching
and insensitive counseling that break my heart. I hear you tell me
that the Quaker community has been a place of solace and refuge,
of peace and growth, and that still even after so many years, my
offering reminds you how deep is the pain that remains. You ask
me if I have a congregation? Are there other rabbis who teach as
I do? Can you remain a Quaker and still find a way to be a Jew?
Is there a way to be a Jew for someone like you?

Then I speak of the Jewish Renewal movement and the new
forms of Jewish spirituality that are emerging (and re-emerging
from quiescence), of the new role of women in spiritual leadership, of new songs and prayers, and of the renewed deepening of
our connection to Torah, Kabbalah, and our people's ancient
wisdom. I speak of a new community of inclusivity, of the great
homecoming that is happening, which doesn't ask us to discard,
but rather to integrate all that we've learned on the other spiritual
paths we've traveled when we were not spiritually nourished at
home. Finally, I speak of the healing of the Jewish soul that our
generation is called upon to do. We are a people that has
internalized the pain of waves of trauma throughout our history.
To be spiritually open means opening wounds, and this is hard to
do. To be healers we must nurture compassion. This is our great
task. I invite you to think of yourself as already having begun to
walk that path.

There are actually two roles I seem to play within Quaker
circles, besides being an affirming presence for Jewish Quakers.
One is as a bridge for Christian Quakers to the spiritual roots of
their own Christian heritage. As one woman, raised Catholic and
now Quaker said to me, "All through my life I've been told about
my 'Judeo-Christian' heritage, but no one until now taught me
anything at all about the Judeo part." "I never understood that
Judaism was alive spiritually," another woman told me. "It always
was presented as dry adherence to long outmoded laws. You've
shown us a vital, alive spirituality that nourishes my own faith."

I am deeply moved by the openness to Jewish teaching that
every Quaker gathering I've visited has shown me. As a community, the Quakers have allowed me to speak from an explicitly
Jewish vantage point about the most profound challenges of the

spiritual quest. As Georgia Peters of Pendle Hill wrote in an open letter after my session there called "Images and Names for God," "I am in a time of exploration concerning the issue of Christology. What Rabbi Prager did was to take me underneath all those questions to the basic faith experience. I was not bound up in an either/or frame of mind about Judaism and Christianity, but saw their commonalities, and new modes for the growth of my own faith."

There is a further area in which I hope my presence will offer some contribution. Within the Quaker community an internal discussion is gently percolating. Here and there Friends are beginning to look again at the role of ritual, liturgy and song. Questions are being raised about whether these can perhaps sometimes aid, not only hamper, spiritual growth, and if so, how? As George Fox's critique of ritualized religion is foundational to the Quaker way, it is exciting and an honor to be invited to share in the "in-house" process of self-reflection which prompts concerned Quakers to explore and question "ritualized ritual-lessness." As ritual creativity from women's spiritual circles (and earth/goddess-centered spiritualities) begins to filter into some overlap with Quaker groups, new questions about the role of myth and ritual are being asked. As a teacher of the Jewish way, I share in the process of bringing a taste of the use of ritual, ceremony, liturgical chant and song, and mitzvot to Friends, just as they share in the process of bringing the spiritually deepening practice of sustained contemplative silent worship to me, and into the Jewish circles which I affect. This is a mutual fertilization of great significance.

I want to close with a blessing. The first part of the blessing is for all those Jews who have found a sustaining and nourishing spirituality in the Quaker house:

May this be for good and for blessing. May your neshamas/ souls bring blessing to all those who have offered you welcome. May the respite and time for healing you've found come back to us. May you come home with wisdom, love, compassion, and renewed hope.

For Quakers of all origins:

May your faith deepen and be a source of strength and joy.

Yours is a path that welcomes all seekers with serenity and grace.
Be blessed.

For the Jewish community:

Now is a time for us to heal so we can go forward with the
enlightened of all peoples towards the One Light. May we deepen
our Torah. May we open our hearts, welcoming home all who
have sought elsewhere for so long. May we have the courage to
craft for them and for us a fitting vessel, deeply rooted in the
historic wisdom of our people and reaching also to the future.
May we have the strength to share the guidance of our path,
neither defensively nor triumphantly, but from a centered place of
wholeness and peace.

Sylvia Boorstein

Spiritual Journey, Teshuvah, and Metta

When I was invited to offer this reflection, I phoned Reb Zalman to ask him what exactly he had in mind for me to write. He said, "Just write about your spiritual journey, and about Teshuvah and Metta." That sounded like three different things to me. But, it has happened to me before that I don't quite understand Zalman's sweeps of mind at first hearing (I think his sweeps of mind are broader by nature than mine are) so I needed to trust that if I started, it would happen.

Ira Progoff, a Jungian therapist who teaches the use of a personal journal as a tool for self-reflection, says that a person should be able to tell the story of their life in no more than twelve sentences, each one being a turning point that charts a new course. Similarly, no more than twelve sentences should be needed to tell the life story of any particular dimension of their lives.

This is my religious history.

1. My grandmother, my principal early life caretaker, had a sweet and steady practice of Sabbath observance throughout my childhood.
2. As a child, I heard stories about "perfect faith" that moved me, but I didn't know exactly what it meant or how I could get it.
3. I taught Sunday School to Kindergarten-age children at Congregation Beth Shalom, in Topeka, Kansas, and I didn't know how to tell them the Abraham and Isaac story.
4. On Yom Kippur, in Kansas, a person standing next to me did a running sotto voce mocking commentary during the recitation of sins, and I felt strange.

5. I spent a decade raising children, going to graduate school, doing peace-work activism, and struggling with increasing existential fear.
6. I met Zalman in 1973 and got excited about spiritual possibility.
7. I met my Buddhist teachers in 1977.
8. In 1985 I had strong experiences in meditation that spoke in the Scripture idiom of my childhood.
9. In 1993 I taught at Elat Chayyim with Miles Krassen who said that he thought that a daily prayer practice, at least a little one, would be good for me.
10. In 1994 I went to Israel for the first time and met some people who shared their excitement of study with me.
11. In my current life I teach Buddhist philosophy and Buddhist meditation, both *Vipassana* (Mindfulness) and *Metta* (Lovingkindness), with great pleasure and delight.
12. In my current life, I am delighting in study and rejoicing in prayer.

Twelve sentences really say it all, but since some of them are enigmatic, and others really cover many years, I'll describe each of them a bit more fully.

My Grandmother, Leah Kanner Schor

My grandmother was really my first dharma teacher as well as my *bubbe*. In our three-generation household, she was my principal caretaker since both my parents worked at jobs outside our home. She was loving and kind, solicitous of any physical need I ever had, and remarkably unmoved by any grumbling of mental discontent that I might express. "Where is it written," she would say, "that you are *supposed* to be happy all the time?" This is excellent fundamental dharma and has stood me in good stead through difficult times.

My grandmother and I spent every Friday making Shabbos preparations, baking challah. We spent every Saturday in shul together. I liked the sound of the men davening and I liked watching them standing and swaying, but a whole morning was a long time for me to sit, so I would go in and out, hanging out with my friends outside, and then coming back in and hanging around my grandmother. Each time I came back, I had to squeeze through to the end of the row to where her chair was, each time creeping over the feet of the other old women in the row. From time to time they would grumble, in Yiddish, "The child is creeping in and out too much!" Unfailingly, my grandmother stuck up for me. "Leave her alone," she would say, "She is fine." This was an excellent beginning.

Perfect Faith

I was born in Brooklyn in 1936, so I was nine years old when those of my father's relatives who had survived in Europe began arriving and staying at our house on their way to farmland in Western Canada. I remember the terrifying stories they told about what it had been like to hide in the forest in Poland through freezing winters, and someone told me that the cousin with swollen ankles with veins that stood out had gotten that way from frostbite. Someone gave me a child's gold ring, and some years later I remembered that no one had said whose it had been, but realized it must have been a child that died. In summer camp, a religious Zionist camp, we sang, "I believe with perfect faith in the coming of the Messiah, and even if his coming is delayed, I still believe." Someone explained that people had been able to say that as they walked into the gas chambers. I guessed that what that meant is that if you had perfect faith that you wouldn't ever need to be afraid. I was afraid of dying, and I was afraid that my mother, whose health was frail, would die. I wished I had perfect faith, but I didn't know how a person got that.

Abraham and Isaac

I was twenty years old, very pregnant, and teaching Sunday School to five-year-olds in Kansas when I realized I didn't feel good about telling them the story of Abraham and Isaac. The story, as I had heard it and understood it in my childhood, didn't sound right to me. It sounds fine to me now, because now I read it as an *instruction for liberation*, a reminder that any sort of attachment to personal ego is a seed of suffering, not as a test of fealty or sub-servience. If it is a test at all, I think it is a test of understanding. Probably what I would teach five-year-olds now is that this is a great story because what it *means* is no matter how frightened we ever might be, or no matter how scary a situation might seem, that remembering about God will make it better. I wish I had known this understanding forty years ago, or even had someone I could have asked about it. Perhaps there were people to ask, and I just didn't know enough to even ask.

Examination of Conscience

It seems strange to me now that I should have felt so dismayed about being mocked as I said the recitation of sins on Yom Kippur. I suppose I felt embarrassed about being caught doing what this other person, a person whom I had thought of as sophisticated, obviously thought was silly. I was trying to be very grown-up and "modern." Also, I remember thinking that I didn't really feel very *guilty*. In my life, through grace or good fortune and good parenting (probably all the same), I have not struggled with guilt very much, but when I even accidentally do something that I regret having done, I have tremendous remorse. Remorse feels to me quite different from guilt. Guilt makes me feel bad about myself. The remorse I feel when I hurt someone, especially inadvertently, makes me feel bad about how difficult *life* is. We try so hard and still there is so much potential for getting it wrong and causing pain.

Existential Angst

Somehow, probably because of the busyness of going to graduate school, establishing a career, raising my children and doing family life, I had managed to keep my lifelong fearfulness and "frailty-of-life alarm" more or less at bay. I had everything in life that was supposed to make a person happy—a family, a career, good health, material security—and although I knew I had a high-level worry system and a tendency to melancholy, I didn't think about it a lot. I think I figured it was just my nature. Besides, I would not have known what to do about it even if I had paid it attention. Religion, at least the kind locally available, had become stranger and stranger, and whatever connections I had to practice had faded as other aspects of my life had emerged more strongly. Then, one morning, two little girls, sisters, one of them a classmate of my daughter, were killed on the way to school by a runaway car just down the street from where we lived and my life-is-too-fragile despair came back in full force and stayed. I became preoccupied with what seemed to me the total meaninglessness of life. If everything hung in the fragile and precarious and apparently capricious balance that was my view of it, I couldn't understand how people could get out of bed in the morning, or do anything at all, or let their children out of their sight for a moment. I looked around me at other people living their lives, seemingly at ease, as if they didn't see the terrible reality that I saw. Everything I looked at seemed broken to me, as if I were seeing the ending of everything in the midst of its liveliness. I felt as if I had gone crazy.

Some years later, back in graduate school yet again, I took a course in Eastern Religions taught by Mary Neill, a Dominican nun, who became and has remained a lifelong friend. It was Mary who first taught me about the Buddha, and it was Mary who taught me the term "existential angst." Mary taught philosophy and introduced me to the work of Kierkegaard and Sartre and Camus. What I read of them validated my vision, so I didn't feel so crazy, but neither did they offer much in the way of hope. Mary was also my introduction to Thomas Merton who had then just recently died. I was tremendously moved by reading his own story, his willingness to share his own spiritual struggle. Here, I think, was my first glimmer of a sense that a life of spirit addressed the pain of the heart. My parents' religious sense had been primarily that of being related to a group, people around you who would support you in times of grief. I had not had the understanding that one could be supported *internally*, by one's own capacity. Perhaps that was the intimation that had moved me as a child about the meaning of "perfect faith." Perhaps I needed to read Merton to get the message about the potential for inner support because Merton was a hermit. I continue to feel inspired reading Merton.

I Met Zalman

I met Zalman in 1973 in Berkeley. He was teaching a workshop on the Tanya, sponsored by the Aquarian Minyon. I fell in love with him immediately, not because of what he said about the Tanya which I really didn't understand, and not because he was a grown-up man who talked about God seriously, as if he believed it, which was very exciting to me, but because when he davened I felt as if his relationship with God was real and intimate, and I wanted to have that for myself. Over the years I have found that there seems to be a secret club of people, nationwide, probably worldwide, who, when you talk to them long enough for it to come out that you know Zalman, they smile softly and say, "Yes, I met Zalman in '75 . . ." or whatever year, and then go on to relate their version of my experience with him. I believe he is a "waker-upper" of people to their hearts. It was, for me, as if a lifelong yearning to trust and to praise and to admit that I *wanted to* spoke up to me and said, "Hey, where *are* you?" I had prayed as a child, and then secretly as an adolescent because my grand-mother was dead by then and no one else I knew mentioned prayer very seriously. I credit Zalman and thank him for validating for me my religious consciousness as an adult.

Here is a Reb Zalman story that is my personal addition to The Teachings of Reb Zalman. One day, early in our friendship when we didn't know each other very well, Reb Zalman stayed with my family at our home overnight and for all the next day. In the evening, as I prepared dinner, he said to me, "I notice that you don't drink any milk. Why is that?" I was surprised! If I had drunk five *quarts* of milk, or only *chocolate* milk, something that was *obviously* different, I would understand interest. But *not* drinking milk you need to notice by its omission. "I don't drink it because

I'm allergic to it," I told him. "Why do you ask?" Zalman replied, "Well, I noticed, and I thought maybe you had a special reason. From every person you can learn something!" Paying attention to everything, being inquisitive, learning without relying on previous concepts, turns out to be the fundamental instruction for Mindfulness practice.

I Meet My Buddhist Teachers

In 1977, without much real understanding of what I was doing, I went to my first two-week, intensive *Vipassana* (Mindfulness) retreat. I think I went mostly because meditation retreats were what people were doing in the 1970s. I had ongoing anxiety and melancholy about life, but I didn't think of meditation as being a way to address that. It was just the "hip" thing to do. Maybe I thought I'd get enlightened, but I wasn't at all sure what that really meant. Everyone talked a lot about enlightenment in those days. Many people I knew were learning to meditate so that they could cultivate exotic altered states without drugs. I think perhaps I thought meditating would be like the scene in the Beatles movie, *Yellow Submarine*, where the mind bursts into color.

It would be a great story, I suppose, if I could say that something marvelous happened on that first meditation retreat, but really nothing dramatic happened with me in terms of exotic mind events. In fact, I was mostly struggling with confusion and sleepiness and my body was in terrible pain. What happened that totally captivated me, and indeed committed me to retreat practice over many equally non-dramatic years of practice, was the message that I heard about the teachings of the Buddha about suffering. Finally, someone was naming just what I was experiencing as the fundamental unsatisfactoriness of life, and promising that there was a way of relating to that in a way that was wise and compassionate. I had spent so many years preoccupied with the notion that I was the only person I knew who saw life as tragically imperfect, and yet here it was as the central teaching of the Buddha. It was such a relief! Finally, here were people who saw life just as I did and were willing to talk about it. This was music to my ears, and even though I was thoroughly daunted by concentration practice and bewildered about what it actually meant to be "mindful," I believed what I heard and I wanted more. I think it helped that my teachers were young, that they were women as well as men, that they had education and backgrounds similar to my own. I thought, "They get it that life is unsatisfactory, and yet they seem content. Even *happy*. Whatever this meditation is, it must have done it for them. And, if they could do it, I can do it!"

This is a good place for a brief explanation of Mindfulness meditation practice. Mindfulness is the aware, balanced acceptance of present experience. It isn't more complicated than that. It is opening to, or receiving, the present moment, pleasant or unpleasant, just as it is, with neither clinging nor rejection. There are two ways, I think, to understand the purpose of practice. One way is to see how it leads to wisdom. As a person is increasingly able to stay alert and balanced from moment to moment, the truths of impermanence, unsatisfactoriness, and of non-separate self will present themselves as "insights." As insight grows, the teachings promise, the habitual tendency of the mind to continue to cling to what is essentially ungraspable diminishes, and suffering lessens. Another way to understand how practice works is that the very practice itself deconditions the mind from its habitual pattern of running from discomfort. Sitting (or standing or walking or eating or whatever) hour after hour, *practicing* remaining calm and alert through the whole range of body states and mind states that present themselves, not doing *anything* to change experience but rather discovering that experience is *bearable*, is itself an antidote to the usual flurried reaction of the mind to each new moment. For a person like myself, for whom, in any moment, a frailty-of-life thought could arise in the mind bringing on an attack of anxiety, it was tremendous to learn that I could sit through anxiety. I did not have to flee from it. It wasn't comfortable, but it didn't last. By sitting through my pain, mental or physical, remaining open to it as fully as I could, not running away from it, at least I didn't complicate things further with the energy of flight. And I learned probably my most important and sustaining lesson: everything *really does* pass. That makes everything bearable—even the worst things.

Metta practice often seems, at least at first glance, like a different practice from *Vipassana*. The technique is different. But, I think they are really quite the same. *Vipassana* practice is relating to all experiences fully, with a balanced and compassionate understanding. *Metta* practice is relating to all *beings* with good will, which means receiving them, or accepting them, without rejection and with compassionate understanding. The technique of the practice is the resolute, non-stop, silent recitation of wishes for the well-being of all beings. One begins with the people one loves most, and using the energy from the pleasure that develops in the mind from wishing well to dearly beloved people, one is able to go on and wish well to people with whom one has conflicts. When I began intensive *Metta* practice I was sure that I had no "enemies," and wondered where I would find people to use in my "conflictual people" category. I was amazed to find what a hidden grudge list I had been harboring in my heart. It turns out that *Metta* practice is a *spontaneous* examination of conscience, and the long list of bad feelings I am holding towards other people (or myself) for whatever infraction, however slight, becomes conscious anytime I am serious in my practice. I often feel as if I have given my internal computer the instruction, "Please give me the list of people I need to make amends to and jobs I need to finish, my uncompleted karma." I don't make that conscious intention, but that is always the way it works out. When it happened the first time, I was somewhat taken aback. I have an image of myself as a grudge-free, splendidly tolerant person, and when it turned out not to be true, my feelings were hurt. Afterwards, I became happy about the fact that practice works that way. I really *do* want practice to be a "Purification of the Heart," which is what it is called, and it is *reassuring* to find that it actually works. And, when I clean up my unfinished karma, with other people and with myself, I *do* feel better. And happier. I did not start to practice intensely because I wanted to be a nicer person. I thought I already was a nice person. I wanted to be less frightened. But it has made me a nicer person. *And* less frightened.

The Iconography of My Heart

I think steady change happened over the first ten years of my *Vipassana* practice, but nothing very dramatic. I felt somewhat calmer, not so frantic, and certainly more able, at least intellectually, to understand my bouts of alarm or melancholy when they arose. I did as much retreat practice as I could while continuing my family life and my career life, since I found silence particularly nourishing. I never struggled about my identity. The questions, "What am I? Am I a Jew? Am I a Buddhist?" never seemed an issue. It didn't seem relevant. My family life with my children and grandchildren remained structured around Jewish holiday observance, which seemed entirely natural. As time went by and I began to teach and became thought of as a Buddhist teacher, or was asked to be the Buddhist delegate or Buddhist spokesperson at various interfaith conferences, that seemed quite natural too.

Retrospectively, there were probably certain prodromal clues to what later seemed a surprising heart-realization. I found that during meditation retreats I would begin to remember to pray. Remembering did not happen in any planned way like, "This would be a good thing for me to do as long as I am here," but actually happened somewhat organically, as if it arose on its own. It began to manifest on the edges of my experience. I found I was saying Kaddish for my mother whose death, many years before, had been very hard for me, and for my father whose death had been more recent. I found I was saying Kaddish many times a day, without a plan. It just happened. I also found that I remembered to bless before I ate. When moments of special beauty or peace or relief in my practice experience happened, my spontaneous response would be thanksgiving for having been sustained in life, enabled to reach that moment. Often, as I sat amongst people whose silent presence supported me in my own practice, my mind would fill with the chant, "Behold! How good and how pleasant it is, to sit together. . . ."

Kundalini experiences, dramatically altered energy experiences, are not typically part of *Vipassana* practice. Certainly they are not the goal of practice, and are not specifically cultivated. When they do arise, students are encouraged to see them as they do other phenomena, as transient and ephemeral. Since these altered states can be quite blissful, seducing the mind into clinging, or quite painful, causing the mind to react with aversion, they are seen as a hindrance to clear seeing and a challenge to practice.

My own energy experiences, developing slowly over years as mild rapture and delight, escalated during a period of intensive practice. I was overwhelmed and overcome with intense, blissful, body energy. I felt myself filled with light and radiating light. My hearing and sight were altered. I felt that my body was a template for cosmic truth, that Genesis was being written in the energy pattern of my body. As experiences presented themselves, lines and images from Scripture came spontaneously to my mind. Although I couldn't see it visually I could feel my connection with all beings. I felt that God was breathing on me. When I told this to my teacher, he said, "Don't reify, Sylvia. Just tell me what your direct experience is." This was a very good response.

What I needed to learn, and continue to need to learn, is that everything changes and all clinging brings suffering. My experience, initially blissful, became so intense as to be painful. I felt like the sorcerer's apprentice, with what I had desired taking over and inundating me. I felt overcome and exhausted with unending energy, and I was often unable to sleep. I felt as if my body were vibrating all the time, quite out of my control. I realized that when my blissful experience began, I had been delighted with it and had hoped that it wouldn't end. I began to appreciate the Buddha's teaching that the cause of suffering is craving. I had craved more, and gotten more, and now I couldn't stop it. It was fully five years before I could depend upon some balanced sense of calm body and calm mind.

I never talked about my experiences, and this is the first time I've written about them. For one thing, they were very special to me, and I felt private about them. For another, I did not want to give anyone (especially myself) the idea that these kinds of experiences are any more valuable or spiritual than other seemingly more ordinary experiences. They are just more exotic. I think I was as concerned that other people might overvalue my experience and that I might do that myself. Fundamentally, it was just an energy experience. Besides, it was blissful only briefly, and after that it was mostly disconcerting and painful.

The reason I choose to tell this story now is that it is pivotal in my reflections on my own development. I can't tell my story without it. Two realizations came from my experience. The first is that it became clear to me that the imagery, the "iconography," of my heart is Old Testament Scripture, and its idiom is prayer-book Hebrew. The second is that that imagery sustains me. For five years my energy system was altered and uncomfortable. I was confused, and dismayed, and disillusioned with practice and/or my ability to manage it. I didn't feel like a normal person who could go places and interact with people in a regular way. I felt weird. It was a crucial period in my practice, and although I learned about desire and attachment and aversion and imperma- nence and suffering and non-self, it was very hard. Secretly, although I knew I was reifying, I was sustained and pleased by the idea that God was breathing on me.

Vipassana *and* Devekut

Teaching with Miles Krassen at Elat Chayyim was both a clarification and a permission experience for me. I had wondered how we would teach together, since we had never met and didn't know each other. I also knew that he is much more a scholar than I am. It didn't matter. Listening to Miles talk about *devekut* as "cleaving" sounded like the *Vipassana* instructions to "rub" the object with the mind." We both knew techniques for gathering and focusing attention and we knew how to share them, and we knew *why* we practiced them. This seems to me the essential question; it is not "What are you?" or even, "What exactly do you do?" but "Why are you doing it?"

Our class went well, we both taught very well, and near the end of the week as Miles and I were privately praising each other, he added, "And, you taught even better the more you let the Jewishness show out." This was important for me to hear. Retrospectively, I thought he was right. It was nothing I had done, or decided to do, in a self-conscious way. Just the opposite. I think feeling confirmed in my understanding allowed me to feel *less* self-conscious and be most plainly myself.

I loved Miles' lack of pretentiousness. When I listened to him teach, I found him always knowledgeable and very kind and yet almost understated in his suggestions. He and I spent time telling each other our stories, teaching each other, and by the end of the week we were friends. He said, in his understated way, "I think a daily prayer practice would be good for you. You could start with something easy. Maybe daven Minchah." I took him seriously.

Jerusalem

I visited Israel for the first time in December of 1993 and spent a month in Jerusalem. I felt very much at home and very happy. Most exciting to me were my meetings with mature, worldly, ecumenical, devout people—women as well as men—who were serious about study as well as prayer. Some of them shared study time with me. The concept, "We studied together," became newly meaningful to me and became part of my life in ways I could not have anticipated.

The Unfolding Present

I like the double-entendre of "present." I hadn't planned it before I wrote it, as I only meant to write a current update, but it really *is* what I want to say. I don't want to say anything more specific only because with my current process, I need to know it more before I share it more. I teach a lot of classes in Buddhist understanding as well as *Vipassana* and *Metta* meditation, and it is a joy for me to practice and to share what I know. And I pray a lot. And I study.

Everyone I know who gives dharma talks, including myself, eventually quotes T. S. Eliot, "We shall not cease from exploration/ And the end of all our exploring/ Will be to arrive where we started/ And know the place for the first time." It is, perhaps, overquoted, so I am a little embarrassed to end with it. But I think it is true. For myself, I do not have a sense of teshuvah as returning from anywhere, or of having gone anywhere. It seems much more like staying here and waking up. *Metta* practice also does not mean going any*where* or doing any*thing*. It means staying here, staying awake, and opening to the fullness of one's heart.

Gershon Winkler, Lakme Elior, and David Carson

Lighting the Story Fires Within: A Shamanic Journey to the Land of Self

Gershon: David, how would you describe the world of shamanism, and how important is the shamanic for everyday, down-to-earth living?

David: Well, rather than call it the "world of shamanism." I'd call it the world of imagination. And we could all use more of that. We need to loosen our subjection to the world of pre-packaged givens and get ourselves acclimated to other worlds, such as the world of fantasy.

Gershon: I agree. In the Kabbalah—the ancient Judaic mystical tradition—they speak of *mokhin de-katnus* and *mokhin de-gadlus*.

David: That's easy for you to say.

Gershon: Not as easy as you might think. *Mokhin de-katnus* literally means "the small mind," meaning that when we are stuck in a limited perception of reality—like, "I can't go beyond ten feet from where we're sitting because there's a wall there"—it's about boundaries that have been defined, not from my Self-Spirit place, but from what I've been taught since childhood. How much of our limitations, of our sense of "this is all I can do" is really our own sense, and how much of it comes from voices within us that are not ours but are those of our parents, our teachers, or the boundaries drawn by society, culture, and religion? Ever notice that when toddlers fall down, they usually don't cry until the adults react with alarm? So the kid gets programmed right then and there that falling down is something really horrendous—I mean, look at the way the adults reacted! This has gotta be tragic and certainly requires a good cry! When I attend a gourd dance among my Dineh (Navajo) neighbors, I'm impressed by how the small kids are running and climbing all over the place amid the drumming and dancing, and when they fall or tumble, the adults kind of pay attention to it but don't express any alarm, and the kids just get right back up again and resume their climbing.

David: And what's the other thing you mentioned?

Gershon: *Mokhin de-gadlus*? Literally it means "the big mind"— That we can move from the world of givens, of limitations, of cant's, to a world of expansion, of open range spirit-grazing. We often call this transcendence. So it means that I will not feel stuck in this room because there's a wall, but that I can either walk right through it or shut my eyes and go beyond the wall in my mind, in my imagination. I can trek to Chaco Canyon while you're sitting here wondering how much it would have cost you to replace your wall had I chosen the former route. So *mokhin de-gadlus* is about accessing those other worlds you were alluding to.

David: And there's a lot of power in those other worlds waiting for us to learn and use them. That's what shamanism is about, being aware that we live and operate simultaneously in many worlds, in realities other than the one we were sold on by so-called normative culture and society. And imagination is one of those worlds, so infinite and full of spiritual empowerment and creative inspiration. So the shamanic path to creativity is that when you sit down to write, for example, try to walk as vividly in the imagination world as you would in the so-called real world. Most people don't think of their imagination places as part of the real world. From the shamanic perspective, they're real. Imagination is not make-believe. It is an essential component to the growth of spirit.

Gershon: In Judaism, too, the realm of fantasy is considered a powerful tool for personal spiritual nurturing. In fact, the fourteenth-century kabbalist, Rabbi Isaac mon de Akko, wrote about a man who was passing the castle of some princess when he heard a woman singing sweetly on the other side of the fence. So he peeked through a hole in the fence to see who it was and he saw the princess herself, bathing . . .

David: Boy, you're getting my imagination going, I can tell you that!

Gershon: It got his imagination going, too, you know. He was so taken by her beauty that he gave himself away and shouted, "God, I wanna be with you!" to which she instantly replied, "In the cemetery!" Her meaning, of course, was that there was no way they'd ever get together in life, only in death. After all, she was a princess and he was a simple commoner, a *schmeggeg*. But in death, everyone goes to the same place— the cemetery—whether you're of royal blood or a peasant. But he took her reply literally and made a beeline for the cemetery to wait for her. And as he waited and waited, his fantasy about how it would be to make love with this very beautiful woman overtook him to such a degree that as days and weeks and months went by, he transformed into a deeply spiritual person, and people from all over started making pilgrimages to the cemetery to receive blessings and healings from this lech-turned-holyman. What had happened, Rabbi Isaac taught, was that since there was no actual physical outlet for his love fantasy about the princess, it eventually got narrowed down to its core essence, which is the longing of the soul to connect with the Creator, the Ultimate Beloved. And so his longing to physically consummate, having no place to go, got translated into spiritual consummation. So it's a story about how the human spirit gets nourished by the imagination.

David: And about how you shouldn't forget your libido.

Gershon: Wow. That would make a terrific bumper sticker: "Remember Thy Libido."

David: On the medicine wheel, the cemetery in that story would be the West. The light is in the East and the shadow is in the West, and that's where we go to face our death. The West is also the keeper of dreams. It's where power and creativity come from—by going inside, into the shadow, and experi-

encing the inner world that we're carrying, which is larger by
far than the outer world we see with our eyes.

Gershon: So you're saying that the root of creation, of creativity, is
in the chaos.

David: Absolutely. And I think a lot of Western people misunder-
stand the idea of a fructifying earth. It's all the excrement,
you know, and the death of things, that bring forth the
flowers. So we're all going through life, but we're headed
toward the West, toward death. It's a place that is generally
overlooked by Western culture because it hasn't dealt with its
garbage. I don't know if many people will buy all that.

Gershon: Well, how much will it cost?

David: How much will you give me?

Lakme: David is right. There seems to be this sense that death is
failure. In the Focusing workshops I do, I teach people to look
at the places within themselves that seem the least fruitful (at
least to the Western mind), the places where you go and you
sit in kind of a dreaming state, but you're not daydreaming,
you're not *making* it happen but are waiting to see what
comes next, what comes out of the shadow. And this is a
difficult process for the Western mindset.

Gershon: According to the ancient Judaic teachings, life and death
share a symbiotic relationship; death is but the seedling for
new life. When we die physically, we start life anew spiritually. When an acorn disconnects from its life on a tree, its
"death" on the ground is but the beginning of yet another
tree. The most sacred period of the Judaic calender year is the
Jewish *new* year, or Rosh Hashanah, which means literally
"Head of the Year," and it occurs in autumn, just when the
leaves are falling and it seems like all that was green and alive
is starting to dry up and die. Yet, this period is about
celebrating new beginnings, in our personal lives and in the
earth that at this time appears lifeless on her surface. Death,
then, is seen not as end but as beginning of something else,
something new. And at the very core of beginnings there is
chaos and death. There is churning of the raw, the unformed
and undefined. While the earth appears lifeless in the dead of
winter, for example, new life is being wombed deep inside
her, waiting to surface in spring. The ancient rabbis taught

that in the middle of winter the sap begins to flow through the trees, and they celebrated this in the Moon of Aquarius with a sacred feast of dried fruits and nuts. And a lot of people, like some of the people who have attended your shamanic workshops on death, David, have experienced this process quite vividly and have found newness in their lives and been transformed by it. You also have it in the Jewish creation story, where each phase of the creation is followed by the mantra, "And it was evening and it was morning the first day . . . the second day . . ." and so forth, to teach that it is in the night, the shadow, the dream place, where new days and new creations get baked.

Lakme: What I see in the Creation story, in the way that it's told by the Jewish tradition, is that first there is an idea to do it, but then there's a long period of darkness, of wombing the idea, during which it is hidden and growing and is nurtured and you can't prove anything. You can't see it. You can't even know, so you can still be scared of it, because you don't know what it is. And then comes morning, when you can see it. Morning in Hebrew is *bo-ker*, which means literally "distinction," because in the light of day all that was one big unseen glob during the night now becomes seen and distinguishable. The chaos of conceiving the idea now achieves the clarity of giving it expression, of bringing it to life. Sort of like the idea of death and *then* life.

David: Where does dreaming come in?

Lakme: Dreaming is part of the merging. Judaism has a special prayer for waking up in the morning and thanking the Creator for returning your soul to your body. In other words, the body is seen as the sacred trust for the journey of the soul in the physical realm. And at night, while the animal plane of soul consciousness remains manifested in your body, keeping it alive, the transcendent spirit plane of soul consciousness is freed enough from physical manifestation to merge with the universe and do spirit journeys or whatever. The experiences of the spirit soul plane of consciousness then manifest as dreams in the animal soul plane of consciousness. And the clarity of their imagery is contingent upon the clarity of consciousness we have achieved in our lives altogether. The morning is when we try to integrate as much as we can of our experiences hanging out in the universal. I suppose that this is why we don't remember all of our dreams, because our finite body-minds can't grasp the totality of where we've been all night.

David: And have you ever had the experience of going to bed haunted by some unsolvable problem and then waking up in the morning knowing what you should do about it? In the Native American path there's a part of the morning called "Hour of the Wolf." It's kind of a twilight of the morning. And that's when the birds sing to the flowers. That's what makes them grow. So the Hour of the Wolf is a growth period. It would be a time to tap into for growing something inside of us. Because this is when we come out of the West, out of the dream, out of the shadow. It is therefore a very powerful time for fostering creativity; to free us from writer's block, for instance. On the medicine wheel the West is also the keeper of dreams. Certain animals such as the bear are poised in that direction, because it corresponds with the hibernating animals. They are the dreaming animals. The West is therefore a place of great power for a writer.

Gershon: What is the East on the medicine wheel?

David: The East is your place of great spiritual light, the place of great teachers and enlighteners. The North is the place of intellect and is associated with winter, the cold and cutting flint of the intellect. When we get fixated in the North, we lose sight of the rest of the wheel. We think we're smart. We forget there's a larger self.

Lakme: And that flinty mind can't tolerate chaos very well. So we lose the creative life force, the place from which all of that comes forth. Because the mind wants to be defined.

Gershon: So I can see how one might tune into the East forces in the morning to receive enlightenment and growth inpetus from the Hour of the Wolf and from the rising sun, and to the West for seeding new ideas or for baking unarticulated feelings.

David: Ancient Native American wisdom has it that everybody has their particular "hour of power," when they can accomplish certain things better than at other times. Generally, it corresponds to the birth power, which is early in the morning. It's not always true, but most of the time it is so. If you're dealing with the whole medicine wheel, you become sensitive to your personal times of power.

Lakme: I was born between three and four in the morning. And whenever I've gotten in touch with my real writing place I have woken up in the middle of the night and not been able to go back to sleep until I wrote. That sense of *"it's* writing me" was incredibly vivid during such times. I mean, it does happen at other times as well, but I've felt most driven to write during the hour that I feel is my personal time of power, the hour I was born.

Gershon: I was born in the middle of the day, but I find it easier to write at night. Probably because I was born in Denmark. That's seven hours later than here. So when it's night here, it's the crack of dawn there, Hour of the Wolf, or the Great Dane. But speaking about animals, David, what about your medicine cards? They teach us of the various animal powers we can learn from, and there is probably a way to tap into the animal power teachings to help us unleash our creative selves.

David: Yeah, but you don't necessarily need the cards to do that. All you have to do is walk outside and get a sense of your environment. The medicine cards never fail to give me some direction, but when you use them, you need to make sure you're asking the right questions. Sometimes you'll get a message that doesn't work for you, so you need to rethink the problem and ask your question differently. Likewise, sometimes you might not feel at ease in your environment, so you may want to look inside to see whether it's the place that is uninspiring or whether there's something's clogging up the plumbing inside of your Self. Like most shamans say, pay attention to every small detail about what's going on around you; what's being told to you is not just being communicated through language but through the whole cosmic field around you. The medicine cards can teach you how to become more sensitive to the powers around you that manifest themselves in animals, in nature. But there is also the danger of getting so caught up in the cards or in a book about nature that you numb your senses to real time, instinctual experiences with nature because of your preoccupation with someone else's teachings about it.

Lakme: You're saying that any time when some wisdom like the medicine cards gets put down in writing, there is a moment in time when that wisdom gets distilled. So you can use the cards as a take-off point, but you shouldn't stop there. So whenever we've written something down, by that very act we've already moved on and beyond.

Gershon: I think that a lot of people have trouble expressing themselves because they're already editing and judging their ideas and wording even before they allow the first sentence to unfold. By being too judgmental about their personal creativity and worrying about how it'll look or sound, they end up obstructing the free flow of what is forthcoming, of the mystery that is creation.

Lakme: And that's the North mind coming in too soon, the mind that likes definiteness, which is good in its right place, but which gets too easily intimidated by chaos, by the place of fresh, undefined creation. And that's a problem we have with this culture. The dominant American culture has the tendency to edit everything before it has a chance to be born.

Gershon: Maybe if you're having that kind of trouble you need to move out of the North and into the West, into the unknown, the world of dream and imagination, the realm of shadow and chaos.

David: Or, if that doesn't work, you might try moving into the South place, the place of earthiness and passion, and kind of get out of your head place by shifting to the opposite direction.

Gershon: So would you advise such an individual to sleep facing south?

David: No, I'd tell them to go to sleep with a rock in their hand, or in other words with something of the South power, something down-home earthy-like.

Gershon: Where is Coyote in the Choctaw tradition?

David: I think he's sitting right in front of me. Quit scratching your ears, Gershon. I saw you staring at that roadrunner.

Gershon: David, how would you apply the teachings and experiences with which you were raised in the Choctaw tradition?

David: That's a pretty important question, because in the Choctaw cosmology we have Grasshopper Mother who came
from the third to the fourth world. The world that we're in
now is the world of separations. That's the fourth world. But
we came from under the earth, which was the third world,
and were shown the way to this world by Grasshopper
Mother. And after all creatures, including humans, were led
out of the third world into the fourth world, the humans
became afraid of Grasshopper Mother. So they killed her and
pushed her back down into the earth. The Choctaw say that
she then became Death Mother, keeper of all the animal
powers, keeper of all the powers of imagination. You see, a
lot of Native American tradition is about facing our death, our
inner world, our dreams, our visions. We have to learn about
our death, and the path to that learning stretches across some
very rich and fertile ground. You might say it's a metaphor for
going into your deepest Self to find your most creative Self.
I'm not pushing this as a cosmology for everyone, but for me
it's been a rich paradigm from which to pull creative ideas.

Gershon: You once led me and Lakme into a meditation where you
had us invite Spider Mother, who you explained was from
the Hopi tradition. She helped us spin webs, actually spin
stories, and moved us into a creative place. How would I
connect with Grasshopper Mother or Death Mother?

David: This is where the drum comes in. In our tradition, the drum
is a vehicle for journeying to the non-ordinary worlds—you
know, to take you there. The drum is the life-mover, the
heartbeat. According to our tradition, we'd be spiritually
stone-dead without the drum. The drum is the pulse of our
inner life, of our Self. We would have no life without the
drum, the heartbeat of our inner Self. The drum is very
powerful from birth to death. The Choctaw tradition says
that the woodpecker is the keeper of the power of the drum.
In our language we call him *wi-sho-nek*, which means "lord of
the drums." So, with proper meditation, and sitting beside a
hole in the earth, for example, the drum can lead the seeker
into the third world where all the animal powers are kept by
Death Mother. You can learn a lot down there. It is a
shamanic realm. The drum can then take you to any world.

And in the Native American tradition we're all related, all
humans, all creations, which means we access all the great
teachers who've ever been. You might therefore want to drum
yourself up to dialogue with Chief Seattle or with Moses.

Gershon: You said your tradition speaks of the present paradigm as
the fourth world. Is there also a fifth world?

David: The fifth world is when we'll realize that we're more than
just humans, that we're also godly—part divine, part mundane, so to speak. It's going to be a world of paradox. So like
the fourth world is the world of separation, the fifth world
will usher in a consciousness of being joined as one with
Great Spirit.

Gershon: That's interesting, because in the Jewish tradition, too,
there are similar teachings about *four* worlds. The first world
is the world of Emanation, *atzilut*. That's the idea place,
where inklings live. You know, like when you "have an
inkling." It's like the plane of inspiration, where you are
struck with that very first "Aha!"—but you can't put it into
words yet. In fact, you can't even picture it yet. That starts to
happen in the second world, the world of Creation, *beriah*.
There, the sputter, the chaos of this initial idea, gets articulated enough so you can start on your outline. The third
world is that of Formation, *yetsirah*. There, the stuff that's
coming through begins to take on a shape, a plot, a direction.
It's starting to flow. It's becoming a story. Finally, in the
fourth world, the piece is practically writing itself into the
finished product. This is the world of Action, *assiyah*, the
plane of manifestation. The inkling has now become fully
manifested; the seed has become the tree.

David: Exactly. You start with a flash of an idea and work it to a
flame of a story, or whatever, through gradual, sometimes
painstaking stages. It's like starting a fire; you begin small and
tedious, first with some kindling, then with some bigger
pieces, then with some logs, until the thing starts taking off
by itself.

Gershon: Is that why you call your workshops "Lighting the Story
Fire Within"?

David: Well, it's more about the fire being the archetype of where
story comes from. I mean, since the dawn of time, people—

all peoples—sat around the fire and spun yarns. It was like an ancient television set. So the story-fire remains an archetype within us which we can tap into and draw out some really good yarns. Today's electro-fire, or TV set, might tell us stories, too, but it doesn't leave us space for *our* stories, whereas the campfire of yesteryear fired up our imagination. So the story-fire within is about getting warm and excited inside about your own stories until they burst forth like volcanic lava. Kind of a pyro learning.

Gershon: In the Judaic shamanic tradition, fire came from water, and became the creative energy of the water, of the womb of Creation. Let's see you beat that one.

David: Sounds like nuclear fusion or something.

Gershon: And that's why fire gets extinguished in water. It's not getting destroyed, it's just going back into its source.

David: Well, that really clears *that* up. I've been thinking a lot about that. I'm serious. I think a lot about where fire came from. In Native American teachings there are many myths about it. Some traditions have it that Coyote brought the fire. Stole it from Great Spirit.

Gershon: Speaking of stealing, seems the Choctaw stole a lot of their ideas from the Jews.

David: Bullshit. You guys ripped it off from *us* . . .

Gershon: Right, two thousand years ago some rabbi wandered through Choctaw country, wrote down what he learned and called it Kabbalah . . .

David: Isn't there something somewhere about the Indians being the lost tribes of the Jews? I think the Mormons said that.

Gershon: I once told that to a Cherokee medicine man back east, and . . .

David: Is that how you lost your hair?

Gershon: . . . he shook his head from side to side and said, "You've got it all wrong. The Jews are the lost tribes of the Cherokees."

David: And the Cherokees are the lost tribes of the Choctaw.

The dialogue went on and on until they fell asleep and were tucked in by Grasshopper Mother who sang a Jewish lullaby and hopped off to the fifth world.

Batya D. Wininger

Jewish Women's Shamanism

A growing number of Jews are using shamanic techniques as part of their spiritual repertoire. This piece is both an explanation of shamanism and an autobiographical narrative of the author's journey into Jewish shamanism. Wininger offers us some fascinating insights into the way Jews lived in Biblical times.

I. A Story
"This Is the Gateway to the Heavens"

The sign said, "This is the Gateway to the Heavens," and so she walked through, parting the heavy, white, woven curtain with her left hand, parting the second curtain, more a lightweight gauzy veil. As she entered, she felt herself grow smaller, less substantial, able to float a bit. She lifted up and found herself among the scrolls, dressed in blue and maroon velvet, with silver breastplates that hung heavily about their necks. Now she was their size, like Alice in Wonderland and the mushrooms, climbing up the stretched finger of the pointer, then the pointer's chain, onto the right horn, slipping a bit on its polished wood. She stood a moment, poised, uncertain, at the top, until a letter floated by. Recognizing it as the beginning of her name, the beginning even of Torah, she jumped, caught the serif on the letter's leg, and swung herself up into its cradling middle part. It floated—barely noticing her presence—upward, ever upward. She felt its safety, its comfort as it slightly rocked, rising.

Suddenly, the letter spilled her out before a gate.

The gate was gold, shining gold, burning with the quality of fire. It was a worked gate, as wrought iron often is, tall, spiked, closed. Beside the gate hung a key, large and heavy, also of worked gold, burning as if with fire. Uncertainly, her hands shaking, she reached for the key, not because she had the desire, but because it was there and called her name. She held it, examined it, heard the lock in the gate call to her, and reached out her hand that held the key.

II. What Is Shamanism?

A story? No, more like an experience.

Let me begin with what shamanism is not. It is not a belief system or a religion. There are, of course, certain beliefs most folks who practice it hold. Most believe, for instance, that there is a spirit side to existence. But there is no list of laws, dogma, prayer, or the like that you must adopt. Each person, after learning the "how-tos," works with it in a slightly different way.

Shamanism is, simply put, the techniques, methodology, and expertise used to move from the world of ordinary reality where we spend our waking hours, into the realm of non-ordinary reality, or the realm of Spirit. As taught by Michael Harner over the last twenty or thirty years, core shamanism boils down the complex, ritual-laden system as found in most Earth-based, traditional (*"primitive"*) societies of the world, so that it is culture-neutral and accessible to those in Western society. One no longer must become Lakota (Sioux), Hopi, Australian aborigine, Siberian, Sami (Lappland) or anyone but one's self to practice shamanic techniques.

In traditional societies there were specific ways in which a person was called to the shamanic path. They usually apprenticed to a successful shaman and learned the specific rituals, prayers, methods, and practices of their own tribe over many, many years. In some societies shamans were also the medicine people; in other societies these were two separate jobs. Either men or women, in most cases, could be a shaman. It is my firm belief that these techniques are accessible to non-traditional people with less time for training, and they're accessible not because we are any better or smarter or more civilized, but because the Earth, the Universe, needs Spirit returned. The very existence of life as we know it requires healing and wholeness, and these sacred paths—once so difficult to attain—MUST be accessed again, now, with no time wasted. The paths remain difficult to follow fully, requiring commitment, life choices and changes, but are accessible as tools for certain purposes without as much struggle as in the past.

The shamanic journey (called such because we go from our world into Spirit's—a distinct and important difference from channelling, where we call Spirit into our world) requires a semi-trance state. Although you are still conscious (through what is often called the "witness"), much of your awareness—kinesthetic, auditory, visual, emotional, psychological, etc.—is engaged in an experience in a foreign world. In the Lower World (You go down to get there—"lower" does not mean "lesser") you most likely work with an Animal Helper. In the Upper World (you go up to get there), you often work with a Teacher in a more or less human form. These are the same Beings with whom you work regularly, and you never do anything in non-ordinary reality without them.

One of the most essential rules is that you journey with a clearly stated purpose and intention, and that you maintain that purpose and intention throughout the journey. You are not a victim or passive explorer. As a shamanic practitioner, you are an agreeing participant, in ultimate control not of the experience, but of your involvement in it. The overall purpose of the work is to bring information or healing back from the Spirit realm to the ordinary world to create more wholeness and/or well-being, and to restore appropriate balance to everyday life.

I have been studying core shamanism with Michael Harner and his assistant Sandra Ingerman for almost seven years. During that time, I have received valuable information from the realm of Spirit about many things, clarifying my own beliefs about how the world is put together, about my own purposes, and about "right action." I have also been gifted with insights into the prayers, ways, and possibilities of my own people—Jewish women. Without asking, I have been given a path to follow, and I walk it with as much care, integrity, and balance as I can muster.

My Jewish shamanic experience began about two years ago, when I spent a rare Shabbat morning in shule, a beautiful little turn-of-the-century place near my home. The ceiling is painted as a sky, the ark is topped by a half-sun, the pews are dark wood, and the windows are stained glass. As I sat, trying to pray in an enclosed space—which has been difficult for me for a long time, I'm much better off out-of-doors—I noticed that above the ark was written the same words as above the ark of my childhood synagogue: "*Zeh Sha'ar HaShamayim.* This is the gateway to the heavens." In my way of working, following the shamanic path, that could mean only one thing: literally, "This is the way to get to the Heavens, to the 'other side.'" I went home and thought about it a long time before trying it.

During my years of shamanic journeying I have learned to be careful before jumping into some new experience or experiment. The spirit world is very real, and contains its own dangers. Journeying is not a game, nor an exercise, nor an "as if" experience. It is not metaphor (it is not ONLY metaphor, though it certainly lends itself to such), and it is not to be played with. Before trying something new, I have learned to ask a lot of questions, explore the details a number of times, and make sure I know how to get back. After all, I am wandering about in a place that is not my usual home.

With all this in mind I began wondering how, once I was in the ark, I could rise up. (Obviously the Heavens were in that general direction.) In my first journey about this, I was told to use a letter from the Hebrew alphabet rather than an Animal Helper. That was fine, but how could the letter rise up? I held this question for many days until, quite unexpectedly, I received the information: "The prayers of the People lift the letters to the Heavens." The understanding often accompanies such messages, and here I understood that it was not the prayer of any segment of the People, nor was it any specific prayer—it was the passion and yearning and intensity of the accumulated prayers of all our People: men, women, children, over the years, in all situations, in all languages.

And so I journeyed again, and was shown the pathway up to the gate, to the key described above. I entered through the ark in that little synagogue. I had recently finished weaving the curtain for the ark for the High Holidays and intimately knew each white, cotton thread and the spaces between them, so going through that curtain was natural to me. The rest of the journey held me quite in awe. That first time I didn't dare open the gate. It was enough to experience the power, the utter magnificence of that gate; its fiery gold, its intricate design, its immensity.

The next time I tried this journey, I did unlock the gate, carefully, and stepped through it to a path that stretched forward surrounded by the non-consuming fire that Moses saw in the bush in the desert. The flames were high, extensive, and as I passed between them, I could hear soft voices of women calling to me, gently, in welcome. I was afraid but not afraid, and I walked forward cautiously. At the end of the path I began to see the faces and forms of the women, of our foremothers, with Sarah at the center. They were the women named and unnamed of the Bible, of my own lineage throughout time. None were totally distinct—except Sarah in the center—but their identities were known by their presence.

Soon after, I journeyed again, asking how to use this pathway in an appropriate manner. I was told not to do this work alone, that it was the work of community, meaning Jewish women, and that it was to be done in order to retrieve the ancient wisdom held by the women and used for healing, for ritual, for prayer. This retrieval is for the benefit of making the community whole again. Instructions were received about a two-day workshop, and I journeyed many times for the details of that experience. Since then, I have conducted the workshop in various forms for women of both Jewish and Christian descent, since the women we meet are far enough back in time to be our common ancestresses. I've done workshops as one-day experiences, or even as a couple of hours for two or three people. Always, no matter who attends, we receive relevant, usable information that makes sense within the context of Judaism as a whole.

I like to picture Judaism as a many-faceted gem. As you turn it, each face represents a different part of our people: one side is Hasidism, one side Reform, one side Kabbalah, one side Reconstructionism, one side. . . . You get the idea. The information we have been bringing back is another turn of the gem, another face, like the dark side of the moon, not seen for much too long.

III. Jewish Shamanism

I don't pretend to know very much about the "shamanic tradition" in Judaism. I know it infused Kabbalah at its beginnings, although the fact that women were traditionally excluded from spiritual study belies the fullness of that form. Bits and pieces throughout our traditions speak of access to the spiritual: Solomon speaking the language of the birds; stories of the Baal Shem Tov walking off into the woods and returning to heal a sick person; further back, Saul seeking out the Witch of Endor (after killing off the other seers). If one reads into the superstitions of our people, we can see vestiges of working with spiritual power. But, for the most part, we have lost our own pathway to it.

IV. Ritual Retrieval

Native Americans and other traditional, Earth-based peoples have ceremonies to enter into their pasts in order to retrieve wisdom, lost rituals, and healings from their ancestors. The Lakota and Plains peoples used the Ghost Dance, for instance. What I learned from my shamanic journeying is similar. Any particular method, when followed carefully, can afford us a way to bring back what we lost in the past and so desperately need now to make our people whole again.

Although I describe some of the method here, there is a depth to the shamanic journey itself that, unless you have been trained and shown to follow this work by your spiritual guides and teachers, I would suggest you not do alone. If done properly, there is no danger; if done haphazardly, or without preparation—as in any serious undertaking—there can be unforeseen problems.

V. Healing Needed: Disenfranchised

As a people, we as Jews have become shattered, existing as only part of our potential. This is not due to the Diaspora, nor the Holocaust, nor acculturation, nor any of the woes we tend to bemoan to each other and the rest of the world. It is not due to the role of "victim" we like to see ourselves in. Instead, our shattering is a result of our own actions, our own beliefs, choices made along our historical path: our women have been disenfranchised, our women are made small, our women are dis-empowered. To be whole again as a people, to be whole again even to approach our God (or Goddess, or however defined), we need healing. And the women in particular need the healing, and need to reclaim our strength, power, abilities, and place. The idea is not to go to the men and ask for this. It is not to go to the men and be like them. It is to find out who we are, who we were, what is ours by birthright. And after our search, we must bring it home with our heads held high, our arms full, our hearts unburdened and bright.

At the first workshop, which was held on two consecutive Sundays, I was told in a journey to hold a space open for healing. I didn't know what that meant, and could get no further detail. As I held the center of the circle, I remembered the words from that first day. As we progressed around the circle, introducing ourselves and our experience with Judaism, a lot of anger was expressed, sometimes with tears, sometimes with a deep, serrated edge to the voice. Not one woman in the circle felt at home in her own religion. The next week when we met, we went around the circle again. This time there were stories about healings: one woman had reconnected with her mother and aunts after a long time; another had attended synagogue for the first time in years; another had decided to enroll in cantorial school.

The need for women to reclaim our spiritual selves has been stated for many years by many people, be they Jewish (Reb Zalman Schachter most recently said this during a personal conversation) or Native American (the spiritual leader of the Canadian American Indian Movement stated it while berry-picking with me), or women ourselves searching for the Goddess. Gaia, our Mother Earth, needs us back, and we must come, wounded but healing, together, as representatives of our own people, re-creating the balance of the worlds.

VI. What We've Retrieved

Since the process of retrieving this information is still at its beginnings, it's not possible to describe a coherent, thorough picture of a body of information in a neat package. Instead, I'd like to present the bits and pieces as they've been brought forth and eventually, allow them to weave their own fabric.

** One of the first things we learned is about shawls (or veils). At the first workshop almost everyone brought one and I was instructed in my preparatory journeys to hang the walls with shawls and materials. In the journeys we saw how the women used shawls to create their own space wherever they were, a private space within a crowd, a safe space for self or infant in blowing sand or storm, a sacred space for inner prayer at any moment. Also, the women carried their jewelry on their shawls and so, made music as they walked along.

** The men and the women prayed in different directions. The men, having the energy of the heavens, prayed down in order to bring that heavenly energy in unison with the Earth. The women prayed upwards, bringing their Earth-connected energy up toward the Heavens. Both genders in prayer were striving to create balance, moving their primary connections, with intention, to the opposite pole. You can see this difference in some of our folk dances, with the men stomping the earth, and women raising their arms upwards.

** Some of the insights to specific prayers I've received include: The purpose of the Mourner's Kaddish is to reach through the veil to the Land of the Dead, to open the way to speak with those who have gone. The way through that veil is by becoming one with the universe. That is done by connecting with the awesome power of "God" or of the universe itself. That is why the Mourner's Kaddish is one of lauding God rather than mourning—it opens the veils to slip through, momentarily, to the other side.

While honoring the directions one morning, as I do, I began to pray about my own participation with those around me and asked that whatever I do or say be in support of the spiritual work of others, that I not get in the way or impede anyone else's spiritual growth. Suddenly the words of the prayer: "May the words of my mouth and the meditations of my heart be acceptable to Thee" became clear—what is acceptable is that which helps the creative force of the universe.

Recently, I was drumming in the moonlight to infuse with healing energy some oils I was going to use as external medicines. After a long time of monotonous drumming, I suddenly thought about the "Thirteen Attributes of God" and "received a message" that these are the qualities required to perform deep healings. When I looked them up, I noted that most of the attributes are about one form or another of compassion and loving-kindness.

** In a shamanic workshop about Death and Dying we journeyed to ask for information about present-day death rituals. I saw how the covering of the new corpse and the immediate saying of a prayer helps to release the spirit from the body and prevent it from lingering so that it may begin its journey onward.

** One of the most important journeys was done about the High Holy Days. I was brought back to the time of the Wandering in the Desert. I saw the camps and tents, and saw that the women of each tribe acted like clan mothers. Even more than at Passover (although maybe this is why we do it at Passover), the women would clean the tents and throw out anything broken or no longer usable before the holidays. Then at night, the tribe's elder woman would go around the tents with a large feather, "dusting" all the debris out of the campsites. This included any energy from the dead that had passed that year. There would then begin a great keening, a mourning, and the women would bring all the tears of the year and all the "dirt" out into the desert beyond the camp and cry out all the rest of the tears, cleansing the camps totally. When they returned, Rosh Hashanah could begin. (In this journey I was told "We'll give you man's teaching also." It seems on each of the ten days between Rosh Hashanah and Yom Kippur, thought and repentance for each commandment was done one at a time, which is why there are ten days. By Yom Kippur, you've addressed all ten.)

** The pre-Maccabean beginnings of Hannukah were found in the desert as well. The women, in charge of the food and the home or the tent, were also in charge of keeping the fire. Each year as the sun reached its weakest point, the female head of each household would bring ashes from her fire (which was carried as they moved from place to place) to a central fire held by the tribe's eldest woman. There she would rekindle her flame for her own household. This also renewed the connection of each of the homes to the others and held unity within each tribe. The little girls would participate in this rite to learn its importance and to understand the sacredness of keeping the flame as the heart and life of the people. The flames were believed to be held in the bellies of the women, as life itself is held and nurtured, and the little clay "pregnant" figurines were shown to me to represent not only fertility, but the potential of fire, as well. When men began to build structures to encapsulate the power of the tribes and the people, they took these flames and created the Eternal Light. Women, however, have retained our connection to this most vital life-maintaining force through lighting the candles to bring in the Sabbath and holidays—the lifeblood of our people.

There are other insights and rituals we have received—some about celebrating, some specific healing rituals—but these are a representative taste.

VII. Creating Community

What it means to me is that there is more of Judaism still to discover—more accurately, to rediscover, and we do not need pickaxes and shovels and pottery shards to find it. While there is value in searching our literature and the soils of Eretz Yisroel, there is "spiritual territory" also available to be explored. As I was told when I began, it is important to do this work as a community, and to bring the information back to our community, so that it can be held, and tried on, and perhaps incorporated into a fuller Judaism to hand on to the next generations.

Diane M. Sharon

The Mystic's Experience of God: A Comparison of the Mystical Techniques and Experiences of a 13th Century Jewish Mystic and a 20th Century Indic Yogi

I. Introduction

Mystical experiences threaten the foundations of religions based on ancient revelation. Ecstatic insight into the nature of the divine implies unmediated access by individuals to the divine source, thereby bypassing established cultic channels.

The ecstatic experience also threatens the uniqueness of any particular religious philosophy. If anyone can achieve a glimpse of the divine by means of specific techniques, then why practice the prescriptions and proscriptions of any particular religion? If all people experience the ecstatic similarly, progressing through similar stages and achieving levels commensurate with their innate capacity for the mystical rather than their relative devotion to a creed, then why bother with a creed at all?

Because of these and other constraints, personal accounts of ecstatic experience, including descriptions of powerful techniques for attaining such experiences, are rare in most cultures, surrounded by taboo, consigned to an esoteric in-group, or whispered privately from master to disciple.

This paper proposes to compare the autobiographical works of two mystics of widely differing cultural backgrounds, religious philosophies, and temporal milieus, and to explore the similarities and differences between their personal ecstatic experiences of the divine. Perhaps an examination of two such widely divergent accounts may cast some light on the nature of the human experience of God and the stages of mystical development which are independent of dogma and creed.

II. Overview

Abraham Abulafia, who died sometime after 1291, is among the most prolific of Jewish kabbalists. He wrote numerous manuals of mystical technique which serve as instructions for achieving ecstatic mystical experiences, guiding his students upward through the various levels. Many of these works still exist today, and although many of them are in manuscript form, Gershon Scholem and Moshe Idel have published many lengthy segments which are available for study.

Swami Muktananda, who died in 1982, is a yogi in the Siddha tradition who established an international following. He left behind a significant number of written works describing his own spiritual evolution, his mystical experiences, and instructions to his students, as well as explications of his theological and cosmogonic philosophies. These have been translated into English by his disciples and published by the foundation that he established.

In spite of vast cultural, philosophical, and temporal gulfs, the stages of the medieval kabbalist's ecstatic development and experiences of mystical union are remarkably analagous to accounts we have of the contemporary yogic master's. These similarities are paralleled in the broad outlines of their respective lives.

Abraham Abulafia was born in 1240 c.e. in Saragossa, Spain, and studied Torah and Gemara with his father until the elder's death when his son was eighteen. Two years later he left home to begin his temporal wanderings and spiritual search, which was documented in his autobiography. This work, 'Ozar 'Eden Ganuz, was composed in 1285 for the purpose of edifying and instructing one of his disciples.

Abulafia's seeking took him from the study of the sciences and mathematics, through philosophy, to Maimonides' *Guide to the Perplexed*, which was to be one of the central pillars of his spiritual life.

The second pillar was the mystical work *Sefer Yetzirah* which he studied, wrote commentaries upon, and taught, along with Maimonides' *Guide*, during the remainder of his life. At about the time of his introduction to the *Sefer Yetzirah* Abulafia experienced a major ecstatic vision which was the beginning of his development as a master of kabbala. Among his students were Rabbi Joseph Gikatilla and Rabbi Moses ben Simeon of Burgos, who were leading Spanish kabbalists in the late thirteenth century.

Swami Muktananda was born in 1908 in Mangalore, India. At the age of fifteen he left home to practice the spiritual discipline of the wandering mendicant, seeking wisdom from holy men and saints throughout his native land, and studying Vedanta and other systems of Indian philosophy, yoga, Ayurvedic medicine, horticulture, music, and the martial arts.

Muktananda received initiation, or *shaktipat*, from his master in 1947, which resulted in a protracted period of ecstatic experiences. He reports attaining God-realization in 1956 after nine years of intense meditation under the guidance of his master, or Guru, Bhagavan Nityananda. He describes these experiences in his autobiography *Play of Consciousness*. Muktananda toured the world three times, teaching Siddha meditation and initiating disciples. Before his death he passed the power of the Siddha lineage on to his disciple Swami Chidvilasananda who continues as a guru in her own right.

The initial uprooting from the natal home is a significant turning point for each master. It is as though the willingness to explore new climes is an externalization of the willingness to explore new intellectual and spiritual terrain. They each express the significance of this initial departure, as both Abulafia and Muktananda apprehend the work of a divine plan in their initial moves away from home.

Abulafia writes of this first transition: "I remained in the land of my birth for two years after my father passed away. At the age of twenty, God's spirit moved me, and I left, heading straight for the land of Israel by sea and by land."[1]

---

1. Aryeh Kaplan, *Meditation and Kabbalah* (York Beach, ME: Weiser, 1982), 66; Gershom Scholem, *Ha-Kabbalah Shel Sefer Hatemunah Veshel Abraham Abul'afiah* (Jerusalem: Academon, 1969), 193.

Muktananda similarly attributes his abandonment of his natal home to destiny: "I was slightly over fifteen when one day I left the love of my mother and father far behind. I should not have done such a thing. But what could I do? I was destined to behave so callously. It was supposed to happen, so it did."[2]

III. Philosophy and Approach

Abraham Abulafia stands in the tradition of the Merkava mystics whose roots are based in the visions of the Hebrew prophet Ezekiel, and he was profoundly influenced by the Ashkenazic Hasidim of the twelfth century. Abulafia's ecstatic approach differs significantly from that of the better-known Sefirotic kabbalah, which he studied and commented upon.

Moshe Idel distinguishes between these two kabbalistic streams, terming the Sefirotic kabbalah as "theosophical-theurgical" because of its concern with the redemptive effect of properly performed mitzvot.

The "ecstatic" kabbalah, on the other hand, focuses exclusively on the individual's mystical experience of the divine, and concerns itself with techniques for achieving ecstatic experience.

The goal of Abulafia's "Path of Names" is a prophetic encounter with the divine. Muktananda expresses the goal of his practice, Siddha Yoga, in similar terms. He writes: "Siddha Yoga is a broad stream through the forest of the world. This stream leads to the realm of oneness, where the individual soul and the Absolute merge."[3]

Muktananda professes the philosophy of Kashmir Shaivism. Very briefly, this philosophy teaches that everything in the universe is the play of the Supreme Power, and an embodiment of the Supreme Deity, or Shiva. The main duty of a seeker who pursues the Truth is to recognize the Supreme Principle, which is the source of everything. It is not possible to recognize this

---

2. Muktananda, *Play of Consciousness* (SYDA Foundation, 1978), xxviii.
3. Muktananda, *Secret of the Siddhas*, (SYDA Foundation, 1980), 58.

Supreme Principle through the senses, but only through purified willpower.

The process of purifying one's willpower and realizing this Supreme Principle is facilitated by one's guru, or master, and takes the form of meditation, or inwardly contemplating the Siddha's (seeker's) identity with the Supreme Principle. Meditation is facilitated by the repetition of the mantra, which consists of the name of God and/or a verse from Scripture. This repetition is thought to purify the mind. Hand movements, body postures, and breathing exercises are part of Muktananda's technique.

Abulafia's technique employs oral and written combinations of the letters of the Hebrew alphabet and of God's name to achieve mystical states. He also prescribes hand movements, head movements, breathing techniques, and chanting techniques reminiscent of various practices in Eastern yoga.

IV. Parallels of Practice

Among the major elements of Muktananda's spiritual practice are meditation, mantra, and discipleship expressed as devotion to the guru. Central to Abulafia's spiritual practice are isolation, combination and permutation of letters, and the importance of the master or teacher. Abulafia cites a few simple preparations, such as bathing, dressing, and securing a private place, preferably at night.

He continues:[4]

> Be careful to abstract all your thought from the vanities of this world. . . . Then take ink, pen and a table to your hand. . . . Now begin to combine a few or many letters, to permute and to combine them until your heart becomes warm.[5]

---

4. Gershom Scholem, *Major Trends in Jewish Mysticism* (New York: Schocken, 1967), 136–137; Gershom Scholem, *Ha-Kabbalah Shel Sefer Hatemunah Veshel Abraham Abul'afiah* (Jerusalem: Academon, 1969), 210–211.

5. Compare B. Uffenheimer's third type of ecstatic experience [B. Uffenheimer, "Prolegomenon of the Problem of Prophecy and Ecstasy" in *Annual of Bar-Ilan University: Moshe Schwarcz Memorial Volume* (Ramat Gan: Bar Ilan, 1987)

Muktananda also prescribes meditative practices to his disciples, and also prefers a time of darkness:

> Get up before sunrise, bathe, and sit quietly for meditation. Face east, or any direction, understanding the direction to be God, become quiet, and sit in the posture. . . . Remember your mantra and synchronize it with the incoming and outgoing breath. Let the mantra fill the mind. If the mind starts to wander, bring it back and concentrate.[6]

The need for a master's guidance, the importance of master/disciple relationships, the whole concept, in fact, of a master's obligation to disseminate to disciples what has been divinely received, is central to both accounts.

Gershon Scholem summarizes Abulafia's manifesto for the obligations of master and disciple. Briefly, the teacher's responsibility to the student, if he is worthy, is to teach him everything the teacher knows, holding back nothing. The master must repeat the material to his disciple once orally, once in outline, and once with full explication. The student must be tested. The teacher's will ought to be to help the student until he truly understands, with a minimum of anger, with much tolerance and compassion for all human beings.

These principles are similar to those described by Muktananda:

> In every field, one needs a guide. In the same way, in spiritual life, one needs a guide who is wise and compassionate, who observes good conduct, who has studied the Scriptures and spiritual philosophies, and who has understood the Truth . . . He must have complete knowledge and be proficient at transmitting energy and removing all obstacles. He should always be pure, simple, and straightforward, capable of bestowing wisdom and making love flow . . .[7]

59–61], which he terms, loosely translated, as the ecstasy of inner apathy. Both Abulafia and Muktananda fit this category, in which the initiate, individually and in isolation, engages in specific activities or techniques to induce a state of the mind separating from the body, which the initiate hopes will result in revelations or unitive experiences.

6. Muktananda, *Play of Consciousness* (SYDA Foundation, 1978), 44.

7. Muktananda, *Secret of the Siddhas* (South Fallsburg, NY: SYDA Foundation, 1980), 59–62.

Both Muktananda and Abulafia refer to sacred texts. Abulafia begins with the study of Torah, Mishnah, and Talmud with his father, but Abulafia does not describe intensive grounding in either Jewish Law or traditional sources once he has left home. He focuses instead on Maimonides' *Guide to the Perplexed*, which he discovers in the course of his travels, and which he studied with a teacher day and night until he had gone through the entire *Guide* many times.

Muktananda wanders for many years across India, seeking the wise men and saints to learn what he can. He stresses repeatedly that the teachings of a living master are the most significant teachings there are.

In fact, the focus of both ecstatics is on mystical experience rather than on intellectual study. Muktananda is delighted that his experiences confirm the sacred writings, and as a result of his ecstatic visions, his faith in the scriptures is strengthened.

V. Parallels of Experience

Abulafia and Muktananda both experience their spiritual enlightenment in stages over the course of many years, and in both cases anguish, fear, the threat of madness and the threat of death characterize progression through the lower stages. Repeatedly they employ similar descriptions of these experiences, beginning with initiation into the mystical experience.

Abulafia implies that his awakening to mystical experience was at the hand of God while he was studying the mystical text, the *Sefer Yezirah*:

> When I was thirty-one years old, in Barcelona, God awakened me from my sleep. . . . My soul awakened within me, and a spirit of God touched my mouth. A spirit of holiness fluttered through me, and I saw many fearsome sights and wonders, through signs and miracles.
>
> But at the same time, spirits of jealousy gathered around me, and I was confronted with fantasy and error. My mind was totally confused, since I could not find anyone else like me, who would

teach me the correct path. I was therefore like a blind man, groping around at noon. For fifteen years, the Satan was at my right hand to mislead me.[8]

Muktananda's initiation is also a profound experience, both euphoric and devastating. Although his initiation is at the hands of his master, which Abulafia lacked, his experience is nonetheless similar. He experiences his initiation as an identification with his guru and with the One:

> For a moment I had an intuition of the One in the many, and I lost the ordinary mind that differentiates between the inner and the outer world, that sees the many in the One. . . . I repeatedly opened and closed my eyes. When I shut them I saw innumerable clusters of sparkling rays, and millions of tiny twinkling sparks bursting within me. . . . I was overcome with awe and ecstasy.[9]

But Muktananda the initiate cannot yet stabilize himself in this blissful state. Shortly thereafter, his rapture is replaced by restlessness, torment, and anxiety:

> My peace of mind had been destroyed, and all my thoughts were leading me into a deep melancholy. My state of mind was just the opposite of what it had been before. . . . torture and anguish returned and grew.
> I cannot write the horrible thoughts that filled my mind, but—it's true—I had them. I was obsessed with impure, hateful, and sinful thoughts. . . . Someone had seated himself in my eyes and was making me see things. . . . It seemed that I was being controlled by some power . . . I no longer had a will of my own. My madness was growing all the time. My intellect was completely unstable.[10]

---

8. This is a difficult passage in the original Hebrew. See Gershom Scholem. I quote here Aryeh Kaplan's reading, in *Meditation and Kabbalah* (York Beach, ME: Weiser, 1982), 67.

On the subject of keeping the commandments, see Gershom Scholem, *Ha-Kabbalah Shel Sefer Hatemunah Veshel Abraham Abul'afiah* (Jerusalem: Academon, 1969), 189.

9. Muktananda, *Play of Consciouness* (SYDA Foundation, 1978), 69–70.

10. Ibid., 72–77.

Muktananda begins to have dramatic visions: the world on fire, the world submerged under water. He is convinced his apocalyptic visions are of reality and is disoriented when he discovers the world is undamaged. He also begins to experience *kriyas*, or involuntary body movements.

Abulafia, too, warns of the emergence of fear and trembling, hair standing on end, and convulsion of limbs in his instructions to the disciple. Mystic disciples in both traditions fear these involuntary effects. Idel writes, "Once the power of the imagination grew, there existed the danger that there would appear before the eyes of the mystic visions which have no connection whatsoever with the intellect. These images, which constitute the primary source of danger in mysticism, are understood as 'messengers of Satan.'"[11]

According to Idel, Abulafia makes it quite clear that the bliss of ecstatic adventure is the aim of mystical experience, making the risks of torment and anguish a small price to pay. Abulafia tries to describe this bliss:

And you shall feel in yourself an additional spirit arousing you and passing over your entire body and causing you pleasure, and it shall seem to you as if balm has been placed upon you, from your head to your feet, one or more times, and you shall rejoice and enjoy it very much, with gladness and trembling; gladness of your soul and trembling of your body, like one who rides rapidly on a horse, who is happy and joyful, while the horse trembles beneath him.[12]

Other sensuous images abound in Abulafia, the most significant being the feeling that his entire body, from his head to his feet, had been anointed with anointing oil. Muktananda describes the mystical experience with a similar image:

When the sun of knowledge rises in the heart and a person experiences the essence of the Self, the universe of diversity with its countless beings and objects is dissolved for him. Duality perishes. The radiant sun of the Self blazes in his eyes. Its flame radiates

---

11. Moshe Idel, *The Mystical Experience in Abraham Abulafia*, (Albany: SUNY Press, 1987), 121.
12. Ibid., 188.

through every pore of his body. As it flashes, his entire body is filled with the nectar of love. Drops of nectar from the stream of love flow from his eyes.[13]

Muktananda also describes fragrances, tastes, sounds and visions which bring him exquisite pleasure in meditation:

I meditated constantly and always saw the sweet, radiant Blue Pearl in its infinite variations. Its luster was more dazzling at each moment, and my enjoyment was forever growing. I . . . was also hearing the divine *nada* (sound, music) of thunder.

As I listened to this thundering, my meditation became so joyful that the desires which remained in my mind were smashed by the thunder and just disappeared. As I listened to this sound for a while I experienced complete union with the taintless Parabrahman.[14]

Abulafia, as a master of ecstatic experience, warns his disciples of what they can expect from their own initiation into his mystical technique. They, too, will experience involuntary physical effects and the fear of death:

All this will happen to you after having flung away tablet and quill . . . because of the intensity of your thought. And know, the stronger the intellectual influx within you, the weaker will become your outer and your inner parts. Your whole body will be seized by an extremely strong trembling, so that you will think that surely you are about to die. . . . And be ready at this moment consciously to choose death.[15]

Death, and the fear of death, are, in fact, intimately bound up with the ecstatic encounter. Abulafia reassures a disciple that only God's grace can protect him, and, as Abulafia notes in his instructions, an initiate must be prepared to surrender to death at the moment of divine contact. Indeed this loss of self in the divine

---

13. Muktananda, *Secret of the Siddhas* (South Fallsburg, NY: SYDA Foundation, 1980), 61.

14. Muktananda, *Play of Consciousness* (SYDA Foundation, 1978), 173.

15. Gershom Scholem, *Major Trends in Jewish Mysticism* (New York: Schocken, 1967), 136–137; Gershom Scholem, *Ha-Kabbalah Shel Sefer Hatemunah Veshel Abraham Abul'afiah* (Jerusalem: Academon, 1969), 210–211.

ocean is a danger of the ecstatic experience for both Abulafia and Muktananda. Muktananda writes of his own experience that he felt that he would die at any moment, and recommends to his disciples that the fear of death during meditation may be transcended by opening to knowledge of unity with the One.

The initiate's fear, panic, and terror at the moment of divine contact are apparently to be expected even if this is the very experience he seeks with his entire being. One can speculate that at the instant of *devekut*, which may be defined as that moment of unwavering union, when knower and known are one, fear arises of the loss of individual ego in an ocean of divinity. The transformation which results from that moment is in fact a death to the self that was before. At the same time that this experience is deeply sought, the approaching moment of transition engenders deep anxiety. The image of the two-edged or revolving sword which appears in Abulafia's writings is thus an apt metaphor for the prophetic experience.

Another of the effects of following an ecstatic spiritual path is apparently the acquisition of magical powers. Both authors allude to a variety of these supernatural abilities, including levitation, clairvoyance, and clairaudience, among others, and both counsel caution in succumbing to the trap of believing these magical abilities to be the goal of the spiritual path.

VI. Symbols and Images

In addition to the concepts already reviewed, many symbols and images occur in both Abulafian writings and Muktananda's. For the purpose of this paper, a simple listing must suffice to indicate their scope.

Both masters refer to metaphysical knots that must be cut or loosened for ecstatic union to occur. Both refer to the ocean as an analogy of God, and the individual as a drop or a cup in the ocean, although Abulafia describes a fear of drowning, while Muktananda embraces a merging into the All.

Both recognize a hierarchy of ecstatic experience, striving to reach the highest point themselves and encourage their disciples to do the same. There is also the idea of the ecstatic encounter as an indicator of salvation or redemption for the individual in both Muktananda and Abulafia. Both counsel the practice of sexual restraint while using sensuous sexual imagery to describe the unitive experience. Both experience visions and hear voices and sounds, but Muktananda emphasizes the value of visual experiences while Abulafia is most comfortable with aural encounters with the divine. Both counsel moderation, and even austerities as part of the spiritual path. And both describe a special kind of meditative sleep that overtakes the seeker at some stages.

This listing is more indicative than inclusive, but it does offer some idea of the variety of parallels between the two mystics in expression and concept of the ecstatic experience.

VII. Conclusion

While the theological and religious frameworks of Abraham Abulafia and Swami Muktananda are very different, and their temporal and cultural milieus could not be further apart, their specific techniques and their descriptions of the stages of mystical growth are remarkably analagous.

Among the many themes in common are the progression through various phases of philosophy and systems of thought, extreme geographic mobility, the importance of the master/disciple relationship in spiritual growth for each, an intimate relationship with God and awareness of divine guidance in the unfolding of spiritual development and achievement of ecstatic experiences as a major transformative experience.

They share an awareness of and exposure to the dangers inherent in these practices; a similarity of imagery in descriptions of ecstatic encounters; and the importance of disseminating the received wisdom in order to lead their students to ecstatic experience.

From a stylistic point of view, the works of both are often autobiographical within the context of illustrating for the reader a model of spiritual evolution, a sampling of the kinds of experiences produced by specific mystical techniques, and a warning of potential dangers. These dangers are specified, and are remarkably alike for each master. Both authors use their own personal experiences as didactic tools in instructing others who will read their words.

Although these similarities do not by any means minimize the vast differences in theology and mythology between these two ecstatic streams, their number and character raise, among other questions, the issues of whether there is a particularly "Jewish" or "Indic" ecstatic experience; whether there is not a universal process in the human experience of the ecstatic which transcends culture and temporality; and whether postulated direct or indirect opportunities for contact between Kabalists and Yogis are necessary to account for parallels of thought and praxis.

References

Idel, Moshe. *Kabbalah: New Perspectives*. New Haven: Yale University Press, 1988.

————. *The Mystical Experience in Abraham Abulafia*. Albany: SUNY Press, 1987.

————. *Studies in Ecstatic Kabbalah*. Albany: SUNY Press, 1988.

James, William. *The Varieties of Religious Experience: A Study in Human Nature*. With an introduction by Jaques Barzun. New York: New American Library/Penguin, 1958.

Kaplan, Aryeh. *Meditation and Kabbalah*. York Beach, Maine: Weiser, 1982.

Muktananda. *I Have Become Alive! Secrets of the Inner Journey*. South Fallsburg, NY: SYDA Foundation, 1985.

————. *In the Company of a Siddha: Interviews and Conversations with Swami Muktananda*. South Fallsburg, NY: SYDA Foundation, 1978.

————. *The Perfect Relationship: The Guru and the Disciple*. South Fallsburg, NY: SYDA Foundation, 1980.

————. *Play of Consciousness*. South Fallsburg, NY: SYDA Foundation, 1978.

————. *Secret of the Siddhas*. South Fallsburg, NY: SYDA Foundation, 1980.

Otto, Rudolf. *Mysticism East and West: A Comparative Analysis of the Nature of Mysticism*. Translated by Bertha L. Bracey and Richenda C. Payne. New York: Macmillan, 1970 <1932>.

Schatz-Uffenheimer, Rivka. *Quietistic Elements in 19th Century Hasidic Thought*. Jerusalem: Magnes, 1968.

Scholem, Gershom. *Ha-Kabbalah Shel Sefer Hatemunah Veshel Abraham Abul'afiah*. Jerusalem: Academon, 1969.

————. *Kabbalah*. New York: New American Library, Meridian, 1978.

————. *Major Trends in Jewish Mysticism*. New York: Schocken, 1967.

————. *On the Kabbalah and Its Symbolism*. New York: Schocken, 1965.

Uffenheimer, B. "Prolegomenon of the Problem of Prophecy and
    Ecstacy." In *Annual of Bar-Ilan University: Moshe Schwarcz
    Memorial Volume*, pp. 45–62. Ramat Gan, Israel: Bar Ilan
    University, 1987.

Nathan Katz

The Hindu-Jewish Encounter
And the Future*

For years, Western scholars of religion have debated whether Buddhism was a religion. They have been reluctant to apply the term "religion" to Buddhism because it has neither a "Creator God" nor sustained cosmogonic interests. In their minds, as in many Western dictionaries, a "religion" is about God, and if some system of thought is not about God, then it could not be called a "religion." These scholars have written about Buddhism as more of a philosophy or "a way of life" than a religion.

Gustavo Benavides, a colleague at Villanova University likes to tell a joke to students in his Asian religions class to disabuse them of this idea, to show them the provincialism of this approach. All religions except for Christianity (and indigenous Chinese religions) are concerned about dietary taboos. To make his point, he jokes about a Hindu who, upon first encountering Christianity, asks about its dietary code. Learning that it has no dietary code, the Hindu concludes that Christianity must not be a religion, but "a way of life."

The academic study of religion emerged in western European universities, which themselves grew out of the church. Small wonder, then, that the interpretative categories which dominate the social sciences reflect the Christian origins of the university. The central theme of this essay is that this condition is especially prevalent in the field of religious studies. As part of a remedy for this imbalance, the possibility of an explicitly Jewish approach to

*An earlier version of this paper was read at a panel on "New Paradigms of 'Religious Tradition': The Case of Hinduisms and Judaisms" at the American Academy of Religion annual meeting, San Francisco, CA, 22 November 1992.

the field of religious studies, interreligious dialogue in particular, is explored. The case in point is the encounter between Hinduisms[1] and Judaisms.

Characteristics of Hindu-Jewish Dialogue

An overemphasis on the "absolute" (as a metaphysic in theology or as an experience in mysticism) tends to predetermine the outcome of interreligious dialogues, often distorting the religious traditions represented. Underlying this search for the absolute is an assumption which values orthodoxy over orthopraxy. Most Hinduisms and most Judaisms, on the contrary, value practice over doctrine, and the primacy of orthopraxy over orthodoxy is the first characteristic of Hindu-Jewish dialogue.

The second characteristic of Hindu-Jewish dialogue is that it is symmetrical. In an intriguing study, Israeli anthropologist Shalva Weil characterized the relations between Christians and Jews in the south Indian state of Kerala as symmetrical, a "pattern of relationship between Christians and Jews in India whereby two communities or ethnic minorities developed along parallel lines in a similar geographic area both in terms of history and tradition and in terms of group image."[2] In this respect, Jewish-Christian relations in Kerala are unique in the world; everywhere else Christians have held a higher social position than, and therefore power over, Jews.

Hindu-Jewish relations, especially outside of India, are symmetrical (except, of course, in Israel). As Indian-Americans and Jewish-Americans begin to discover one another in the workplace and in the public arena, one of the first discoveries is of their

---

1. Throughout this essay, we are using the term "Hindu" in its etymological sense of "Indian," rather than implying any sort of doctrinal, textual, cultic or mythic continuity, as has been suggested by the Vishwa Hindu Parishad. Thus, as we are using it, the term "Hindu" includes all religions of Indian origin— Buddhism, Jainism, and Sikhism, as well as what we commonly call Hinduism.

2. Shalva Weil, "Symmetry between Christians and Jews in India: The Cnanita Christians and the Cochin Jews of Kerala," *Contributions to Indian Sociology* 16: 2 (1982), 175–196.

similar social positions, their symmetry in the context of American society. Such symmetry bodes especially well for dialogue.

Hindu-Jewish dialogue is quite different than Hindu-Christian dialogue. While concepts of and practices leading to the "absolute" are part of Hindu-Jewish dialogue, these aspects tend to recede into the background. Foregrounded are historically rooted realities. This means that many of the problems which have bedeviled Hindu-Christian dialogues have no relevance to the Hindu-Jewish encounter.

For example, as Indian Catholic theologian and self-professed Hindu, Raimundo Pannikar, has observed,

> the Hindu-Christian dialogue has never been a round-table conference, not merely a theoretical exercise in *brahmodya* (theological disputations). It is embedded in particular socio-political circumstances and takes place within a certain elusive myth. The first phase was that of a tiny minority finding its own identity: Christians dialoging with the Hindu majority in order to establish their own identity. No wonder the dialogue was not one of great theological speculations, as it has been noted. It was the *Christian* dialogue with Hinduism. The second phase reverses the roles. Demographically, the Hindus were the majority, of course, but the power was on the other side. Hinduism had to establish its identity, and awaken from an alleged slumber that had permitted first the Muslim and later the Christian conquests. The so-called Hindu Renaissance is witness thereof. It was a *Hindu* dialogue with Christianity.[3]

The symmetry which characterizes the Hindu-Jewish encounter is not only an issue within the context of India, but within the world at large. While Hindus were and are obviously more powerful than Jews in India, and the converse would be true in Israel, more significant is the relative lack of power of both groups during the five hundred years of European ascendancy in world politics and economics, the age of imperialism. This point, too, is best illustrated by a story.

As fate would have it, one day I found myself in Rome in the

---

3. Raimundo Pannikar, "Foreword—The Ongoing Dialogue," in *Hindu-Christian Dialogue: Perspectives and Encounters*, ed. Howard Coward (Maryknoll, NY: Orbis, Faith Meets Faith Series, 1989), xvi.

company of a good friend from Thailand, a leading Buddhist monk at the royal monastery, Wat Bovoranives in Bangkok. We decided to visit the Vatican's Museum of World Religions. The museum is arranged according to a Christian hierarchy of religions: first were the pagans, then the Hindus and Buddhists, then the Muslims, the Jews, and finally the non-Catholic Christians. As we came to the displays of Buddhist art, my companion stopped short. His eyes widened and nostrils flared as he stared at a large Thai *Buddharupa* (image of the Buddha). Inquiring as to his obvious distress, he stammered, "That *rupa* was stolen from my monastery. For years I had heard that some Christians had taken it, but I never believed that story. What kind of person would steal a sacred object from a temple? But here it is." And he pointed out the Thai inscription beneath the *rupa*, identifying it as from Wat Bovoranives. I commiserated with his pain, and after a time we continued our tour. Then it was my turn for shock. In the Judaism section of the museum, we saw Torah scrolls displayed. One of them was identified as originating in the Great Synagogue of Budapest, which was the home of my mother's family on both sides. Quite possibly, my own unknown cousins who had been slaughtered in the Holocaust and read from that very scroll. I knew more deeply what my Buddhist friend had experienced when confronted with the "stolen" Buddharupa, just as he understood the anguish this display of a Torah scroll prompted.

This too is part of Hindu-Jewish dialogue. This too is the symmetry between our religions, a symmetry occasioned by the religious oppression meted out against our peoples.

The symmetry that characterizes the Hindu-Jewish encounter exemplifies one of Catholic theologian Leonard Swidler's ground rules for interreligious dialogue: "Dialogue can take place only between equals, or *par cum pari*, as Vatican II put it."[4] While Swidler was not referring specifically to socio-political equality so much as an equal openness and willingness to learn, nevertheless this more historical aspect of symmetry cannot be overlooked; it is a necessary component—perhaps a starting point—for the contemporary Hindu-Jewish encounter.

---

4. Leonard Swidler, "The Dialogue Decalogue," *Journal of Ecumenical Studies* 20: 1 (Winter 1993), 3.

The Issue of Idolatry

Before describing an agenda for Hindu-Jewish dialogue, there is one preliminary concern which must be mentioned, and this is entirely an internal Judaic issue: idolatry. While an analysis of Judaic attitudes towards Hinduism is well beyond the scope of this paper, the issue of idolatry is, for Jews, a necessary preamble. Put in traditional terms, the question is whether Hinduism conforms to the seven Noahide *mitzvot* (commandments) as articulated in rabbinic literature. There should be no difficulties with the five ethical Noahide *mitzvot*: to establish courts of justice, to practice sexual morality, and to avoid bloodshed, robbery, and tearing a limb from a living animal. As far as ethics go, there can be little doubt that Hindu traditions exceed Judaic requirements. But what of the two doctrinal *mitzvot*: avoiding blasphemy and idolatry? Is there a way to reconcile the Hindu use of images (*murti*) with the avoidance of idolatry?

David Novak recently summarized Judaic views on purported idolatrous practices among gentiles:

> the rabbis . . . insisted that the ban on idolatry was binding on both Jews and gentiles, [but] they recognized a difference in degree. Thus the important third-century Palestinian authority Rabbi Yohanan ben Nappaha . . . stated that "gentiles outside the Land of Israel are not idolaters but are only practicing ancestral customs." . . . [T]he key to understanding this statement of Rabbi Yohanan is his choice of the scriptural proof text. The heavenly bodies are called "signs," that is, the nations of the world approach God through the mediation of nature, even through the symbolization of created nature in images. Israel, because of its unique historical relationship with God, must approach him directly through revealed commandments. Here we see the beginnings of the notion . . . that the difference between Israel and the rest of the nations of the world is not that Israel worships the one God and the gentiles worship *other* gods altogether. Rather, the difference is that Israel worships God directly, for the covenant makes that direct relationship with God the only acceptable one for them.

The nations of the world, being outside this direct covenant with Israel, are not wholly separated from God but are farther removed from him. Therefore, they are justified in approaching him through visible intermediaries, which are now seen as functioning symbolically . . . Philo prohibited Jewish ridicule of pagan cults because their ultimate intent is not in essential opposition to monotheism.[5]

In summary, Novak held that ". . . if gentiles are permitted to acknowledge God through mediation, then as long as God is the ultimate object of their concern, they may swear by these intermediaries and not transgress the Noahide prohibition of idolatry."[6]

Apart from this specifically Judaic concern about idolatry, there is also the secular issue of imposed definition vs. self-definition: Swidler's principle that only a Hindu can define what it means to be Hindu, while the rest of us can only describe it from the outside.[7] In other words, how could we know whether Hinduism were idolatrous a *priori*? Wouldn't that understanding only emerge out of dialogue, not prior to it? A traditional Jew who is serious about interreligious dialogue must avoid imposing his or her own definitions on the dialogue partner, and "idolatry" surely is not the way anyone would describe their own religion. Even if we do not wish to be so liberal-minded as Novak's rabbinic sources, at a minimum we should be able to agree that the question of whether or not Hinduism is idolatrous must be bracketed, since any authentic answer could only emerge out of such a dialogue.

This being said, I can relate a conversation with a swami resident at Kataragama, the sacred complex in southern Sri Lanka. Hoping to understand better my own tradition, I asked the swami his view of the Judaic abhorrence of idolatry. Much to my surprise, he replied that he agreed with it "one hundred percent."

---

5. David Novak, *Jewish-Christian Dialogue: A Jewish Justification* (New York: Oxford University Press, 1989), 40–41.

6. David Novak, *Jewish-Christian Dialogue: A Jewish Justification* (New York: Oxford University Press, 1989), 47. Cf. Nathan Katz, "The 'Jewish Secret' and the Dalai Lama: A Dharamsala Diary." *Conservative Judaism* 43:4 (Summer 1991), 45.

7. Leonard Swidler, "The Dialogue Decalogue," *Journal of Ecumenical Studies* 20: 1 (Winter 1993), 2.

In his view, the use of the *rupa* or *murti* was an unfortunate concession to popular Hindu religiousness, and that Hindus would do better to adore the formless and transcendent rather than the incarnate. Therefore, he concluded, Hindus should pay heed to Judaic chastisements! The swami's unanticipated comment was very strong evidence for Swidler's principle: "Each participant must come to the dialogue with no hard and fast assumptions as to where the points of disagreement are."[8]

An Agenda for Hindu-Jewish Dialogue

If Hindu-Jewish dialogue is not the same as Hindu-Christian dialogue, what is it? What is the agenda? Based on my own experiences over the past twenty years, I offer the following as an agenda:

1. The Hindu-Jewish dialogue *is* about the absolute and practices which lead to the absolute. To maintain, as I do, that it is a mistake to focus upon orthodoxy to the neglect of orthopraxy, so too is it a mistake to neglect doctrines and mysticism entirely. For example, an important aspect of the historic Tibetan-Jewish dialogue in 1990 was about mysticism and meditation. While the Dalai Lama and most Tibetans had long viewed Jewish exile and return after two thousand years as a model for their own experience, he was surprised to learn about Judaism's rich esoteric traditions. At the conclusion of the intensive dialogue, the Dalai Lama commented, "As a result of our meeting, to speak quite frankly I developed much more respect for Judaism because I found there a high level of sophistication."[9] As I wrote of that encounter, and as I continue to believe, "[Jewish esotericism has] a crucial role in this dialogue. Tibetan Buddhism is a tradition especially rich in esotericism, and Tibetans suspect that a religion

---

8. Leonard Swidler, "The Dialogue Decalogue," *Journal of Ecumenical Studies* 20: 1 (Winter 1993), 2.

9. Nathan Katz, "The 'Jewish Secret' and the Dalai Lama: A Dharamsala Diary." *Conservative Judaism* 43: 4 (Summer 1991), 43.

which is not likewise esoteric might be superficial. Much of the overlap between our traditions lies in esotericism . . ."[10]

It is not only in the domain of mysticism that comparative studies of religious ideas should be undertaken. We need more along the lines of Arnold Kunst's study of Talmudic and Hindu logic,[11] Barbara Holdrege's book on how Scripture is understood,[12] and Hananya Goodman's edited volume on Hindu and Jewish religious concepts.[13] However, this type of research is most often not dialogical but individual.

2. The Hindu-Jewish dialogue is also about something so apparently mundane as dietary laws. As traditions which emphasize orthopraxy, it should not be surprising that the area of dietary laws has actually been on the forefront of Hindu-Jewish religious interactions in America. Any number of enterprising Tamil restaurateurs in New York City sell "kosher doshas," proudly display hechshers from Orthodox rabbis, and in fact Hindu "brahmin" restaurants afford a kosher dining alternative for the most scrupulous Jew.[14] Not only that, one often finds the latest in kashruth research in newspapers which serve America's Hindu community.[15] While Hindu and Jewish dietary codes do not coincide, they do overlap, and these are areas in which communication and cooperation can be developed. A faithful Hindu is as concerned as

10. Nathan Katz, "The 'Jewish Secret' and the Dalai Lama: A Dharamsala Diary," in *Conservative Judaism* 43: 4 (Summer 1991), 39.

11. Arnold Kunst, "An Overlooked Type of Inference," in *Bulletin of the School of Oriental and African Studies* 10 (1932–42), 976–991.

12. Barbara A. Holdrege, *Veda and Torah* (Albany, NY: State University of New York Press, forthcoming).

13. Hananya Goodman, *From Benares to Jerusalem*, ed. Hananya Goodman (Albany, NY: State University of New York Press, forthcoming).

14. "Brahmin" restaurants serve food which is consumable by brahmins, the hereditary priests of Hinduism. Not only is their food strictly vegetarian (lacto-vegetarian, to be precise; it contains neither eggs nor fish), but it is prepared and served by brahmins themselves, following the dietary principle of the caste system that "the cook must be as pure as the eater." [Louis Dumont, *Homo Hierarchicus: The Caste System and Its Implications* (Chicago and London: University of Chicago Press, 1973), 139.] On the interactions between Jewish and Hindu dietary codes in south India, see Nathan Katz and Ellen S. Goldberg, "Asceticism and Caste in the Passover Observances of the Cochin Jews," *Journal of the American Academy of Religion* 57: 1 (1989), 53–82.

15. See, for example, *The India Times* (July 15, 1992), 13.

is the observant Jew about the chemistry of rennet, or the presence of lard in baked goods, and therefore would be interested in learning about the mysterious code of O-U and Kof-K, and of Fleishig/Milchig/Pareve, as well as in supporting kashruth research.[16]

The issue of diet is also a spiritual issue, although it's not usually recognized as such. Divine dietary codes are about the sanctification of food, the archetypal mundane issue. Food can be kosher, just as it can be *prasadam*,[17] and a study of Hindu and Jewish reflections on the meaning of food regulations would itself be worthwhile, beyond the practical issues of hechshers and food research.[18]

3. The Hindu-Jewish dialogue is also about our experiences of oppression and intolerance, as my Thai Buddhist monk friend and I understood viscerally at the Vatican's museum. We Hindus, Buddhists, and Jews can better understand our own history—especially the less savory aspects of intolerance at the hands of powerful religions—by comparing notes with one another.

4. The Hindu-Jewish dialogue is also about preserving culture in the face of diasporization and modernization.

Diaspora, or exile, was the issue which compelled the Dalai Lama to invite Jewish scholars to his palace for the historic Tibetan-Jewish dialogue in 1990. In fact, Jews have been exemplars in the minds of the Tibetan people ever since their forced exile in 1959. Soon after they established themselves in temporary

---

16. Observant Jews are concerned about whether rennet is an animal product, in which case it could not be eaten with dairy products. Lard, also an animal product, is found in many bakery products in America, much to the dismay of many Jews, Hindus, and vegetarians. O-U and Kof-K are well-known *hechshers*, rabbinical certifications that a product is kosher. The system of kashruth divides foodstuffs into animal products (Fleishig in Yiddish, Basari in Hebrew), dairy products (Milchig; Halavi), and "neutral" (pareve) products containing neither animal nor dairy products. Today's food industry is highly sophisticated, and categorizing a product requires a sophisticated understanding of biochemistry; "kashruth research" investigates and tests foodstuffs continually.

17. In some Hindu traditions, food is offered to a deity before it is eaten. This "sacred transaction" between the deity and the devotee entails first the gift of the food to the deity, then the return of the leftovers to the devotee as a gift from the deity known as *prasadam*.

18. Rabbi Jacob N. Shimmel and Satyaraja Dasa Adhikari, *Om Shalom: Judaism and Krishna Consciousness* (Brooklyn: Folk Books, 1990).

quarters in India, they commemorated the 2100th anniversary of the independent Tibetan state by publishing Jamyang Norbu's pamphlet, "An Outline of the History of Israel." Norbu, the militant president of the Tibetan Youth Congress, wrote that "[W]e need to derive a source of inspiration from a people whose determination and hard work achieved their long-awaited goal . . . Israel, whose people had struggled for two thousand years under many difficulties and hardships to get their land and freedom back."[19]

Today we see two kinds of diaspora: the forced exile of the Tibetans, Vietnamese and Cambodians, and the voluntary exile of American Hindus. We Jews experienced the first variety until 1948, but since the establishment of Israel, *galut* has become our home voluntarily. Our struggles over nearly two thousand years may inspire Tibetans and Vietnamese, but many American Hindus rightly or wrongly see American Jews as role models for their gentle exile in America: we are taken as fully participating in American life while simultaneously maintaining religio-cultural traditions. Our Hebrew day schools, federations, newspapers, self-defense organizations such as the ADL, youth summer camps, and lobbying organizations for both domestic and international issues are serving as models for other minority peoples who fear assimilation and the loss of traditions. Just this past summer, two Tibetan educators were sent by the Dalai Lama to observe Jewish summer camps, with the goal of adapting this institution to the situation of Tibetans in India.[20]

For many newly diasporized peoples—such as Tibetans and Indochinese-Americans—diasporization and modernization are simultaneous. In some senses, the two phenomena are interrelated. Diasporization shatters the premodern sense of a nation as a confluence of land-people-language-religion. If one is landless, then the fusion of these four separable factors unravels. Similarly, the essence of modernization is pluralism wherein one's sacred canopy is seen as a human cultural product rather than sacred,

---

19. Jamyang Norbu, *I-si-ral gyi rgyal-rabs snying-bsdud bsgyur-bsgrib-pa* (Dharamsala, India: Information and Publicity Office of the Dalai Lama, 1973), 1. My translation from the Tibetan.

20. Sarah Blaustain, "Tibetas Seeks Help in Survival," in *Forward* (August 21, 1992), 5.

eternal meanings. Diasporization confronts one with the other, with a pluralism of meanings. So does modernization, and in this sense the two phenomena are related. Jews are seen as the first diasporized *and* the first modernized people, even if in our case the former preceded the latter by sixteen hundred years. Peoples who are just now become diasporized and/or modernized tend to look to Jews for guidance.

5. The Hindu-Jewish dialogue in America has concerns specific to life as a minority religious culture in this country. For example, both ethnic groups have a vested interest in maintaining a strong public education system. The secular character of public institutions, especially schools, is a concern to both groups. Both communities can and do strive against discrimination in housing, the workplace, and in schools, as well against the threat of violence from the resurgent Klan and other Nazi-like organizations. Parents in both communities fear unscrupulous missionaries. For both, calls for the "Christianization of America" are viewed with alarm. Finally, both American Hindus and Jews have deep ties to their countries of origin, and both groups would like the American government to reflect their sentiments in "special relationships" with India and Israel. Therefore, there are many avenues for cooperation in the political arena.

6. The Hindu-Jewish dialogue is itself multicultural; that is, there are and have been Hindu-Jewish dialogues in America, in India, and elsewhere. The Hindu-Jewish dialogue in India may well take forms different from that in the United States. The long and happy Jewish diaspora among Hindus ought to be recalled as a background for the contemporary dialogue.[21]

The long overdue establishment of ambassadorial relations between India and Israel, so enthusiastically welcomed by Hindus as well as Jews, is another, contemporary aspect of Hindu-Jewish dialogue. When coupled with the Hindu-Jewish dialogue in America and recalling the long, happy and continuing encounter in India, this new, diplomatic relationship between our two homelands may bring about a flowering of cooperation in culture, commerce and technology, and international cooperation.

---

21. Nathan Katz and Ellen S. Goldberg, *The Last Jews of Cochin: Jewish Identity in Hindu India* (Columbia, SC: University of South Carolina Press, 1993).

7. It should be recognized that what we have been calling "Hindu-Jewish" dialogue is both Hindu-Jewish and Hindu-Judaic; or perhaps Hindu-Judaic and Indian-Jewish. The point is that it involves both religion and ethnicity (the latter a distinctly American formulation). While any one given dialogue session might emphasize one aspect, we need to be clear about which aspect we are discussing.

8. Finally, I offer an admonition as to what Hindu-Jewish dialogue is not. First and foremost, it is not a monologue among Jews; both parties must be present. This may be obvious, but this basic principle of dialogue is often the casualty of convenience and ignorance. A negative example of this type of monological dialogue is Catholic theologian Hans Küng's recent book, *Christianity and the World Religions: Paths of Dialogue with Islam, Hinduism, and Buddhism*, which claims to be "the transcript of an actual dialogue that took place in the summer semester of 1982 at the University of Tübingen."[22] In Küng's book one finds no Muslims, Hindus or Buddhists, but only three (Christian) scholars who speak for the "other" half of the world. I wish this were purely a Christian problem, but it is not. I was asked recently to review a book manuscript on Hindu-Jewish dialogue for an academic publisher, a collection of essays by Jewish writers. And there are similar cases of a synagogue or a Hillel Center which wants to sponsor a "Buddhist-Jewish" dialogue between a rabbi and a Jew who practices meditation! As a prerequisite to our participation in Hindu-Jewish dialogue, perhaps we need to remind ourselves that dialogues must involve real people, not our imaginations and surely not our projections. We must realize that the issue of Jews who practice Buddhist meditation or Hindu yoga is an internal Jewish issue, not to be confused with the Hindu-Jewish dialogue.

---

22. Hans Küng, *Christianity and the World Religions: Paths of Dialogue with Islam, Hinduism, and Buddhism* (Garden City, NY: Doubleday, 1986), xiv.

Conclusions

Hindu-Jewish dialogue is not some new fad; it is truly an ancient encounter which dates back more than two millennia.[23] A retrieval of links between Hindus and Jews, which is an aspect of the contemporary Hindu-Jewish dialogue, reconfigures not only our understandings of Judaism and Hinduism, but the very manner in which we go about doing interreligious dialogue is modified; more than that, how we study religious traditions is changed. Indeed, our understanding of the very concept of "religion" becomes modified when Hinduism and Judaism are allowed to meet symmetrically.

---

23. See Nathan Katz, "Contacts Between Jewish and Indo-Tibetan Civilizations through the Ages: Some Explorations," in *The Tibet Journal* 16: 4 (Winter 1991), 90–109.

References

Blustain, Sarah. "Tibetans Seek Help in Survival." *Forward* (August 21, 1992). 5.

Coward, Harold. *Hindu-Christian Dialogue: Perspectives and Encounters.* Ed. Howard Coward. Maryknoll, NY: Orbis, Faith Meets Faith Series, 1989.

Dumont, Louis. *Homo Hierarchicus: The Caste System and Its Implications.* Chicago and London: University of Chicago Press, 1973.

Goodman, Hananya. *From Benares to Jerusalem.* Ed. Hananya Goodman. Albany, NY: State University of New York Press, forthcoming.

Holdrege, Barbara A. *Veda and Torah.* Albany, NY: State University of New York Press, forthcoming.

Katz, Nathan. "The Jewish Secret and the Dalai Lama: A Dharamsala Diary." *Convervative Judaism* 43: 4 (Summer 1991): 33–46.

———. "Contacts Between Jewish and Indo-Tibetan Civilizations through the Ages: Some Explorations." *The Tibet Journal* 16: 4 (Winter 1991): 90–109.

Katz, Nathan, and Ellen S. Goldberg. "Asceticism and Caste in the Passover Observances of the Cochin Jews." *Journal of the American Academy of Religion* 57: 1 (1989). 53–82.

———. *The Last Jews of Cochin: Jewish Identity in Hindu India.* Columbia, SC: University of South Carolina Press, 1993.

Küng, Hans. *Christianity and the World Religions: Paths of Dialogue with Islam, Hinduism, and Buddhism.* Garden City, NY: Doubleday, 1986.

Kunst, Arnold. "An Overlooked Type of Inference." *Bulletin of the School of Oriental and African Studies* 10 (1939–42), 976–991.

Norbu, Jamyang ('Jams-dbyang Nor-bu). *I-si-ral gyi rgyal-rabs snying-bsdud bsgrib-pa [An Outline of the History of Israel].* Dharamsala, India: Information and Publicity Office of the Dalai Lama, 1973. [In Tibetan]

Novak, David. *Jewish-Christian Dialogue: A Jewish Justification.* New York: Oxford University Press, 1989.

Pannikar, Raimundo. "Foreword—The Ongoing Dialogue." In *Hindu-Christian Dialogue: Perspectives and Encounters.*, ed. Howard Coward. Maryknoll, NY: Orbis, Faith Meets Faith Series, 1989.

Shimmel, Rabbi Jacob N., and Satyaraja Dasa Adhikari, *Om Shalom: Judaism and Krishna Consciousness.* Brooklyn: Folk Books, 1990.

Swidler, Leonard. "The Dialogue Decalogue: Ground Rules for Interreligious, Interideological Dialogue." *Journal of Ecumenical Studies* 20: 1 (Winter 1993).

Weil, Shalva. "Symmetry between Christians and Jews in India: The Cnanite Christians and the Cochin Jews of Kerala." *Contributions to Indian Sociology* 16: 2 (1982), 175–196.

Index

About the Editor

Shohama Wiener, D. Min., is president of The Academy for Jewish Religion, the multidenominational seminary that ordains both rabbis and cantors. Following her ordination as rabbi by the AJR, she received honorary ordination from Rabbi Zalman Schachter-Shalomi. She is coeditor of *Worlds of Jewish Prayer*, and writes and teaches widely on Jewish spirituality, meditation, and healing.